Using the *Teach Yourself in 24 Hours* Series

Welcome to the *Teach Yourself in 24 Hours* series. You're probably thinking to yourself, "What? They want me to stay up all night and learn this stuff?" Well, no, not exactly. This series introduces a new concept in teaching you about exciting new products: 24 one-hour lessons, designed to keep your interest and keep you learning. By breaking the learning process into smaller units, you will not be overwhelmed by the complexity of some of the new technologies being introduced in today's market. Each hourly lesson has a number of special items, some old, some new, to help you along.

10 Minutes

In the first 10 minutes of the hour, you will be given a complete list of all of the topics and skills you will have a solid knowledge of by the time you finish the hour. You will be able to know exactly what the hour will bring, with no hidden surprises.

20 Minutes

By the time you have delved into the lesson for 20 minutes, you will know what many of the newest features of the software application are. In the constantly evolving computer arena, knowing everything a program can do will aid you enormously, if not right now, then definitely in the near future.

30 Minutes

Before 30 minutes have passed, you should have learned at least one useful task, oftentimes more. Many of these tasks will take advantage of the newest features of the application. These tasks take the hands-on approach, and tell you exactly which menus and commands you need to step through to accomplish the goal. This approach is found through each lesson in the *24 Hours* series.

40 Minutes

As you will see after 40 minutes, many of the tools you have come to expect from the *Teach Yourself* series are still here. Notes and Tips offer you quick asides into the special tricks of the trade to make your work faster and more productive. Warnings give you the knowledge to avoid those nasty time-consuming errors.

50 Minutes

Along the way, you may run across terms that you haven't seen before. Never before has technology thrown so many new words and acronyms into the language, and the New Terms elements you will find in this series will carefully explain each and every one of them.

60 Minutes

At the end of the hour, you may still have questions that need to be answered. You know the kind— questions on skills or tasks that may come up every day for you, but weren't directly addressed during the hour. That's where the Q&A section can help. By asking and answering the most frequently asked questions about the topics discussed in the hour, Q&A will possibly not only get your specific question answered, it will definitely provide a succinct review of all that you have learned in the hour.

Teach
Yourself
Access® 97

in 24 Hours

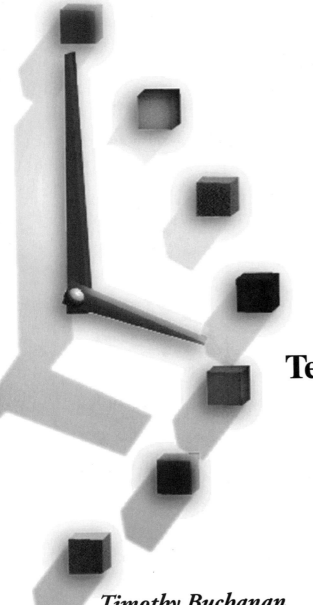

Teach Yourself
ACCESS® 97
in 24 Hours

Timothy Buchanan
Craig Eddy
Rob Newman

SAMS
PUBLISHING

201 West 103rd Street
Indianapolis, Indiana 46290

To Stacy, for her understanding, strength, and guidance,
and to my family for all of their support.
—Tim Buchanan

Copyright © 1997 by Sams Publishing

FIRST EDITION

International Standard Book Number: 0-672-31027-9

Library of Congress Catalog Card Number: 96-71493

2000   99   98   97   4   3   2   1

Interpretation of the printing code: the rightmost double-digit number is the year of the book's printing; the rightmost single-digit, the number of the book's printing. For example, a printing code of 97-1 shows that the first printing of the book occurred in 1997.

Composed in AGaramond and MCPdigital by Macmillan Computer Publishing

Printed in the United States of America

Trademarks

All terms mentioned in this book that are known to be trademarks or service marks have been appropriately capitalized. Sams Publishing cannot attest to the accuracy of this information. Use of a term in this book should not be regarded as affecting the validity of any trademark or service mark.

Publisher and President   Richard K. Swadley
Publishing Manager   Rosemarie Graham
Director of Editorial Services   Cindy Morrow
Managing Editor   Mary Inderstrodt
Assistant Marketing Managers   Kristina Perry, Rachel Wolfe

Acquisitions Editor
Corrine Wire

Development Editors
Kristi Asher
Marla Reece

Production Editor
Heather E. Butler

Copy Editors
Fran Blauw
Kris Simmons

Indexer
Cheryl Dietsch

Technical Reviewer
Dick Cravens

Editorial Coordinator
Katie Wise

Technical Edit Coordinator
Lorraine E. Schaffer

Resource Coordinator
Deborah Frisby

Editorial Assistants
Carol Ackerman
Andi Richter
Rhonda Tinch-Mize

Cover Designer
Tim Amrhein

Book Designer
Gary Adair

Copy Writer
Peter Fuller

Production Team Supervisors
Brad Chinn
Charlotte Clapp

Production
Georgiana Briggs
Mike Henry
Ayanna Lacey
Carl Pierce
Gene Redding
Becky Stutzman

Overview

Contents

About the Authors

Timothy Buchanan has been working and developing with Microsoft Access for more than four years. Many of the database applications that he has designed have been licensed and distributed nationwide. He also runs his own consulting firm that supplies programming and database design assistance.

Craig Eddy currently resides in Richmond, Virginia, with his wife and two children. Craig holds a B.S. degree in electrical engineering from Virginia Tech. He is currently employed as Senior Developer for Pipestream Technologies, Inc., where he is responsible for the continuing development of ContactBuilder and Sales Continuum. He is also the architect and chief programmer for the two-way synchronization between SQL Server and remote versions of Pipestream's sales force automation products. Craig specializes in Visual Basic, SQL Server, and Access development. He has been an author for *Access 95 Unleashed*, *Office 95 Unleashed*, *VBScript Unleashed*, and *Access 97 Unleashed*, as well as co-author of *Web Programming with Visual Basic*. Craig's hobbies include private business development and relaxing at the Outer Banks in North Carolina. Craig can be reached at craige@richmond.infi.net.

Rob Newman is a contract consultant residing in Federal Way, Washington. With more than 11 years experience working with computers, Rob has developed applications for clients in the military, banking, and healthcare industries and for Fortune 100 companies such as AT&T, Microsoft, and Weyerhaeuser.

Introduction

Welcome to *Teach Yourself Access 97 in 24 Hours*, your teach-yourself guide to learning a powerful, easy-to-use database system. This book explores Microsoft Access 97. The book is divided into 24 chapters that can be completed in about an hour each.

Access 97 is an exceptional database system and the best of the Windows databases available today. This book covers everything you will need to know about Access 97 up to a moderately advanced level. We start with the basics, so it is no problem if you have no experience with any database systems, yet even those with some database experience will find a large amount of information to learn about Access 97 and database systems in general. The book starts with the basics and builds on each previous chapter. Many chapters will require the knowledge learned in previous chapters to fully comprehend the topics in the current chapter. In this case, we review the topics you need to understand to continue to the next chapter. While each chapter is an important piece of the book, each chapter can also stand alone. If you have previous knowledge of Access, you can skip ahead to the chapters that contain the topics you want to learn.

The examples in this book are based on a database included with Access 97, so there is no need for an additional disk. These examples are based on the tables, queries, forms, and reports that will be familiar to most people who are creating databases for common business applications. We have included tips and hints to help you understand the different aspects of Access 97.

We hope you enjoy using the book as much as we enjoyed writing it for you. Thank you, and good luck with Access 97.

Tell Us What You Think!

As a reader, you are the most important critic and commentator of our books. We value your opinion and want to know what we're doing right, what we could do better, what areas you'd like to see us publish in, and any other words of wisdom you're willing to pass our way. You can help us make strong books that meet your needs and give you the computer guidance you require.

Do you have access to CompuServe or the World Wide Web? Then check out our CompuServe forum by typing GO SAMS at any prompt. If you prefer the World Wide Web, check out our site at http://www.mcp.com.

JUST A MINUTE

> If you have a technical question about this book, call the technical support line at (800) 571-5840, ext. 3668.

As the publishing manager of the group that created this book, I welcome your comments. You can fax, e-mail, or write me directly to let me know what you did or didn't like about this book—as well as what we can do to make our books stronger. Here's the information:

Fax: 317/581-4669

E-mail: enterprise_mgr@sams.mcp.com

Mail: Rosemarie Graham
            Sams Publishing
            201 W. 103rd Street
            Indianapolis, IN 46290

PART
I

Introduction to Access 97

Hour

Hour 1

Introduction to Access Databases

by Craig Eddy

You are about to embark on a 24-hour journey through the heart of Microsoft Access 97. When you have completed this journey you will have a firm handle on how to use Access 97 to solve your needs. Whether you're a business professional, an engineer, or simply someone who has been told to use Access 97 in your work, you'll find Access is an easy to use but full-featured database development tool.

Access can be used for everything from a simple list keeper to a full-featured accounting tool. Of course, what you can do with Access depends on what you put into the databases you develop. The purpose of this book is to provide you with the necessary knowledge and skills to effectively use Access to meet your needs.

In this first hour of your journey you'll find an introduction to just what Access 97 is and does. You'll learn about relational databases, the components that make up an Access database, and a little about the capabilities and limitations of Access 97.

 A *relational database* is a database that allows you to group its data into one or more discrete tables that can be related to one another by using fields common to each related table.

This journey is intended to give you a thorough introduction to building and using databases with Access 97. After completing the first hour of the journey, you'll have the confidence and knowledge necessary to sail through the remainder of the journey smoothly.

Access 97: A Relational Desktop Database

What is Access 97? That question can be answered in three simple words. Access 97 is a relational desktop database. This section will break those words apart and demonstrate to you how each word applies to Access 97. By the end of this short section, you'll understand why Access is a relational desktop database.

First, Access is, obviously, a database application. Databases allow you to collect any type of information for storage and later searching and retrieval. Access excels at being able to collect information through the use of either a datasheet view or a custom form. The Datasheet view, which you'll delve into in-depth in Hour 5, "Using the Datasheet View," provides a spreadsheet similar to Microsoft Excel. You can create custom forms that look like all other Windows 95 applications and use these to gather and retrieve information. You can also create custom reports for printing or exporting the information stored in the database.

Second, Access is a desktop database. This means that Access is designed to be used on a desktop computer. You can place an Access database file on a network file server and share the database with other users on your network. It is not, however, a true client/server database because the Access database is a file stored on a hard drive, not a running application.

 Client/server is a term that describes two applications, typically running on two different computers, which communicate with one another in a sort of master-slave relationship. One computer, the server, provides data and other services for multiple other computers, the clients. Microsoft SQL Server is an example of a client/server database.

The fact that Access is not a client/server database might seem like a disadvantage, but it really isn't. When Access is used in the proper environment, it has distinct advantages over client/server databases. First and foremost, it is very easy to administer. There aren't a lot of complicated settings or network and security issues to muddy the waters. You also don't need

a Pentium 200 with 64MB of RAM to run Access 97 (although it runs really well if you have such a system!). So, if you're a one-man shop or you need a database which only a few people must access at a time, Access 97 is the perfect choice because it's a desktop database.

Finally, Access is a relational database. Relational databases are one of the most versatile types of databases ever developed. In a relational database, you can define relationships between the different data tables contained in the database. These relationships can then be used to perform complex searches and to produce detailed reports.

reduce redundant

Another advantage to relational databases is that they eliminate the need to store redundant information. For example, a mail-order business may use a relational database to track their customers and orders. Because the customer data already contains a customer's address and phone number, the database does not need to repeat that information with the order data. Instead, each order is related to a customer by using a special field known as a key field. A key field is really no different from any other field in the table except that the data stored in the field can be used to look up a record in another table. For example, there may be a field named CustomerID that is found in both the order table and the customer table, as shown in Figure 1.1. This CustomerID field is the key field that defines the relationship between the two tables. Relationships are discussed in detail in Hour 16, "Planning and Designing Your Access Database."

Key field

 A *key field* is a field that can be used to look up a record in another data table. The data stored in a key field must uniquely identify a single record in order for the relationship to be valid.

Figure 1.1.
An illustration of related tables.

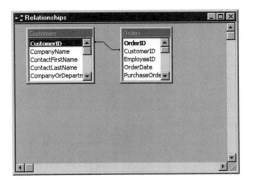

customer info in one area

As you can see, the fact that Access 97 is a relational desktop database brings with it many advantages. You have the ease of use of a desktop database and the power of a relational database all in one package.

The remainder of this hour will provide an introduction to indexes and relationships, provide an overview of the many components of an Access database, and finally discuss the capabilities and limitations of an Access database.

The How and Why of Indexes

Another feature that gives Access 97 some added horsepower is the use of a database concept known as indexing. An index, to Access, is similar to the index at the back of this book. Just like you use the book's index to quickly find a topic of interest, Access uses an index to quickly locate the record for which it is searching. A book's index decreases the amount of time it takes a reader to find the necessary information and Access's indexes decrease the time it takes Access to perform its work.

NEW TERM An *index* is an ordered list of the data contained in a field or a group of fields within a table.

Access uses indexes to assist in performing its searches or lookups. When an index is provided and you attempt to search on the field that defines the index, Access does not need to look at each record in a table. Instead, it can use the index to quickly locate the value you are searching for and then obtain the data necessary to uniquely identify the records that match the search.

Let's look at an example. The Customers table is shown in Figure 1.2. The Customers table has an index on the Company Name field. If you were searching for all the customers whose company name started with the letter L, Access would not have to look at each customer in the table. Instead, Access would move directly to the Ls in the Company Name index's ordered list. It would then see that the customers with Customer ID values 1 and 4 begin with L. These two records would then be returned as the results of your search.

Figure 1.2.

The Customers table in Datasheet view.

Customer ID	Company Name	Contact First Name	Contact Last Name	Billing
1	Let's Stop N Shop	Jaime	Yorres	87 Polk
2	Old World Delicatessen	Rene	Phillips	2743 Be
3	Rattlesnake Canyon Grocery	Paula	Wilson	2817 Mi
4	Lenny's House of Suds	Lenny	Leazer	2815 Mi
*	(AutoNumber)			

Record: ⏮ ◀ | 1 | ▶ ⏭ ▶* of 4

Granted the data shown in Figure 1.2 is not very extensive. Even a mere human can quickly locate the customers whose Company Name begins with L in this list. However, Access is quite capable of storing tens of thousands of customers. Even a computer could not examine each record quickly enough to be useful as a search engine. Indexes are the key to making searching vast amounts of data possible in a timely manner.

1

CAUTION

Too much of a good thing can be dangerous as far as indexes are concerned. You should take care not to create too many indexes on your tables because this can seriously degrade performance. You should only have indexes on fields that are most commonly queried upon.

Components of an Access Database

Because you already know that Access is a database, you know that it provides an object into which the data you want to store is placed. However, Access is more than just a database. It's also a full-featured application development environment. This section discusses the objects included in Microsoft Access that provide you with the capability of developing a complete database application.

Don't let the number of different objects available in Access 97 scare you off. Access provides wizards which are very helpful when you're creating your database's objects. You'll see wizards covered extensively throughout your journey. In fact, the Order Entry database discussed earlier was created using the Database Wizard. This wizard steps you through the entire process of creating a database and will even populate your new database with sample data. It's a great way to get started using Access 97. In Hour 14, "Creating a Database Using Wizards," you'll learn about wizards in-depth.

Tables

The most obvious component of any database is the table object. This is where the actual data being stored is kept. A table is a collection of records that can be divided into fields. Each field holds a single piece of information about the record in which it resides.

Access 97 tables can be viewed in either Datasheet view (see Figure 1.3) or Design view (see Figure 1.4). In Datasheet view you enter the data for each record in the table. In the Design view you define how the table operates.

The Datasheet view, as you can see in Figure 1.3, is similar to an Excel spreadsheet. The columns in the datasheet represent the fields in the table. There is one row for each record stored in the database. In Figure 1.3 you can see that there are four rows, just as there are four customer records currently in the database. You'll learn more about using the Datasheet View in Hour 5.

The Design view is used to set the properties for the entire table and for each individual field. These properties include the field names, the datatype used for each field, and the indexes defined for the table, among other items. In Hour 10, "Modifying an Existing Table," you'll learn more about the Table Design View window.

Figure 1.3.

*The Customers table in
Datasheet View.*

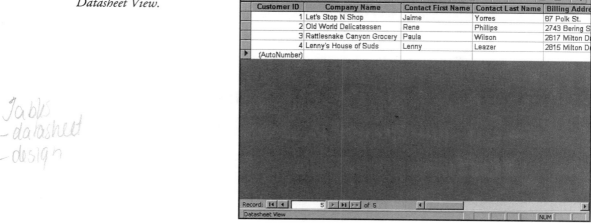

Figure 1.4.

*The Customers table in
Design View.*

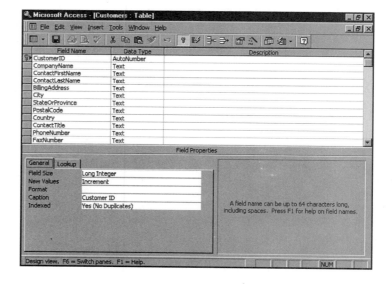

Queries

Queries in an Access 97 database are used to search, view, and modify the data that exists in
the tables. You can also use queries to modify the structure of the tables or to access data that
is external to the Access database file.

The typical query is used to return data that meets specific criteria. These queries can be viewed in Datasheet view or can be used as the source of data for forms and reports that are created in the database. In addition to providing the ability to search on specific criteria, queries can also be used to summarize and analyze data. For example, you might want to see how each employee is doing in the sales area. The Order Entry database I created with the Database Wizard has a query named Sales by Employee Subquery. This query summarizes data from the Orders and Order Details tables to produce the Datasheet view shown in Figure 1.5.

Figure 1.5.

The Datasheet view for the Sales by Employee Subquery query.

Employee ID	Order Date	Freight Charge	Sales Tax Rate	Total Sales	Total Units
Davolio, Nancy	4/9/95	$3.00	0.00%	31.6	4
Davolio, Nancy	4/18/95	$2.00	0.00%	144.65	7
Fuller, Andrew	2/18/95	$2.00	0.00%	52.3	2
Fuller, Andrew	5/1/95	$3.00	0.00%	136.65	3
Fuller, Andrew	5/11/95	$2.00	0.00%	52.3	2
Fuller, Andrew	5/21/95	$3.00	0.00%	11.3	2
Leverling, Janet	3/26/95	$2.00	0.00%	137.1	2
Leverling, Janet	6/25/95	$2.00	0.00%	42.45	3
Peacock, Margaret	2/25/95	$3.00	0.00%	11.3	2
Peacock, Margaret	4/15/95	$5.00	0.00%	13.5	2
Buchanan, Steven	2/1/95	$3.00	0.00%	5.65	1
Buchanan, Steven	2/2/95	$2.00	0.00%	231.95	15
Buchanan, Steven	3/14/95	$3.00	0.00%	87.3	6
Buchanan, Steven	4/1/95	$2.00	0.00%	32.65	3
Buchanan, Steven	6/12/95	$3.00	0.00%	51.2	2

Record: 1 of 15

Datasheet View

JUST A MINUTE

If you look at the Orders and Order Details tables in Design view you'll notice that they do not have fields for the employees' names. They do, however, make use of a feature known as Lookup Fields which allows you to define a more user-friendly means of populating the data in a field. In the Orders table, the EmployeeID field uses a Lookup to display the employee's name in a drop-down list box, as you can see in Figure 1.5. You'll learn more about Lookup Fields in Hour 17, "Creating Tables."

Like tables, queries also have a Design View window. Actually, queries have two different Design views: the Design Grid (see Figure 1.6) and the SQL View (see Figure 1.7). The Design Grid provides you with a user-friendly means of creating and modifying queries. The SQL view allows you to modify the actual code used to define the query using Structured Query Language. This is a computer language that is used when, surprise, you create database queries. You'll learn more about these views in Hour 7, "Using Existing Queries."

Figure 1.6.

A query's Design Grid View.

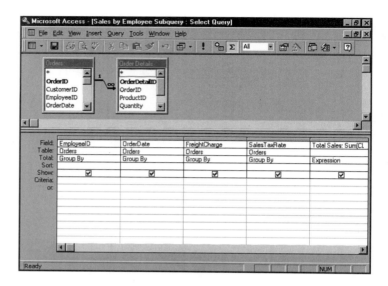

modifying queries

design SQL

Figure 1.7.

A query's SQL Grid View.

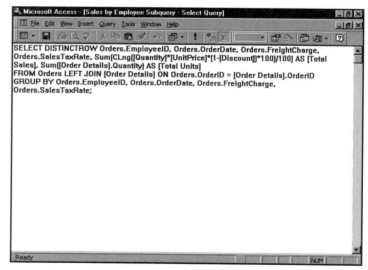

Structured Query Language

Forms

One of the most powerful features of Access 97 is the capability to create forms that can be used to enter, edit, and search your data. After a form is created, it looks and operates like a Windows 95 application. A sample form that the Order Entry database created with the Database Wizard is shown in Figure 1.8.

1

Figure 1.8.

The Order Entry database's Orders by Customer form.

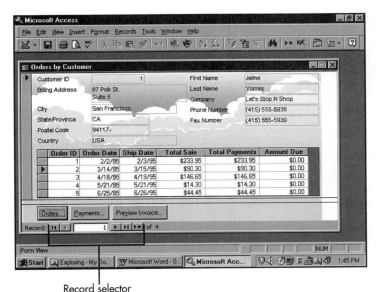

Record selector

As you can see in Figure 1.8, the form contains text boxes for data entry, labels to identify the various elements on the form, and buttons to perform other actions.

The form also has a record selector. This is the series of buttons on the bottom edge of the form. The record selector allows you to navigate among the records in the underlying data. The form in Figure 1.8 uses the Customers table as its data source. Using the record selector will move you from one customer to another and change the data on the form accordingly.

You'll learn more about forms in Hour 8, "Editing Data in Forms," and in Hour 12, "Modifying an Existing Form Design."

Reports

What good is all the data you enter into a database if you can't share it with someone else? Reports allow you to output to any number of places in an easy-to-read format. You can use reports to print to a printer or you can export the report to any number of formats. You can even publish your reports on the Internet or your company's intranet.

Reports, like forms, use an underlying data source, either a table or a query, to provide the actual data. The report's design dictates how the data will be presented when the report is printed, previewed, or exported. Figure 1.9 shows the Print Preview window for the Order Entry database's Sales by Employee report. This report combines the Sales by Employee Subquery that we looked at in the "Queries" section with the Employees table to retrieve the needed data.

Figure 1.9.

The Sales by Employee report in the Print Preview window.

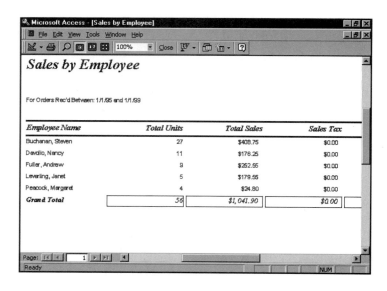

You'll learn more about reports in Hour 9, "Displaying Data in Reports," and in Hour 13, "Modifying an Existing Report."

Macros and Modules

Finally, Access databases can also have macros and modules. These help produce the action side of a database. They provide a means of acting upon and utilizing the tables, queries, forms, and reports that exist within a database.

Macros are simply a set of actions in which each action performs a specific task. You can define a macro to open a specific report in the Print Preview window, for example. So, macros are useful in automating the use of Access 97. You'll learn more about macros in Hour 21, "Creating Macros."

Modules are collections of Visual Basic for Applications (VBA) procedures. Access 97 comes with a built-in programming language essentially identical to Microsoft's popular application development tool, Visual Basic. VBA in Access 97 allows you to create your own custom functions and procedures. You can also programmatically control Access 97's underlying database engine. This allows you to work with data one record at a time and perform some operation on each record, for example.

Modules and VBA are beyond the scope of this particular book. However, if you would like more information on them, *Access 97 Unleashed*, also published by Sams, has excellent coverage on these topics.

1

The Capabilities and Limitations of Access 97

Hopefully by the time you've gotten to this point in our first hour you've come to realize that Access 97 is a powerful database development tool. However, there are some definite limitations and drawbacks to keep in mind when using Access 97. You should consider some of these points when choosing how you will deploy your database.

For example, Access 97 has no built-in backup process. Microsoft SQL Server has built-in backup capabilities and does not require all users to exit the database before the backup can proceed. Access does require the database file to be closed by all users before it can be manually backed up. If you're using mission-critical data, you might want to consider this point. Of course, there are automated backup procedures that can back up the database file as long as all users have closed their connection to the database.

Second, Access has a limit of 1.2 gigabytes of data per database. For a desktop database, that's a lot of data. For an Order Entry and Inventory database for a large corporation, that's probably not going to be enough storage space.

Third, Access 97 has a limit of 255 total users. Again, if you're in a large network environment with hundreds or even thousands of users who must have access to the data, you'll probably need to choose a different database system.

There is an excellent article on the Microsoft Developer's Network Web site which compares the capabilities and limitations of Access 97 with Microsoft's Visual FoxPro and SQL Server databases. The article can be found at http://www.microsoft.com/msdn/library/choosing.htm and is entitled "Choosing the Appropriate Database Development Tool."

Summary

This hour has provided an introduction to Access 97 and its components. By now you should be in a position to move on to the next hour, "A Quick Tour of Access 97," where you'll learn about installing and starting Access 97. If you weren't working along with the examples in this hour you might want to return here later and do so.

Workshop

The Workshop is designed to help you anticipate possible questions, review what you've learned, and begin thinking ahead to putting your knowledge into practice. The answers to the quiz are in Appendix A, "Quiz Answers."

Q&A

Q How did you create the Order Entry database?

A Run Access 97. In the initial dialog box, select the **D**atabase Wizard option button in the Create A New Database Using option group. Select the Order Entry icon in the new database dialog that appears next and follow the steps the Database Wizard provides. If you do not see the Database Wizard choice, you did not install that wizard when you installed Access 97. Refer to Hour 2 for details on doing so.

Q Do all the tables in my database need to be related in some way?

A No. You can have tables that are not related to any other table. However, you'll find that this will be a rare case because your data will almost always be inter-related in some way.

Q Does creating an index for a field require that the field contain unique values throughout all the data stored in the table?

A No. You can create indexes on fields regardless of the data that will be contained in the field. However, you can create a unique index that requires such uniqueness. This is a property of the index. A special index known as a primary key is a unique index that can be used to identify each record in a table.

Q I have a form which I would like to use to print the data for more than one record. Can this be done?

A The best way to do this is to create a report based on this form. You can do this easily by selecting the form in the database window, right-clicking the mouse, and selecting Save As Report from the shortcut menu. The form will be converted to a report that can be used like any other report.

Quiz

1. In three words, describe Access 97.
2. What is the primary purpose for using an index?
3. What is the primary purpose of a query?
4. What is the maximum size of an Access 97 database?

1

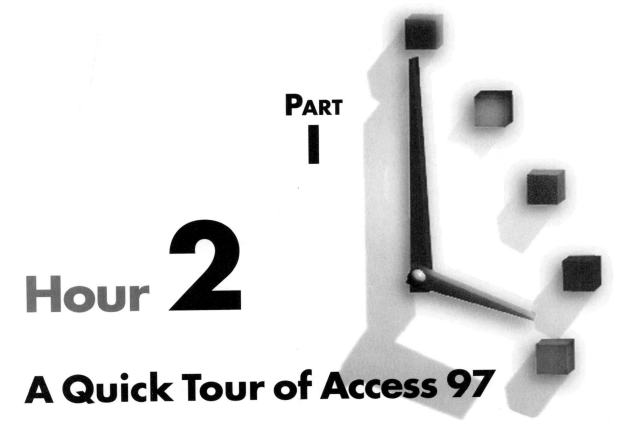

Hour 2

A Quick Tour of Access 97

by Timothy Buchanan

This hour gives you a quick tour of the various windows and dialog boxes that Access 97 uses. Even if you already are familiar with previous versions of Access, it is a good idea to take a look at the changes that Access 97 brings.

The highlights of this hour include

- ☐ How to install Access
- ☐ Different ways to start Access
- ☐ Opening databases
- ☐ Looking around the database window
- ☐ Main database objects and their relationships
- ☐ Closing, saving, and backing up a database
- ☐ Exiting Access

Before You Install Access 97

Access 97 will need to be installed on your computer before you can begin to use it. The whole process is simple, and you should be using Access 97 within 30 minutes of when you first start the installation process. The Access installation process is similar to other Windows 95 products.

JUST A MINUTE

> Although this is an easy thing to do, if you are installing Access on your company's computer, there might be some considerations you need to know about before you begin. It is a good idea to check with the department that handles your computer systems to see whether any special circumstances exist.

Software and Hardware Requirements

To run Access 97 comfortably and successfully, you need an IBM or compatible computer with a Pentium or higher processor and 12 megabytes (MB) of RAM. We recommend a Pentium or better with at least 16MB of RAM. The more RAM you have, the more applications can be run simultaneously and the better your overall performance will be. You also need between 14 and 45MB of hard drive space, depending on what you choose to install. You will also need room for all the databases you will be creating. Access 97 also requires a VGA monitor, although an SVGA monitor would be much better, and a fast video card is recommended. A mouse or other pointing device is required to do any work with Access 97, and if you want to print anything from Access, a printer or access to a printer across your network is required.

JUST A MINUTE

> Access 97 requires that Windows 95 be installed on your computer. Windows 95 does not come with Access 97; it must be purchased and installed separately.

Upgrading to Access 97 from Access 2.0 or Access 95

If you already own a copy of Microsoft Access 2.0 or Access 95, then you can purchase and install an upgrade version of Access 97. If you do not own any of the previous versions of Access, you need to purchase a regular copy of Access 97. Before you decide to upgrade any databases that were created in previous versions of Access, there are a few things you must consider. First, although you can still run a database that was created in a previous version of Access, you cannot make any changes to that database until it has been converted to Access 97. After you convert the database, it cannot be converted back to a previous version of Access. If you will be working with other people who will still be using a previous version of Access, you might want to install the older version in a separate place on your computer; that way you can work with both versions of your database.

Installing Access 97

Now you should be ready to install Access 97. If you are installing from a CD-ROM, insert the disc into your CD-ROM drive, or if you are using floppy disks, insert the disk in your drive. Now select **R**un from the Windows 95 Start menu.

1. Either type in the default setup path to run the Access 97 Setup program, which is usually D:\setup, (with D being the letter of your CD-ROM or floppy disk drive), or run Windows Explorer, select the proper drive there, and run the Setup program. Some Windows 95 programs will interfere with the installation process, so the Setup program will warn you if you have any other applications running, and ask you to shut down these applications.

2. Now click the Continue button to continue the setup process, or click E**x**it Setup to cancel the installation. You can close the other applications and run Setup again.

3. The Setup program asks you for some information. It asks for your name and company name to customize your copy of Access. The next screen gives your product I.D. number. Make sure you write down this number; you will need it if you ever need to call Microsoft for support.

4. Setup asks you where you want to install Access on your hard drive. The default will usually be C:\ACCESS or C:\MICROSOFT\ACCESS, or if you are installing Access along with Office 97, C:\Program Files\Microsoft Office\Office. If this location is acceptable, then select OK to continue. If you do not want to install Access in this location, simply type in a new drive and directory name. If you type in a name that does not exist, Setup will create it for you.

5. Setup will check to make sure you have room on your hard drive and to see whether any existing copies of Access are on your system. After that, Setup asks you to choose between three types of installations. You can choose from the following three options:

    ☐ **Typical:** Installs Access 97 with the most common options, in the directory you specified.

☐ **Co**mpact: Installs the minimum number of files needed to run Access 97. It is usually used for laptop installations and for users who have low hard drive space.

☐ **Cu**stom: Lets you choose which files you want to install. You can install other options later by rerunning Setup.

JUST A MINUTE

> To install the sample databases needed to run the examples in this book, you need to select the **C**ustom installation.

6. To install the sample databases, click the Microsoft Access check box, and make sure the Sample Databases check box is selected. If you want any other options to not be installed, deselect their check box. The check will disappear, and that option will not be installed.

7. Setup determines which disks and files it needs to copy to your hard drive, and then the installation begins.

If you are using floppy disks, you are asked to insert the required disks. If you are using the CD-ROM, the installation automatically continues. Depending on what options you have selected, the installation could take anywhere from 20 to 40 minutes. While the installation is taking place, a series of pictures and notes appears on your screen telling you various information about different features of Access 97, and how you can use them. When the installation is complete, you are returned to the Windows 95 desktop. A new program in your Start menu is named Microsoft Access.

Starting Access 97 and Opening a Database

There are several ways to start Access 97. The four easiest ways are the Windows 95 Start menu, a shortcut icon, an Access icon, and the Windows Explorer. If you have Microsoft Office, you can also start an Access database from the Office toolbar.

Windows 95 Start Menu

When you install Access 97, Windows 95 automatically adds Access to the Start menu's program selection area. The easiest way to start Access is to click the Start button, select Programs, and then select Microsoft Access. This starts Access 97 and displays the Access startup screen.

2

Access Shortcut Icon

You can set up a shortcut icon that will always be displayed on your desktop. You can either drag the Access for Windows 97 icon from the `Program Files\Microsoft Office` folder, or right-click on the desktop to set up a shortcut. Double-clicking the shortcut icon easily launches Access.

Access Icon

If you installed Access as part of Office 97, you will have a folder for MS Office located in `C:\Program Files\Microsoft Office`. Inside this folder is another folder named `Office`. The actual icon for `MSACCESS.EXE` is located in this folder, as shown in Figure 2.1. You can double-click this icon to start Access 97.

Figure 2.1.

The Access icon allows you to load Access quickly and easily.

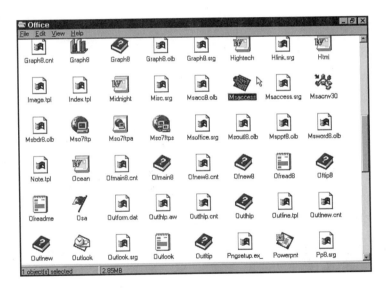

Windows Explorer

You also can select the database you want to load using Windows Explorer. Simply select the database you want to load, and double-click the filename, and Windows 95 will start Access 97 with the database you selected open. Access 97 databases usually have the `.MDB` file extension. If you already have Access running when you double-click a database file in Windows Explorer, Windows 95 will start another copy of Access 97 and open the database you selected. However, it will not let you start two copies of the same database.

Microsoft Office Toolbar

When you install Microsoft Office, an Office shortcut toolbar will automatically load whenever you start Windows 95. There are two ways to start Access 97 from this toolbar. You can either select Start a new document and choose Blank Database, or you can select Open a document and select a database you have already created.

Opening a Database from Within Access

When you load Access, the first thing Access asks you is whether you would like to open a database or create a new database, as shown in Figure 2.2. From this menu, you can select the circle next to **B**lank Database to create a new database. If you select **D**atabase Wizard, a wizard will run that asks you different questions about the database you want to create, and helps you get the basic elements created. If you select **O**pen an Existing Database, Access asks you which database you want to open. If the database you want is not shown in the list, select More Files… and Access allows you to choose which database you want to open.

JUST A MINUTE

Don't worry about that strange looking paper-clip character on the bottom of your screen. That is the new Office Assistant, and you will learn about it in Hour 3, "Getting Help with Help Systems." You can click Cancel at this screen and still open a database later.

Figure 2.2.

Access 97's opening menu.

Opening a Sample Database

The sample database we use in this book is included with Access 97, and is called Northwind. To open this database, select the **O**pen an Existing Database option, and double-click the More Files... option. The Northwind database default location when Access 97 is installed with Office 97 is `C:\Program Files\Microsoft Office\Office\Samples`. You can see this location in Figure 2.3.

Figure 2.3.

*Northwind database
Open menu.*

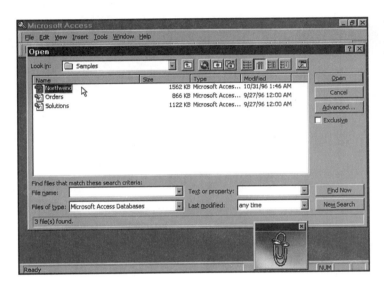

TIME SAVER

If you cannot find the Northwind database in this location, or you installed Access 97 without Office 97, you can select New Search to find Northwind. If it is not on your hard drive anywhere, you have to install Access again, and this time select the Sample Databases option under the Custom Installation option.

Clicking the Northwind database file and selecting the Open button, or just double-clicking Northwind, opens the Northwind database. The Northwind Traders opening screen loads, as shown in Figure 2.4.

This is a splash screen designed to tell you that you have opened the Northwind database and to explain a little about the database. You can either click OK to continue, or if you don't want to see this screen the next time you open the Northwind database, select the check box next to Don't show this screen again, and click OK.

Figure 2.4.
*Northwind Traders
database splash screen.*

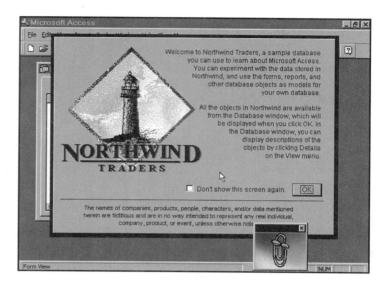

The Access Window

The screen you see in Figure 2.5 is an example of the Access window. This is the Northwind database with the database window maximized. The Access window is the center of all activity regarding your database and consists of several items.

Figure 2.5.
The Access window.

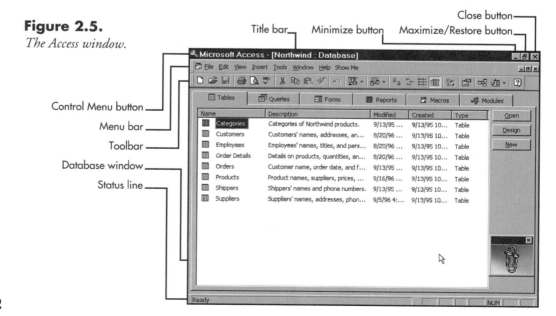

Title Bar

The database window always displays the name of the currently open database in the title bar.

Control Menu Button

The Control Menu button is located in the upper-left corner of the application window, and has a picture of a key on it. When you click this button once, a menu appears that allows you to perform certain tasks, such as restore, move, size, minimize, maximize, and close Access. When you double-click the Control Menu button, Access closes automatically.

Minimize and Maximize Buttons

The minimize button is located in the upper-right corner of the screen, and has a picture of a line on it. When you click this button, your application is still running, but it is minimized. You can reactivate it by selecting it from the taskbar. The maximize/restore button can be used to maximize your application if it is only taking up part of the screen, or it will restore the screen to its previous size if it is already maximized.

Close Button

The button in the upper-right with the X on it is the close button. This will close Access when clicked.

Menu Bar

The menu bar contains all the various menu choices. When you click one choice, a menu drops down with more choices. The choices will depend on what you are doing in Access at that time.

Toolbar

The toolbar is located directly below the menu bar, and is a group of picture buttons that provide shortcuts to many of the menu bar commands. Depending on where you are in Access and what you are doing, the pictures will vary. The toolbar can be resized and moved to different places on the screen. By selecting **View** | **T**oolbars, you can show, hide, select new, or customize other toolbars, and pick between large and small icons.

Database Window

The database window has three main parts. There are six object tabs along the top in a horizontal row, three command buttons along the right side, and a list of objects. The object tabs allow you to select the type of object you want to work with. The Tables tab is the default selection, and you see the different tables that the Northwind database uses. The command buttons are used to place the database object in a different view. You can open, design, or create a new object with these buttons. The list of objects displays a list of all the existing objects of that type in the current database. To display or design an object, you select the name of the object from that list.

JUST A MINUTE

> You also can change the way you view the objects in the list by selecting **V**iew from the database window menu bar. The four choices are Large Icons, Small Icons, List, and Details.

Status Line

The status line is located at the bottom of the screen. The left side is reserved for displaying information helpful to whatever you are doing at the time. The right side displays the status of various keyboard settings, such as Caps Lock and Num Lock.

The Six Main Access Database Objects

To understand how to use Access, you must first understand a few basic database concepts. A database is a collection of information regarding a certain topic. A database will help you organize this information in a logical manner for easy understanding. The database in Access is a term for the container that holds all the data and its associated objects. The six main objects in Access include tables, queries, forms, reports, macros, and modules. While some other computer database programs may call the database the object that actually holds the data, Access calls this object a table.

Access can only work with one database at a time, but in that database can be hundreds of objects, such as tables, queries, and forms. They all are stored in one Access file. The heart of the Access database is the table.

2

Tables

A table is used to hold the raw data of the database. You enter data into tables in logical groupings of similar data. Then the table organizes this data into rows and columns. The table list is the default view when you open a database in Access.

like excel

Queries

A query is used to extract only certain information from a database. A query can select groups of records that fulfill certain conditions. Forms can use queries so that only certain information will appear on the screen. Reports can use queries to only print certain records. Queries can be based on tables or on other queries. Queries can be used to select, change, add, or delete records in your database. A list of the queries in the Northwind database is shown in Figure 2.6.

exact

Figure 2.6.

Northwind database query list.

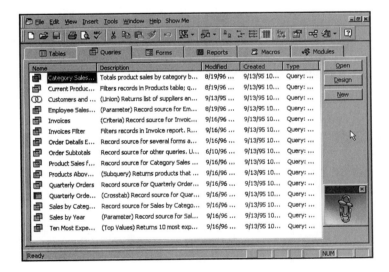

Forms

Forms can be used in a variety of ways, but the most common ways are as data entry and for display. Data entry forms are used to help users enter data into tables quickly, accurately, and easily. Forms display data in a more structured way than a normal table does. You can change, add, delete, or view records from a table using a form. Display forms are used for the selective display of certain information from a given table. A list of the forms in the Northwind database is shown in Figure 2.7.

Figure 2.7.
Northwind database forms list.

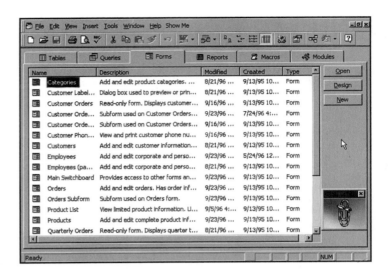

Reports

Reports present the data you select in a printed format. Reports can be based on tables to show all the data from the given table, or they can be based on queries to only show information that meets certain criteria. The reports can also be based on multiple tables and queries to show complex relationships that exist in your data. Access has many default reports that you can easily create to display your data in any way you might require. A list of the reports in the Northwind database is shown in Figure 2.8.

printed format

Figure 2.8.
Northwind database reports list.

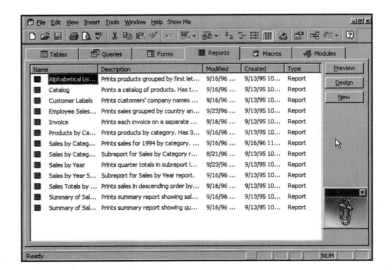

Macros

Macros help automate repetitive tasks without having to write complex code or learn a programming language. You will be introduced to macros in Hour 21, "Creating Macros."

Modules

Modules are user-written functions using Visual Basic for Applications. This book does not cover modules. A good source to learn about modules is *Access 97 Unleashed* by Sams Publishing.

Relationships

There are a few things you have to think about before you design your first database. One very important tool is relationships. This can be a tricky topic, but it is important to the overall design and function of your database. I will go into more detail later, but for now here are a few items to think about. Tables should be related to each other so that information in one table can be accessible to other tables. Most of the time, you will have several tables related to one another. These tables are related by having certain fields in each table that share common values. The field names do not have to be the same, but the values have to match. Using good table and relationship design helps prevent you from storing the same data in two different places. Not only is that a time-saver, but it helps keep your data accurate as well. This may seem complicated right now, but keep it in mind as you continue throughout the book.

table.
relates
values must match.

Saving, Backing Up Databases, and Exiting Access

When you are done working on your database, there are several ways to quit Access. You can choose Exit from the File menu, click the Close button at the top right of the title bar, or double-click the command button. Just make sure you never just turn off your computer. You will corrupt your database, and you might lose data. If you want to turn off your computer when you are done with Access, you must first exit Access, select Start, and then Shutdown to avoid a loss of data. It is always a good idea to back up your database often. If you keep a copy of important databases in two different locations, the chance of a complete loss of information is greatly reduced. You will also want to back up the Northwind database before you begin to work with it. To back up this database, you need to run Windows Explorer. In Explorer, select the Northwind files, as shown in Figure 2.9. Click on the database file you want to back up, and drag it to the directory in which you want to save the database files. It is also a good idea to back up very important databases on a floppy disk, or onto your network hard drive, if you have access to one. Keep a copy on floppy disk at a different location than your PC in case of fire or other damage.

Figure 2.9.

The Northwind database Access files in the Windows Explorer.

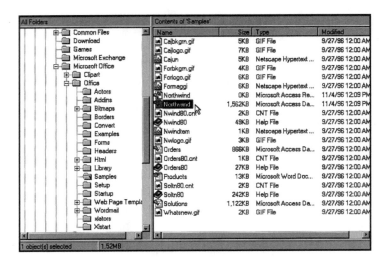

CAUTION

Remember to always exit Access properly, or you run the risk of losing data!

Summary

This hour provided a quick tour of what Access 97 has to offer. The various windows and dialog boxes that Access 97 uses were sampled, as well as a few topics you should think about before designing your first database. You should now know how to install Access, open a database, close a database, and exit Access. Keep in mind that Access 97 has many more things to offer.

Workshop

The Workshop is designed to help you anticipate possible questions, review what you've learned, and begin thinking ahead to putting your knowledge into practice. The answers to the quiz are in Appendix A, "Quiz Answers."

Q&A

Q Why are tables so important to Access?

A They not only hold the raw data that all objects use, they also use relationships to maintain data integrity and accuracy.

Q Why do I need to exit Access before I shut off my computer?

A Access has many different internal files open when Access is running, and if you shut off the computer before saving and exiting Access properly, these files are left open, and database corruption and data loss can result.

Q Can I run Access 95 and Access 97 at the same time?

A You can have both versions on your computer at one time, but databases created in Access 97 cannot be used in any previous versions of Access. Also, any databases created in earlier versions of Access can only be viewed as read-only in Access 97 until you convert them.

Quiz

1. How much hard drive space do you need to install Access 97?

2. What are the six main database objects used in Access 97?

3. How do you save your database in Access 97?

Hour 3

Getting Help with Help Systems

by Timothy Buchanan

In this hour, I explain how to find topic information using the online help systems. After you complete this hour, you will be able to find help and more information on any Access 97 topic. Topics for this hour include the following:

☐ Using the Office Assistant
☐ Getting help using the standard Help menus
☐ Browsing Help using Contents and Index
☐ Using the specialized help system in the Northwind database

Examining Ways to Get Help

Now that you know the basics of starting Access, you probably need some help learning more about the program. Online help systems provide a reference tool and information about various Access tasks. The questions you might have can be answered in many ways, and several online functions are available to help you:

- ☐ Office Assistant
- ☐ Standard Windows Help menus
- ☐ Screen tips
- ☐ Solutions database

JUST A MINUTE

Hour 2, "A Quick Tour of Access 97," explained how to start Access and open the Northwind sample database. To open the Northwind database, start Access, select the Open an Existing Database option, and double-click the More Files option. The Northwind database default location when Access 97 is installed with Office 97 is `C:\Program Files \Microsoft Office\Office\Samples`. It may be in a different location on your PC.

TIME SAVER

One good shortcut involves the right mouse button. Although previous versions of Access made little use of the right mouse button, Access 97 uses it for many different options. Right-clicking different parts of the database gives you several shortcut options for that part of the database. Experiment with the parts of the database to see what shortcuts you can use.

Using the Office Assistant

One of the first things you notice when starting Access 97 is a new, curious-looking paper clip at the bottom right-hand corner of the screen. This is the *Office Assistant*—a new feature in all the applications in the Office 97 suite. After you click the Office Assistant, press F1, or select Help | Microsoft Access, a menu is displayed by the Office Assistant listing several options, as shown in Figure 3.1. Your list may look slightly different, depending on your setup. You can also use the hot key F1 by itself to open the Office Assistant.

3

Figure 3.1.

Using the Office Assistant menu.

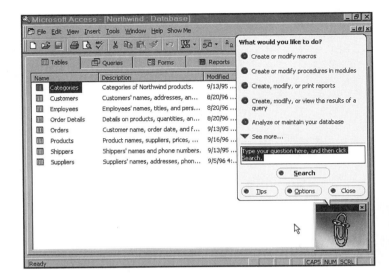

JUST A MINUTE

The screen shots in this book may look different from the screen on your PC. Different resolution settings, colors, and choice of Office Assistant can make the screen shots different from what you are viewing on your own PC. Don't worry about the differences; just concentrate on the information we discuss.

Under the heading "What would you like to do?," a few context-sensitive help topics are listed that are relevant to what you currently are doing in Access. Here, you have the option to see more context-sensitive help by choosing the See More option. Below this option is a text box with room for you to type a request or help question. If you need help but are not exactly sure which help topic you should select, this is a good place to start. You can type a question using plain English, without relying on technical language. Or, you can just type one or two words related to the help topic for which you are searching, as shown in Figure 3.2. After you finish typing, click the **S**earch button. You then see help topics that are related to the question you typed.

The next button on the Office Assistant menu is **T**ips. After you click this button, Access displays the Tip of the Day, as shown in Figure 3.3. These tips give you special advice and tricks you can use with Access 97. You can click the **B**ack button in the tip box to browse through previous Tips of the Day.

Figure 3.2.

Searching for a help topic.

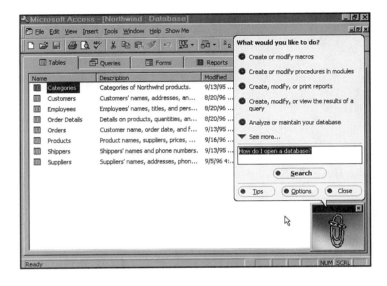

Figure 3.3.

Viewing the Tip of the Day.

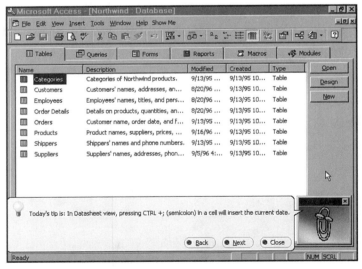

You can click the **O**ptions button to change the capabilities and functions of the Office Assistant. You click Close to close the Office Assistant menu, but the Office Assistant window stays open. You can close this window by clicking the X icon in the upper-right corner if it is in the way, and you can reopen it by pressing F1 or choosing **H**elp | Microsoft Access **H**elp.

3

JUST A MINUTE

The default Office Assistant is Mr. Paper Clip, but you can change your Office Assistant by right-clicking him or by clicking him and clicking **O**ptions. You can choose from an Albert Einstein assistant, a bouncing rubber ball, a two-dimensional cat, or William Shakespeare! They all work the same, so play around with them and see the different animations they each provide.

Using the Help Topics Dialog Box

In addition to the Office Assistant, the standard Windows 95 help systems are available. You can choose **Help** | **Contents** and Index to display Access's Help Topics dialog box, as shown in Figure 3.4.

Figure 3.4.

The Help Topics dialog box with the Contents tab selected.

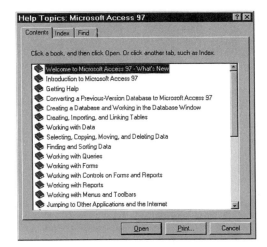

The Help Topics dialog box shows you a few ways to get started with Access 97. This dialog box offers three options:

☐ **Contents:** Displays the default view in the table of contents, as shown in Figure 3.4. After you click a topic, a menu of subtopics appears.

☐ **Index:** Displays an alphabetical listing of the help topics available to you. You can scroll through the list or type the first few letters of the topic on which you want to get help.

☐ **Find:** Gives you a much more detailed listing of help topics than the index. You start by entering a single keyword. A list of potential topics appears. You can select one of these potential topics to see a list of related help topics.

TIME SAVER

If you have used a previous version of Access, you might want to use the default Help menu, which provides information on the new features of Access 97. This information is listed under the What's New topic.

The Contents Tab

The list of help topics under the Contents tab is very general. Book icons designate general topics. Double-click a book icon to display more specific topics. You can double-click an open topic to close it. Double-clicking the general topics leads you to specific help topics, which are indicated by open-book icons and page icons, as shown in Figure 3.5.

Figure 3.5.

Viewing specific topics indicated by the book and page icons.

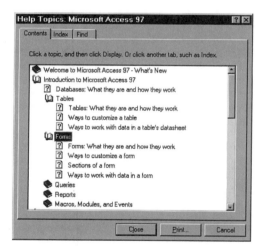

The Index Tab

You can click the Index tab to search for help alphabetically. Type the first few letters of the help topic for which you are searching, and the menu jumps to the topics that start with those letters, as shown in Figure 3.6. Double-click a topic, or select the topic and click the **D**isplay button, to view the help topic.

When a help topic is displayed, some words appear green and underlined, as shown in Figure 3.7. After you click these words, which are called *hyperlinks*, a help screen appears with more information on that specific word or topic. This temporary screen disappears after you click the underlined word again. When viewing these help topics, you can click the **B**ack button to return to the previous help topic. You can click Help **T**opics to return to the main Help menu.

3

Figure 3.6.

Using a shortcut to search for help.

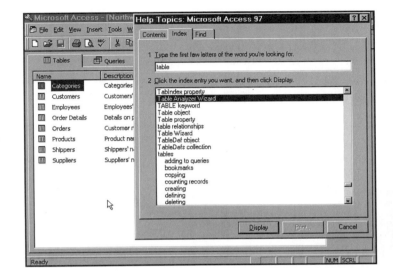

Figure 3.7.

Using hyperlinks to get more information on a topic.

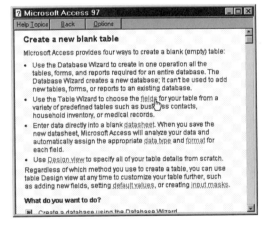

The Find Tab

You can use the Find tab in the Help Topics window to locate more detailed help topics. After you select the Find tab, you can type the topic for which you want more information. After you press Enter, a list of potential topics related to what you typed in the box appears. You can select any of these topics to see a list of related help topics.

Tool Tips

You can get help on using the toolbar tools by viewing tool tips. When you move the mouse pointer to one of the toolbar tools and leave the mouse pointer on the tool for a moment, Access displays the name of the selected tool in a small box next to the pointer. This is a *tool tip*, as shown in Figure 3.8.

Figure 3.8.

Placing your cursor over an icon to preview the action that the icon performs.

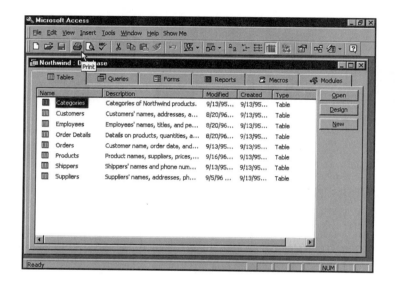

Screen Tips

Screen tips are similar to tool tips but usually provide more information than tool tips. *Screen tips* give you a short explanation about the various parts of Access. They consist of text only, displayed in a rectangle. Screen tips provide a paragraph about the topic, whereas tool tips consist only of a word or two. You use screen tips by clicking the Help icon on the toolbar or choosing **Help** | What's **This**. You then click the area of the screen that you want information on, and Access displays a screen tip consisting of a paragraph of text about the item you selected, as shown in Figure 3.9.

Time Saver

> You also can press Shift+F1 to access screen tips related to the part of the screen where your cursor is located.

3

Figure 3.9.

Using screen tips to learn about the Tables tab.

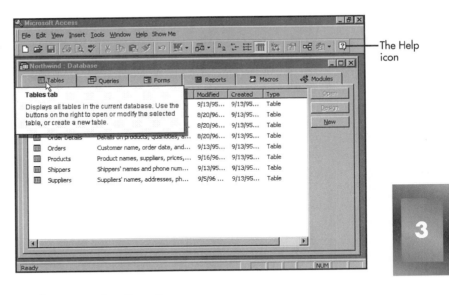

The Help icon

The Microsoft on the Web Option

You might have noticed an option on your **H**elp menu called Microsoft on the **W**eb. If you have Internet access, you can select one of the options from the submenu shown in Figure 3.10. Access will log onto the Internet and take you to the Web page with help related to the topic you selected.

Figure 3.10.

Using the Help menu to access the Internet and view help related to a specific topic.

Using the Solutions Database

The Northwind database is installed by default in C:\Program Files\Microsoft Office\Office \Samples. It may be in a different location on your PC. The Samples directory has three databases:

- ☐ NWIND.MDB: Northwind sample file used in Access documentation
- ☐ ORDERS.MDB: Sample order entry system also used in the Access documentation
- ☐ SOLUTIONS.MDB: A teaching database

The first screen you see when you open the Solutions database is shown in Figure 3.11. After you open the Solutions database, a Help menu is displayed. Global topics appear at the top, and related subtopics follow. After you select a global topic, subtopics are displayed that are related to that topic. After you double-click a subtopic, an example from the Northwind database appears with a small help screen. This feature enables you to see examples of complicated topics, and you can use it to solve a particular problem you might have in Access.

Figure 3.11.

Getting information on various topics.

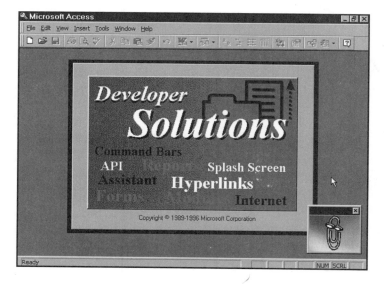

JUST A MINUTE

There is one more new item in Access 97 that you can use to get help. In the three sample databases, Northwind, Order, and Solutions, an additional menu selection appears on either the toolbar, the menu bar or within the Help menu. It's called Show Me. You can use the Show Me option to find out what is going on behind the scenes in many of the sample tasks. This help option is available only in the sample databases, but is a feature you can add to more advanced databases you may write.

3

Summary

In this hour, I explained how to find topic information using the online help systems. There are many different ways to get help using Access 97. The most popular and easiest ways to get help are covered in this hour.

Workshop

The Workshop is designed to help you anticipate possible questions, review what you've learned, and begin thinking ahead to putting your knowledge into practice. The answers to the quiz are in Appendix A, "Quiz Answers."

Q&A

Q What other Office Assistants are available for use?

A Access 97 gives you nine different Office Assistants: Clippit, The Dot, The Genius, Hoverbot, Office Logo, Mother Nature, Power Pup, Scribble, and Will. They all perform exactly the same, but each provides a way to make your desktop unique.

Q What kind of help is available on the Microsoft Web pages?

A All kinds of help and news on Microsoft products are available on the Microsoft Web pages (http://www.microsoft.com). Tips, free software downloads, and more information is available.

Quiz

1. Where can you get help on the Internet?
2. How do you access help?
3. Can you browse for help?
4. What is the Tip of the Day?

PART

II

Editing Data in an Existing Database

Hour

Hour 4

Understanding Someone Else's Database

by Timothy Buchanan

This hour helps you learn to quickly understand the basic design of a database that someone else has developed and to make changes to that database as necessary. You learn about the following topics in this hour:

- ☐ Examining startup options
- ☐ Reviewing security levels
- ☐ Understanding existing relationships
- ☐ Establishing referential integrity
- ☐ Using encryption
- ☐ Using the Database Documenter

JUST A MINUTE

> Several concepts covered in this hour are too complicated to be discussed completely within the scope of this book. I will cover the basic topics related to adapting an existing database.

Viewing the Splash Screen

You might have noticed when loading the Northwind database that a splash screen appears first when you load the database. This screen simply tells you a little about the database, but this feature also can be used as a security measure. Some databases use the Autoexec option or the Startup macro to display the splash screen in order to prevent you from accessing other parts of the database. You can skip this opening screen by pressing Shift while the database is loading. This prevents the Autoexec macro from executing.

JUST A MINUTE

> A macro is an Access database object that allows several menu item actions to take place at once. The Startup macro executes automatically when the database is opened, usually running a splash screen and opening forms. You'll learn about these and other types of macros in Hour 21, "Creating Macros."

Looking at the Types of Security

Two general types of database security are available in Access 97. The first and simplest is *password security*. Databases that have this type of security display a Password Required dialog box when you try to load the database, as shown in Figure 4.1.

Figure 4.1.

Entering your password so that you can load the database.

If you do not enter the correct password, you cannot open the database. If you type the correct password, you are allowed to open the database, and you also are granted rights to view and edit all objects in the database.

CAUTION

If the database you tried to load displays a Password Required dialog box when you open it and you do not have the password, you must get the correct password from the database designer before you can log on. You will not be able to open the database until you get the password.

The second type of security is *user-level security,* and it is more flexible and extensive than just setting a password. This form of security is similar to a network system's security. Users have to enter a user ID and password when they open these databases. These users will have been defined as members of a group in the workgroup information file. Each group is given permissions that regulate what it is allowed to do with each object in the database. See Hour 23, "Database Administration," for more on permissions.

JUST A MINUTE

It can be difficult to access all parts of a database if user-level security has been used with the database you are trying to change. The easiest thing to do is to contact the original database designer and have him remove the security. If you cannot do that, there is a way to remove user-level security, but it is beyond the scope of this book. You can find more information about this by searching for the help topic "Removing User-Level Security."

4

Working with Encrypted Databases

Encrypted databases are another potential problem when working with someone else's database. Encrypted databases have been compacted and made indecipherable to a word processor or utility program. Access can still open encrypted databases. To decrypt a database, you first must exit the database but remain in Access 97. Choose **T**ools | **S**ecurity | **E**ncrypt/Decrypt Database. Then, specify the database you want to decrypt and click OK. Next, specify the name, drive, and folder you want for the decrypted database, and then click OK.

CAUTION

Encrypting a database does not restrict access to any of the database objects. You must implement user-level security in order to restrict access.

Examining Relationships

After you can open and change the objects of the database, the next topic you need to consider is the relationships between the objects in the database. As you might remember from Hour 2, "A Quick Tour of Access 97," *relationships* are the way objects are linked together to ensure data integrity. To view the relationships of objects, you can open the Relationships window. Make sure that the database is loaded and that the Database window is active. Press the F11 key if you do not know whether the Database window is active. Click the Relationships button on the toolbar or choose **T**ools | **R**elationships from the menu. If any relationships exist in this database, the Relationships window is displayed. If no relationships are defined, the Add Table/Queries dialog box appears. Figure 4.2 shows the Relationships window for the Northwind database.

Figure 4.2.

Viewing the Northwind database Relationships window.

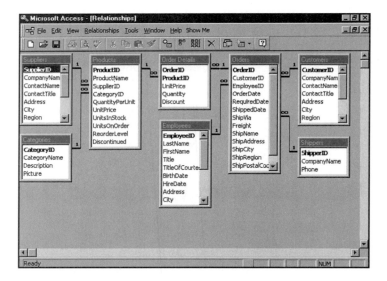

You can use the Relationships window to see which tables and fields are related to one another. You can use this information to build a blueprint of how the database is designed. The different symbols represent the types of relationships that exist between the database objects. The 1 symbols represent one-to-one relationships, and the infinity symbols represent one-to-many relationships.

There are many reasons why relationships are so important to the overall design of a database. Relationships between objects are used to maintain referential integrity. *Referential integrity* refers to a system of rules that Access 97 uses to ensure that relationships between records in related objects remain valid and that related data is not accidentally changed or deleted. A well-designed database uses referential integrity to insure data validity.

4

You must have enough disk space for both the original database and the decrypted database. For example, if the database is 5MB, you need at least 10MB of hard drive space or you get an error.

Using the Database Documenter

The Database Documenter is a tool that first was included with Access 95. You can use it to easily explore the database design and objects. You can view the table design for a table in your database by choosing **T**ools | Anal**y**ze | Documenter, as shown in Figure 4.3. You can also print the table design after viewing it.

Figure 4.3.
*Viewing Northwind's
table design in the
Database Documenter.*

After you open the Database Documenter, a form appears in which you can choose which database objects you want to analyze. You can select the All Object Types tab to display a list of all the object types in the database. You also can select different options for printing. You can click the **O**ptions button to access additional options that enable you to select the information to print about your database. You can print all the field names, their properties, and their indexes. After you select the information you want to display, Access displays this information in a report. You then can simply view this information or print it.

*object
types*

You can use the Database Documenter to create a table of all the database objects and properties you specify. Choose **F**ile | Save **A**s Table, as shown in Figure 4.4. You then can use this table to document all the tables, queries, forms, and other objects to tell you more about the database with which you are working.

Figure 4.4.

Choosing File | Save As
Table to create a table of
database objects and
properties.

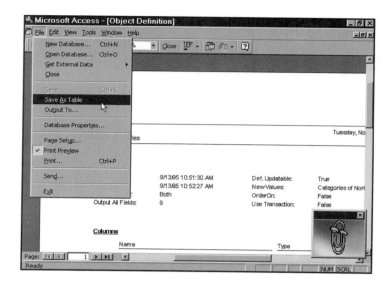

Summary

This hour discussed ways to quickly learn and understand the basic design of a database that someone else has developed and to make changes to that database as necessary. Security and encryption of databases were also covered.

Workshop

The Workshop is designed to help you anticipate possible questions, review what you've learned, and begin thinking ahead to putting your knowledge into practice. The answers to the quiz are in Appendix A, "Quiz Answers."

Q&A

Q What can you do with a Startup macro?

A You can use the Startup macro to open any database object such as forms, reports, queries, or tables. Any action performed by the menu can be performed in a macro.

Q Why should you use relationships?

A Relationships are the main feature that a database program has to offer. Relationships ensure that your data is valid and that there is no unnecessary duplication of data.

4

Quiz

1. How do you skip the startup screen when a database loads?
2. How can you look at the relationships in a database?
3. Can you save the results of a database documentation?

Hour 5

Using the Datasheet View

by Craig Eddy

Access 97 provides a variety of ways to view and work with the data stored in its tables. There are forms, datasheet views, print preview windows, and printed reports. This hour provides an introduction to the datasheet views, which you'll probably use more often than any other window in Access 97. The introduction provided here is by no means a thorough discourse on datasheet views. It is, however, a base to build future hours upon.

An Overview of the Datasheet Windows

Datasheet views are very similar to Excel spreadsheets. An example is shown in Figure 5.1. As you can see, data is displayed in a row and column format. Each row represents a single record in the table or query results. Each column represents a field in the table or returned by the query. Tables, queries, and forms all have datasheet views available.

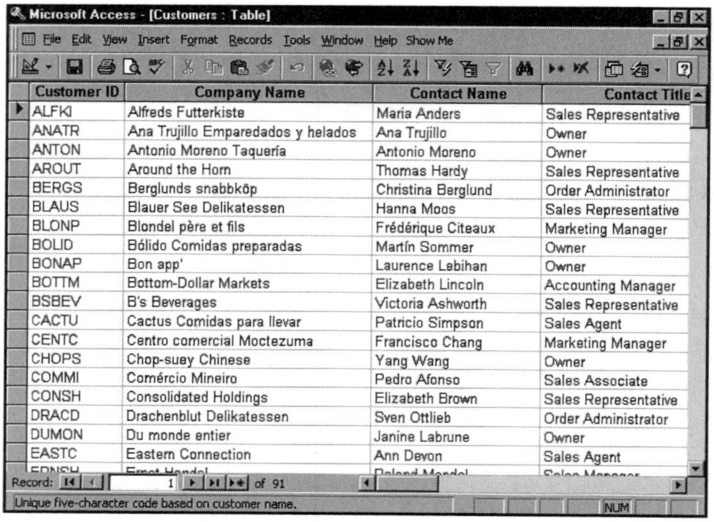

Figure 5.1.

A typical datasheet window.

You can use the row and column headings for various editing functions or to sort and filter the information. You can also format the way the data is displayed within the datasheet, as well as print or export that data.

JUST A MINUTE

Certain form properties will prevent a form from displaying in datasheet view (for example, forms with their Modal property set to Yes cannot be viewed in datasheet view).

The remainder of this hour will cover the basics of working with the datasheet views. If you want to work along with the text, open the Northwind sample database that you installed with Access 97.

5

Toolbars Used

In Access 97, as well as most other Office 97 products, you'll make heavy use of the toolbars. These are the rows of buttons just below the application's main menu. They provide a way to use common features with a single click of the mouse. This section will provide you with an introduction to the more useful toolbar buttons present while a datasheet view is active. The remainder of this hour discusses each of these toolbar buttons and how they operate.

The datasheet toolbar is shown in Figure 5.2. Table 5.1 follows with a brief explanation of each button. This hour we'll only be concerned with the buttons specific to datasheets, so our discussion will start with the Sort Ascending button.

Figure 5.2.

The datasheet view toolbar.

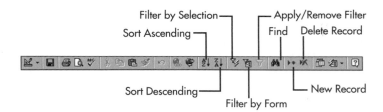

Table 5.1. The toolbar buttons of the datasheet views.

Button		Description
![Sort Ascending icon]	Sort Ascending	Sorts the datasheet's records from first to last using the selected or current column to sort on.
![Sort Descending icon]	Sort Descending	Sorts the datasheet's records from last to first using the selected or current column to sort on.
![Filter by Selection icon]	Filter by Selection	Filters the datasheet so that only records having the same value in the selected field will remain in the datasheet. If only a portion of the field's value is selected then any records that have the same matching portion will remain.
![Filter by Form icon]	Filter by Form	Filters the datasheet based on data you enter into a form which is opened when you click this button. This allows you to filter on more than one field at a time.

continues

Table 5.1. continued

Button		Description
	Apply/Remove Filter	If a filter is not active, applies the last defined filter. If a filter is active, removes the filter and returns the datasheet to its original contents.
	Find	Searches the currently selected column for a value which you specify. The matching records are found one at a time.
	New Record	If the datasheet is updatable, allows you to enter a new record into the database.
	Delete Record	If the datasheet is updatable, allows you to delete the currently selected record or records.

record it a time (handwritten margin note)

Sorting the Datasheet

One of the most useful features of a database application is its capability to sort data. Access 97, likewise, has a powerful sorting tool you can use with the click of a button.

The records displayed in the datasheet window can be sorted on one or more columns merely by clicking the appropriate toolbar button. You can sort the data in either ascending (first to last) or descending (last to first) order. To sort on more than one column, the columns must be adjacent to one another in the datasheet window. Access will sort the records starting with the leftmost column.

You can sort any type of data except fields that have data types of Memo, Hyperlink, and OLE Object. The Memo and OLE Object data types do not lend themselves to efficient sorting and the Hyperlink data is really not in a format that can be sorted. Hyperlink fields contain addresses of objects stored in a variety of places and in a variety of formats.

There are two toolbar buttons that are used in sorting: the Sort Ascending button and the Sort Descending button. If the column on which you want to search has the focus (that is, has the cursor in it), you can click these buttons to sort the data. You can also use the **R**ecords | **S**ort flyout menu and select either Sort **A**scending or Sort Des**c**ending.

If you want to sort on multiple adjacent columns, simply select the columns by Shift+clicking in the column header for each column and then click the appropriate sort toolbar button or use the appropriate menu item.

not memo hyperlink ole (handwritten margin note)

shift+click ole (handwritten margin note)

To return the datasheet's data back to its original sort order, use the **R**ecords | **R**emove Filter/ Sort menu item.

To try out some sorting, open the Northwind sample database that you should have installed when you installed Access 97. Open the Customers table in datasheet view by selecting the Customer table on the Tables tab of the database window and clicking the **O**pen button. Let's first sort on the Contact Name field. Select the column by clicking on the words Contact Name in the column header. Now either click the Sort Ascending toolbar button or click the right mouse button and select Sort **A**scending in the shortcut menu. The data is now sorted by the Contact Name field. Return the datasheet to its default sort order by using the **R**ecords | **R**emove Filter/Sort menu item. The data is now back to the way it was before you sorted it.

Finding and Filtering Records

Another feature that makes databases useful tools is the capability to find and to filter data. Being able to find and to filter means that you can locate and work with the specific information that you're interested in at a particular time. The difference between finding and filtering in a datasheet view is that when you perform a find, you'll locate a single record at a time. Enacting a filter, however, will find multiple records by narrowing down the data displayed in the datasheet to the records that match your filter specifications.

First let's look at how the find feature works. Open the Northwind database's Customers table again. Click in the first record's Contact Title column. Click the Find button on the toolbar. The Find in Field dialog appears, displaying the field name in its title bar. (See Figure 5.3.)

click on then column, then find

Figure 5.3.

The Find in Field dialog box.

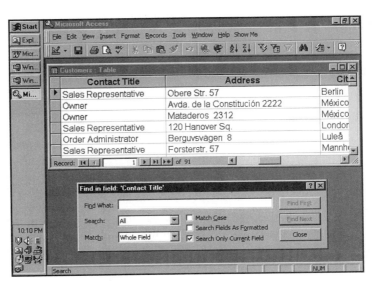

Enter Owner in the Find What text box and click the Find First button. The first record with Owner in the Contact Title field is selected. Click Find Next to locate the next record with Owner in the Contact Title. Keep going until you've located all of them (not really, but I'm trying to make a point here, as you'll see in the next paragraph).

As you can see, finding records is a bit tedious. And you really can't do a whole lot with the records you do find because they're being located one at a time and as soon as you move to the next record, you've lost touch with the previous record you found. Here's where filters come to the rescue: Filters will weed out any records that do not match your criteria. The datasheet will be populated with only the records matching the filter. Let's try it.

If the Find in Field dialog is still open, close it. Click in the Contact Title column for one of the records which has Owner in this column. Click the Filter by Selection toolbar button. Now the datasheet should appear as in Figure 5.4. Only the records whose Contact Title equals Owner are left in the datasheet. You can now print this datasheet or export the data to some other file. A little more useful than Find, don't you think?

Figure 5.4.

The Customers table filtered by Contact Title equals Owner.

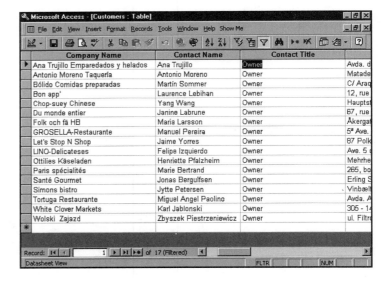

Click the Remove Filter button to return the datasheet to its original contents. Now, click it again to see that the previous filter's criteria is still active.

Now let's look at the Filter by Form feature. This allows you to filter across multiple fields at once. Click the Filter by Form button. The window changes to a single row grid with Customers: Filter by Form in the title bar. Notice that in the Contact Title the Owner criteria is already present. Scroll over to the Country field using the horizontal scrollbar at the bottom of this window. The drop-down list boxes are populated with the current data from all

5

customers in the database. So, if you open the drop-down list box in the Country field, you'll see that it's filled with all the different countries represented by the customers in the database. Select USA in the drop-down list for Country. Click the Apply Filter toolbar button (it's the same button as on the normal datasheet toolbar, just in a different location). Now the datasheet contains only two records, both of which have Owner in the Contact Title and USA in the Country.

Working with Records in the Datasheet

Now that you have the data in which you are interested displayed in the datasheet, it's time to do some work with that data. This section discusses how you edit the data in a datasheet.

Most of the editing discussed in this section requires that the datasheet in question be updatable, that is, that you are allowed to update the records. Some queries that you can execute in Access 97 produce a resulting set of data which cannot be updated. Unfortunately, Access does not provide any visual cues that a datasheet is not updatable. If you try to type in one of the fields you'll hear a beep and the status bar at the bottom of the Access window will display the following message: This Recordset is not updatable.

Adding, Editing, and Deleting Records

To add records to an updatable datasheet, click the New Record toolbar button. The cursor is moved to a blank row at the bottom of the datasheet. You should now enter the data for this record. Moving to a different row or closing the datasheet window will cause Access to save your new row. You can also use the **R**ecords | Save Rec**o**rd menu item.

To edit data in a datasheet, simply select the record and field you want to edit by clicking in its row and column. Make your desired changes and either move to a different row or use the **R**ecords | Save Rec**o**rd menu item to save the changes. If you have violated a rule imposed by the database's design, Access will display a message informing you of the problem. You must either correct the data problem or cancel the edits you've made by pressing the Esc key.

To delete a record from the datasheet, click in the row for that record and click the Delete Record toolbar button. You can also use the **E**dit | Delete **R**ecord menu item or select the row (by clicking in its row header in the far left column), right-clicking the mouse and selecting Delete **R**ecord from the shortcut menu. Again, if there is a database rule that requires this record to be in the database you will receive a message from Access informing you of this fact.

Copying, Cutting, and Moving Records

In some instances you might want to copy an entire record and modify only a few of the fields. First, select the record to be copied by either clicking in the record's row header or by using

5

the **Edit** | Select Record menu item. Then either use the **Edit** | **Copy** menu item or right-click the mouse and select **Copy** from the shortcut menu. The record has now been copied to the Windows 95 Clipboard. To add the new copy to the current datasheet, use the **Edit** | **Paste Append** menu item. To add the copy to a different datasheet (but with the same fields as the current datasheet), open that datasheet and use the **Edit** | **Paste Append** menu item.

To copy a record to the Clipboard and delete it from the current datasheet, use the **Edit** | **Cut** menu item or right-click the mouse and select **Cut** from the shortcut menu. The record has now been deleted and copied to the Windows 95 Clipboard. You can now use the **Edit** | **Paste Append** menu item in another datasheet to move that record to the other datasheet. Again, the fields must be identical between the two datasheets.

Data Entry Shortcuts

Table 5.2 shows a few of the available shortcut keys you can use when editing data in the datasheet.

Table 5.2. Data entry shortcut keys.

Action	Keystroke
Insert the current date	Ctrl+semicolon (;)
Insert the current time	Ctrl+colon (:)
Insert the default value	Ctrl+Alt+spacebar
Insert the value from the same field in the previous record	Ctrl+apostrophe (')
Add a new record	Ctrl+plus sign (+)
Delete the current record	Ctrl+minus sign (–)
Save changes	Shift+Enter
Toggle between values in a check box or option button	spacebar
Insert a new record	Ctrl+Enter

Formatting the Datasheet

Not only is the datasheet a handy way to view your data, it can also be a well-formatted way to do so. Access 97 has many features that allow you to adjust the look and feel of the datasheet window. This section will touch upon a few of these features.

Changing Cell Formatting and Fonts

By changing the cell formatting you can change elements such as the background color and how the cells are displayed graphically. To access these elements, use the Format | Cells menu item. The Cells Effects dialog shown in Figure 5.5 appears.

Figure 5.5.

The Cells Effects dialog.

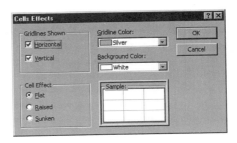

On this dialog you can choose whether or not to display the horizontal and vertical gridlines, what color to use for the gridlines and the cell background, and whether to make the cells appear flat, raised, or sunken. The Sample frame of this dialog shows how the datasheet will look if you click the OK button.

You can also change the font used for all text displayed in the datasheet. Use the Format | Font menu item to access the Font dialog shown in Figure 5.6.

Here again there is a Sample frame that displays the results of your font changes.

Figure 5.6.

The Font dialog.

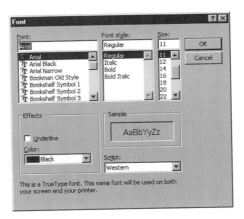

Changing Column Width and Row Height

You can also change the width of individual columns and the height of all rows in the datasheet. Doing so involves moving the cursor to the line in the column or row headers that separates the columns and rows. Doing so causes the cursor to change from a pointer to a sizing cursor. For the column header, this cursor is a vertical line with arrows pointing left and right. For the row header, this cursor is a horizontal line with arrows pointing up and down. You can drag this cursor in the desired direction to either expand or contract the row or column sizing.

In addition to this method, you can also double-click the mouse when the sizing cursor is active. This will cause the row or column to be sized to fit the data currently displayed in the datasheet. Also, you can use the **Format** | **C**olumn Width and **Format** | **R**ow Height menu items to display dialog boxes.

JUST A MINUTE

Access will print the datasheet using the column widths and row heights the same size as they are on the datasheet window.

To move a column to a different place in the datasheet, simply click the column header, hold the mouse button down, and drag the column to its new location.

Printing the Datasheet

Now that you've seen a basic introduction to using the datasheet views, it's time to learn how to print the data. Printing in Access 97 is about the easiest operation you'll perform (next to closing a window, which we'll touch on in the next section), so this won't take long.

After you have your datasheet loaded with the data you'd like to print, use the **File** | Page Set**up** menu item to set the output page's margins, paper orientation, and paper size.

Next, use the **File** | Print Preview menu item to display the output in the print preview window. This gives you a chance to see just how the printout will look and to make any adjustments if necessary. You can click the Print toolbar button if everything is in order and the datasheet will be output to your default printer.

To print using a dialog to choose the printer, select the print range, and set the number of copies to be printed, use the **File** | **P**rint menu item. The Print dialog box appears where you can set these properties to meet your current needs.

Closing the Datasheet

When you've finished working with the datasheet, you need to close the window. Click the close button in the upper-right corner of the window. You can also use the **File | Close** menu item.

If you have modified any of the formatting for the datasheet, such as the column widths, font, and so on, Access will prompt you asking whether you want to save these format changes. If you select **Yes**, then the next time you open that datasheet it will look just like it does now. If you don't care to save the formatting changes you've made, select **No**.

Summary

This hour has introduced you to the basics of working with the datasheet views. It's a pretty important topic because throughout the rest of this venture in learning Access 97 you'll be using datasheets quite a few times.

The next hour teaches you how to work with existing tables in a database. Here you'll rely heavily on datasheets to get through the hour. If you need to, review the material in this hour and perhaps work through the examples with a different datasheet than the one I used.

Workshop

This section contains a question-and-answer section as well as a quiz to test your knowledge of queries. The quiz answers are contained in Appendix A, "Quiz Answers."

5

Q&A

Q **What causes Access to display a message box about not being able to delete a record when I attempt to do so?**

A Because Access is a relational database, it is possible to relate rows in one table to rows in another table. This relationship is usually based on a key field in common between the tables. In order to maintain your data's integrity, it is necessary to maintain this related data throughout the database. Otherwise, you will produce orphan records which are records in one table that point to a record in another table that no longer exists.

Q **Can I change the font of an individual cell in the datasheet?**

A No. Font changes apply to the entire datasheet.

Quiz

1. Which is more useful when you want to print a specific set of records in a datasheet: Find or Filter?

2. Can you sort the datasheet based on more than one column?

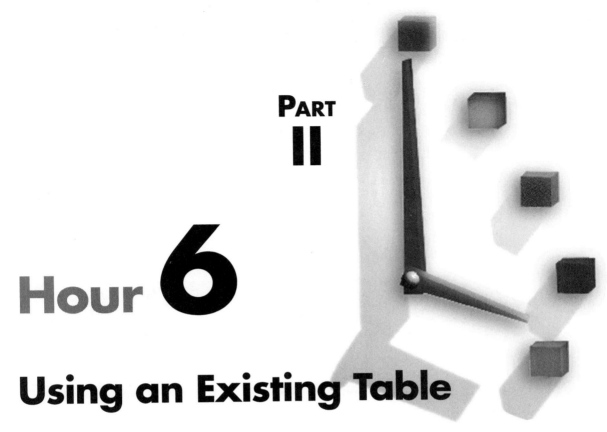

Hour 6

Using an Existing Table

by Craig Eddy

Tables are the basic building blocks of any database. Tables serve as the repository where information such as names, addresses, product cost, and so on is actually stored. A database without some sort of table does not really serve much of a purpose.

tables

I've found that the best way to learn how to design and implement databases is to examine existing databases. This is even more helpful when the database being examined performs a function similar to your current needs.

As you saw in the last hour, you can use the Datasheet view to view and edit the data held in a table. In this hour, you'll learn the basics of working with tables that already exist in a database, and you'll learn the basics of a table's structure. The highlights of this hour include the following:

- ☐ Opening tables
- ☐ Using the Design and Datasheet views
- ☐ Looking at the basic structure of tables

Opening Tables

When working with an existing database, the place to start is usually with the tables in the database. Tables contain the data being stored in the database. Access uses a *relational database model*—the database can contain more than one table, and the tables in the database can be related to one another.

To open an existing table, activate the Access 97 Database window. Then select the Tables tab. The List view on the Tables tab displays the names of all the existing tables in the open database. Figure 6.1 shows the Tables tab for the Northwind sample database that ships with Access 97.

Figure 6.1.

The Tables tab of the Database window.

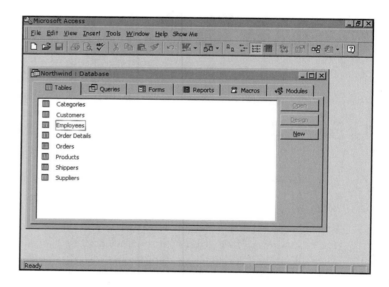

Click the name of the table you want to work with. After you select a table, you can perform many different actions on it. You can use the buttons on the Tables tab to open the table in Datasheet view or Design view. To open the table in Datasheet view, click the **O**pen button. For Design view, click the **D**esign button.

You can right-click a table name to see a larger list of available activities useful for existing tables. Right-clicking causes a pop-up menu to appear. In addition to **O**pen and **D**esign, which perform the same functions as the buttons on the Tables tab, this menu contains items such as the following:

☐ **Print and Print Preview:** Enable you to print the data in the table.

☐ **Cut and Copy:** Enable you to use the Windows Clipboard to cut and paste or copy and paste an entire table—data and all. You can paste a copied or cut table into the currently open database or into a completely different database.

☐ **Save As/Export:** Enables you to perform essentially the same function as Copy and Paste.

☐ **Create Shortcut:** Enables you to create a Windows 95 shortcut to the selected table. You can place the shortcut on your desktop or in any location you specify.

☐ **Delete:** Enables you, surprisingly, to delete the table, as well as any data it contains. Access warns you if the table is involved in any relationships with other tables. You then can instruct Access to remove these relationships and delete the table.

☐ **Rename:** Enables you to rename the table. You also can rename a table by clicking its name after selecting it.

☐ **Properties:** Displays the properties of the current table. You also can view the table properties by choosing **V**iew | **D**etails. Figure 6.2 shows the Details view for the Tables tab.

Figure 6.2.

Using the Tables tab in Details view.

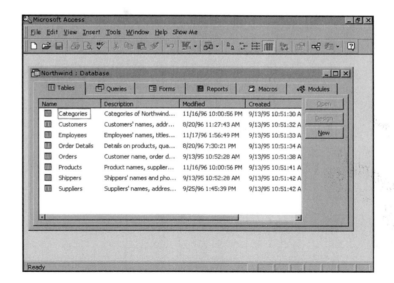

You also can perform all these functions by using Access 97's main menu. You can create a Windows 95 shortcut by choosing **E**dit | Create **S**hortcut, for example.

Using the Design and Datasheet Views

In this section, you'll see how easy it is to view the design and data of existing tables. Make sure that you have the Northwind database open so that you can follow along with the text. Also, activate the Database window by clicking its title bar or choosing **W**indow | **1** Northwind: Database.

In this section, you'll examine the Employees table, so click Employees in the Table list.

Design View

After you select the Employees table, right-click and choose **D**esign or simply click the **D**esign button. This opens the Design view for the Employees table, as shown in Figure 6.3.

Figure 6.3.

Looking at the Employees table in Design view.

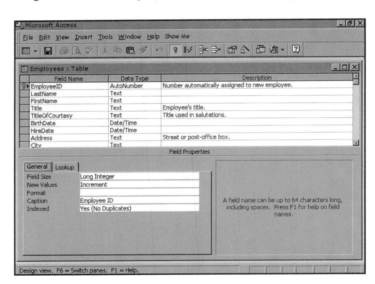

You can use Design view to examine the structure of the table—the fields contained in the table, as well as the data types and properties of those fields. This topic is examined further in "Examining the Basic Structure of Tables," later in this hour.

Design view is set up in a form/subform arrangement. The grid at the top of the Design View window lists all the fields in the table, their data types, and an optional description for the field. The tabs at the bottom of the form display other properties for the field that is selected in the grid.

6

To view the details of another field, simply click anywhere in the grid row on which it appears. The information displayed in the tabs changes to match the properties for the newly selected field. The leftmost column of the grid at the top of the Design View window displays an arrow on the row of the currently selected field.

If the leftmost column of the grid displays a key icon, that field is being used in the primary key for the table. The relational database model requires that every table have a field or fields that can be used to uniquely identify each record stored in the table. This field, or set of fields, is known as the *primary key* for the table.

The tabs at the bottom are divided into General and Lookup. The General tab contains miscellaneous properties for a field. The Lookup tab is used to determine whether the field is related to another table in the database. If it is, the information on the Lookup tab describes how the field's data is entered whenever the field is displayed on a form or in Datasheet view. Select the TitleOfCourtesy and ReportsTo fields and click the Lookup tab to see how this process works.

When you click anywhere in the Design View window, the text at the bottom right of the window changes to describe the currently selected item. Click in the Description column, for example, and the text changes to describe how the Description column is used. For additional information about any item, you can press F1 for context-sensitive help.

You'll visit the table Design View window in more depth in Hour 10, "Modifying an Existing Table."

Datasheet View

Next, you'll look at the Datasheet view. Datasheet views were covered in depth in Hour 5, but I'll review the specifics of the table Datasheet view here.

If you've been following along through this hour and still are looking at the Employees table in Design view, simply choose **View | Datasheet View** to open the Datasheet view. Otherwise, activate the Database window, select the Tables tab, and click Employees in the List view. Then click the **O**pen button. You also can double-click the table name and open the table in Datasheet view. Figure 6.4 shows the Datasheet view for the Employees table.

Datasheet view displays the data, using a grid or spreadsheet format. The columns represent the fields in the table. The rows are the data records stored in the table. In the Employees table, each row represents an employee.

Figure 6.4.

Looking at the Employees table in Datasheet view.

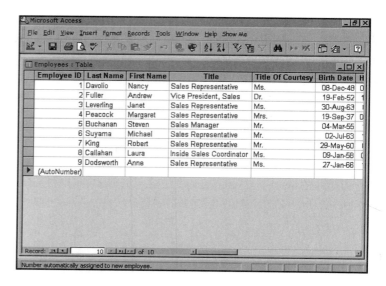

To move around the datasheet, you can use the mouse or the keyboard. Using the mouse, you can click in any cell in the datasheet. Using the keyboard, you can press Tab and Shift+Tab to move from field to field. When you reach the last field in the current row and press Tab again, you are taken to the first field of the next record. The same applies to the first field; if you press Shift+Tab when the cursor is in the first field, you move to the last field of the preceding record. You also can use the arrow keys to move up and down in a column; this moves you from record to record within the same field.

To add text to a highlighted field, press F2. Alternatively, you can click on the field you want to edit. To highlight the entire contents of the field, press F2 again. Pressing F2 toggles between Edit and Highlight mode.

CAUTION

If you do not press F2 or you don't click in the field before typing, you will replace the previous data in the field. To undo this, press the Esc key.

To select an entire record, click the leftmost column of that record's row (the column with the arrow that signifies the current row). You then can cut, copy, or delete an entire record of data.

To add a new employee to the table, click in the last row of the datasheet and enter the appropriate data. You also can append a new row by copying a row and choosing **E**dit | Paste Append.

You should look at a few special fields in the Employees table. First, click in the Title Of Courtesy column. Notice that the edit box changes to a drop-down list box. Click the button with the down arrow to display the available titles in the drop-down list. Click one of the titles, and the field's value changes to the value you selected. Likewise, the Reports To column displays a drop-down list. The names in this list are actually the names contained in the Employees table. You can see how this is set up by returning to Design view (choose **View | Design View**), selecting the ReportsTo field, and clicking on the Lookup tab at the bottom of the Design View window.

Another special field is the Photo field. Notice that for every record in the table, the value is Bitmap Image. This signifies that an image object is being stored in the field. Access 97 can store binary data and OLE objects in fields in the database. To view the image while in Datasheet view, double-click the cell for the employee whose photo you want to view. Microsoft Paint (or possibly another application that has been installed to handle bitmap files) opens, and the photo is displayed.

Examining the Basic Structure of Tables

In this section, you'll learn all about how a table is constructed. As I said earlier, the best way to learn about database design is by studying existing databases. Here, you'll examine the design of the Employees table in more detail.

If you've been following along with the text, you'll be looking at the Employees table in Datasheet view. If so, choose **View | Design** View to return to Design view. If you haven't been following along, open the Employees table in Design view by activating the Database window, clicking the Tables tab, selecting the Employees table, and clicking the **Design** button.

Field Names

The Field Name column specifies a name for the field (surprised?). The name can be practically anything you want it to be, but you can't use the same name twice in the same table. The field name is set in the leftmost column of text in the grid at the top of the Design View window. In the Employees table, some of the field names are EmployeeID, LastName, FirstName, HireDate, and ReportsTo.

Field names must follow certain rules. They can contain up to 64 characters and can include any combination of letters, numbers, spaces, and special characters except periods, exclamation marks, accent graves, or square brackets. Field names cannot start with spaces or control characters (ASCII values 0 to 31).

6

JUST A MINUTE

Although spaces may appear in a field's name, it's not advisable to use them. Doing so necessitates the use of square brackets ([]) around the field's name whenever the field is referred to in a query or another expression. Instead of spaces, most database designers use mixed case, as in the LastName and HireDate fields in the Employees table.

Data Types

The Data Type column, which is next to the Field Name column, specifies the type of information stored in the field. The edit box for this column is a drop-down list box. The list contains all the available data types, as well as a Lookup Wizard entry. The available data types include the following:

- **Text:** A string of characters used to store alphanumeric data.
- **Memo:** Stores long text fields. No maximum is specified by the user, but Access imposes a limit of 64,000 characters. The Notes field is a Memo field.
- **Number:** Stores numeric data.
- **Date/Time:** Stores dates and times. HireDate and BirthDate are Date/Time fields.
- **Currency:** A special numeric data type used for monetary values because it prevents round-off errors during calculations.
- **AutoNumber:** A special numeric data type that can be used for primary key fields. Fields of this data type always are read-only, because Access automatically inserts the next number in the sequence or a random number when a data record is created. The EmployeeID field is an AutoNumber field.
- **Yes/No:** Stores Boolean data, which can contain only one of two values, such as On/Off, Yes/No, or True/False.

- **OLE Object:** A special type of object or component provided by a Windows OLE server. The Photo field is an OLE Object type.
- **Hyperlink:** Stores the text for a hyperlink address. Access enables you to store addresses to Web documents, network files, and local files. The hyperlink also can contain more detailed information, such as a bookmark in a Word document, an object in an Access database, or a range of cells in an Excel spreadsheet. After a Hyperlink field is clicked, Access attempts to load the referenced file or document using the appropriate viewer.

As you can see, there's a data type for just about every occasion. By examining the Employees table, you can get a good feel for which data types are appropriate for your needs.

6

The *Lookup Wizard* is a wizard that guides you through the steps necessary to populate the Lookup tab. You will never see a field with the data type set to Lookup Wizard, even if the wizard was used to help populate a field's Lookup tab properties.

describes

Description

The Description column is where a short description about the field can be entered. The description should provide future viewers of a table's design (such as yourself) with a complete explanation of the purpose the field serves.

If the field is added to an Access form, Access uses the text in the Description column as the text displayed in the form's status bar area.

Properties

Each field in a table has its own set of properties that further define the field and how it's used in the database. Although an exhaustive look at the different properties is not necessary at this time (field properties are covered in more detail in Hours 10 and 17), a brief look at a few important properties is in order.

The available properties change, depending on which data type is chosen for a field. To verify this, make sure that the General tab is active and select fields with different data types in the grid at the top of the Design View window. You'll see the Properties list at the bottom of the window change.

Now take a look at some of the more useful properties.

Field Size

The `Field Size` property is available for the `Text` and `Number` data types. For `Text` fields, the property specifies the maximum number of characters that can be stored in the field for a single record. Access 97 uses only enough disk space to store the data actually entered in the field—not the amount of space required to hold the number of characters specified by the `Field Size` property. For `Number` fields, `Field Size` specifies the type of number that will be stored in the field. The available choices are Byte (a number from 0 to 255, whole numbers only), Integer (–32,768 to 32,767, whole numbers only), Long Integer (–2,147,483,648 to 2,147,483,647, whole numbers only), Single (can store a very large number and fractional numbers), Double (stores numbers larger than Single), and Replication ID. The choice made in this case does affect the amount of disk space Access uses to store the field, so `Field Size` should be appropriate to the data being stored. The most common choices you'll see are Integer, Long Integer, and Double. Long Integer fields can store numbers larger than Integer. Double fields can store data with numbers to the right of the decimal point.

Caption

The Caption property specifies a string to be displayed as the column heading whenever the field is displayed in Datasheet view. Also, if the field is added to a form, this value is used as the caption for the label that is added along with the field. In the Employees table, the Caption property is used to put spaces in field names that use mixed case, such as LastName and FirstName.

Default Value

The Default Value property specifies a value that will be inserted into the field if one is not specified when a record is added to the table. None of the fields in the Employees table specifies a value for the Default property.

Validation Rule **and** Validation Text

The Validation Rule property specifies a test to be performed on any data entered into the field. If the data does not pass the rule, a message box appears that displays the text specified in the Validation Text property.

In the Employees table, the BirthDate field specifies a Validation Rule property of <Date(). This forces any dates entered into this field to be less than the current date.

Required

The Required property specifies whether the field is required to have a value entered in it. If this property is set to Yes and you attempt to change the field to be empty, Access displays a message informing you that a value is required in the field. The LastName and FirstName fields are both required in the Employees table.

Summary

In this hour, you took a somewhat detailed look at the Employees table. You saw how to view and modify data in the table, as well as how to determine the structure of the table. Some of the concepts learned here will be greatly expanded on in upcoming hours. For now, make sure that you understand how to work with the Design view to access the properties of the fields. Also, make sure that you know how to add and edit data in the Datasheet view. You will use both these skills heavily during the remainder of this book.

In the next hour, you'll learn how to work with existing database query definitions. They're essentially dynamically created tables and, like tables, they have both a Design view and a Datasheet view.

Workshop

The Workshop is designed to help you anticipate possible questions, review what you've learned, and begin thinking ahead to putting your knowledge into practice. The answers to the quiz are in Appendix A, "Quiz Answers."

Q&A

Q Why is the column heading in Datasheet view different from the field name shown in the Design view for a table?

A Every field, regardless of data type, has a `Label` property. You use this property to specify the default caption for the field. This caption is used in the Datasheet view. It also is the default caption for the label that is placed on a form when the field is added to the form.

Q When I add a new employee, I get a message informing me that the `FirstName` field cannot contain a `Null` value. Why is this happening?

A Most fields have a property called `Required`. If this property is set to `Yes`, you must enter a value for every record stored in the database. If the data is really not required, you can set this property to `No`.

Q When I attempt to delete an employee, I get a message informing me that the record cannot be deleted. Why is this happening?

A Remember that Access 97 uses a relational database model. This means that you can relate a record in one table to a record or records in another table. After you create such a relationship, the information pertaining to the relationship must be kept intact. In the Northwind database, for example, you can create an Orders record that has an Employee record related to it—the employee who took the order, perhaps. If you then deleted that Employee record, you'd leave a hole in the Orders table. Access 97 enforces this data integrity by disallowing deletions in this instance. As you'll see in Hour 10, however, Access 97 can instead be instructed to delete any records related to the record you're attempting to delete.

Quiz

1. How can you determine which fields make up the primary key for a table?
2. Which field property allows you to control what data can be entered into a field?
3. Can a field name contain spaces?

6

Hour 7

Using Existing Queries

by Craig Eddy

In the preceding hour, you learned how to work with existing tables in a database. In this hour, you'll learn how to use existing queries. A query in Access 97 produces results similar to a table, in that you can view data that has been stored in the database. Unlike a table, though, queries can display data that is stored in multiple places in the current database or even outside the current database. With a query, you can specify which fields from different tables are displayed. More important, you can control what data is displayed by specifying the criteria that individual data records must match in order to be included in the query's result set.

NEW TERM A *query* is an object in an Access database that returns records from or performs actions on one or more tables in the database.

The highlights of this hour follow:

☐ Opening queries

☐ Using Datasheet view

- ☐ Using Design view
- ☐ Looking at the basic structure of queries
- ☐ Using toolbars

Opening Queries

Opening an existing query is similar to opening an existing table. The first step is to open the database in question and move to the Database window's Queries tab. Figure 7.1 shows the Queries tab for the Northwind sample database.

Figure 7.1.

The Queries tab for the Northwind database.

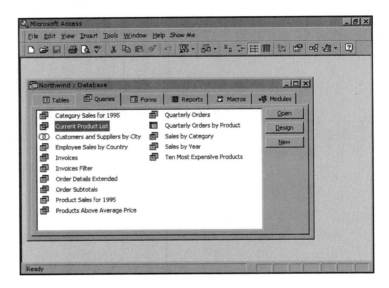

In Figure 7.1, you see several types of queries that are in the database. The types are denoted by different icons next to the query name in the list. To help decipher which icon goes with which query, you can switch the Queries tab view to Details view by choosing **View** | **D**etails. The Queries tab now appears as shown in Figure 7.2. The Details view works like the files pane in Windows Explorer. You can size the columns by moving the pointer between the column headers and, when the pointer changes to the sizer cursor, clicking and dragging the pointer to size the column. You can also sort the list using a column by simply clicking the column heading.

To see each query's type, use the horizontal scrollbar at the bottom of the list, and move the elevator box all the way to the right. The Type column is the last column that appears in Details view, as you can see in Figure 7.3.

Figure 7.2.
The Queries tab in Details view.

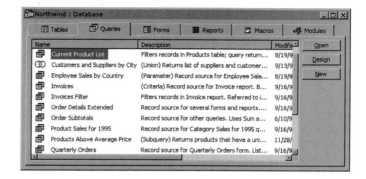

Figure 7.3.
Viewing the Type column.

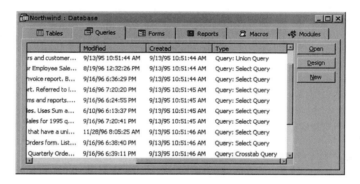

Although most of the types of queries available are beyond the scope of this hour, you will learn about the more common types:

☐ **Select queries:** These are the most common queries. By using a simple select query, you can retrieve data from many tables based on criteria specified in the query's definition. The Category Sales for 1995 query is an example of a simple select query.

☐ **Crosstab queries:** These queries are a special type of select query and are similar to pivot tables used in Microsoft Excel. You can view data summarized over different categories. For example, the Quarterly Orders by Product query in the Northwind database provides a quarterly summary of product sales for each product in the database. This query provides the sales in each quarter for each product.

> **NEW TERM** A *crosstab query* has row headings as well as column headings. Crosstab queries typically summarize data that is grouped by a specific category or date range.

☐ **Top *n* queries:** These are another type of special select query. Top *n* queries are designed to return only a certain number of the top records. The 10 Most Expensive Products query returns the names and unit prices of the 10 most expensive

(1) Union Query
corresponding
fields from
multiple tables
into single field

products in the database, for example. By reversing the sort order of the query, you also can view the 10 least expensive products. You'll learn more about Top *n* queries in Hour 11, "Modifying and Using Existing Queries."

☐ **Union queries:** These queries combine corresponding fields from multiple tables into a single field returned by the query. The same number of fields must be returned from each table involved in the union. You might create a union query to return the CompanyName fields from both the Customers and Suppliers table in the Northwind database, for example.

JUST A MINUTE

Notice in Figure 7.2 that the Description column for some of the queries in the Northwind database starts with a short description of the type of query in parentheses. This is not a requirement, and it is not automatically placed there by Access. The designer of these queries thought it would be a good idea to help better explain each query's purpose. This is a practice I highly recommend.

Like the Tables tab discussed in Hour 6, "Using an Existing Table," the Queries tab offers an Open button and a Design button. Clicking Open opens the selected query in Datasheet view. Clicking Design opens the query in Design view.

A shortcut menu appears after you select a query and right-click it. This menu contains the options Open and Design, which perform the same functions as the buttons; it also contains the other options listed in Table 7.1.

Table 7.1. Options on the Query shortcut menu.

Option	Function
Open	Opens the selected query in Datasheet view.
Design	Opens the query in Design view.
Print	Prints the data returned by the query.
Print Preview	Displays the query results in the Print Preview window. The contents of this Preview window are identical to what will appear in an actual printout.
Cut	Cuts the query's definition and pastes it to the Windows Clipboard. You can then paste the query into the currently open database or into a completely different database.
Copy	Copies the query's definition and pastes it to the Windows Clipboard. You can then paste the query into the currently open database or into a completely different database.

7

Option	Function
Save As/Export	Performs essentially the same function as Copy and Paste, but also allows you to export the query's results to an external file. You can save the query results in any number of formats, providing you installed the export file format when you installed Access 97. The more popular formats are text files or Excel files.
Create Shortcut	Creates a Windows 95 shortcut to the selected query. You can place the shortcut on your desktop or in any location you specify when you create the shortcut.
Delete	Deletes the query.
Rename	Renames the query. You also can rename a query by clicking its name once after you select it.
Properties	Displays the properties of the current query. You also can view some of the query properties by choosing **View**	**Details**.

You also can perform all these functions by using Access 97's main menu. You can delete a query by selecting a query on the Queries tab and then choosing **Edit** | **Delete**, for example.

The following two sections discuss how to use a query after you open it—whether in Datasheet view or Design view.

Using Queries in Datasheet View

Opening a query in Datasheet view produces a display very similar to that produced when you open a table in Datasheet view. To open a query in Datasheet view, select the query on the Queries tab and then click Open. Figure 7.4 shows the datasheet for the Category Sales for 1995 query.

Figure 7.4.

The Datasheet view of the Category Sales for 1995 query.

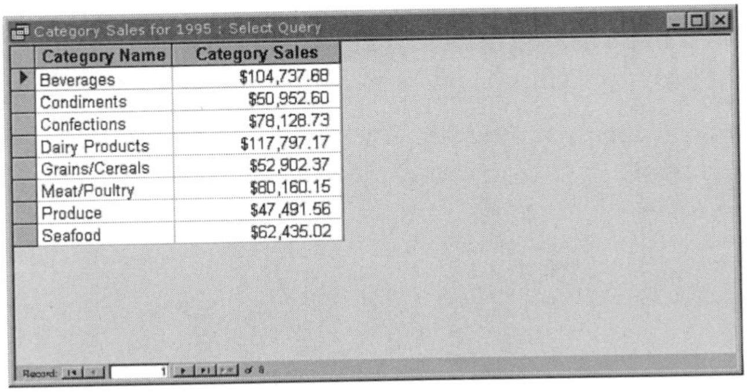

Category Name	Category Sales
Beverages	$104,737.68
Condiments	$50,952.60
Confections	$78,128.73
Dairy Products	$117,797.17
Grains/Cereals	$52,902.37
Meat/Poultry	$80,160.15
Produce	$47,491.56
Seafood	$62,435.02

As you can see, the datasheet has columns representing the fields in the query and rows representing the records returned by the query. The unique aspect of this query is that the Category Sales column is not a field in the database. Instead, the query has created a sum of all the sales for each product category. This sum is displayed in the Category Sales column. That's the power of queries: You can select specific records and perform summations (totals, averages, minimums, maximums, and so on) on the data in those records.

Because of the nature of the data returned in this query, you cannot perform any updates, inserts, or deletions on the rows in the datasheet. After all, this data is merely a summary of a lot of underlying data from other tables in the database. If you modify the Category Sales column, what underlying data should be modified—the product sale on January 12 or the one on March 7? Because Access can't determine the answer to that question, it doesn't enable you to update the data in this type of query.

If you open the Products Above Average Price query shown in Figure 7.5, however, you can modify the data in either column. That's because this is a simple select query with no summations in the returned data columns. It doesn't show all the products—only the ones that have an above-average price. You then can modify the data of some of the products to bring them in line with the average-priced products.

Figure 7.5.

The Datasheet view of the Products Above Average Price query.

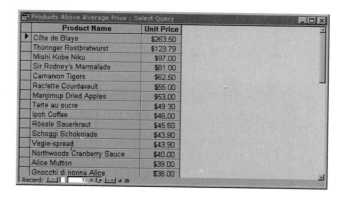

You can use the **Records | Sort** fly-out menu to sort the records in the datasheet. To see the lowest-priced products first, for example, choose **Records | Sort | Sort Ascending**.

You also can create a filter to apply to the query's data. Choose **Records | Filter** to create a filter. The current query doesn't have much to filter on, however.

Using Queries in Design View

Queries, like tables, also have a Design View window. This is where you can view how the query is defined, as well as the properties of the columns returned by the query. Queries actually have two design views: the Design Grid (labeled as Design View on the menus and toolbar), which allows you to use *Query by Example* (QBE), and the SQL View. In this section, you'll learn how to open a query in Design View and how to work with queries in the Design Grid and in SQL View.

NEW TERM *SQL* is an acronym for Structured Query Language, which is used to define a query with words. Like other computer languages, SQL has a specific format and keywords.

Whether both design views are available for a query depends on what the query does and how it is defined. A union query, for example, has only a SQL view, because it is actually a combination of two or more SQL SELECT statements.

To run a query, which opens the query in Datasheet view, you first must be in one of the Design View windows. Click the Run button (the Exclamation Mark icon) on the toolbar, or choose **Q**uery | **R**un.

The Design Grid and Field List

The Design Grid is the Design view you see when you open most queries in Design view. Figure 7.6 shows the Design Grid for the Current Product List query.

Figure 7.6.
The Design Grid for the Current Product List query.

Run Query button

Tables in Query

Table Pane

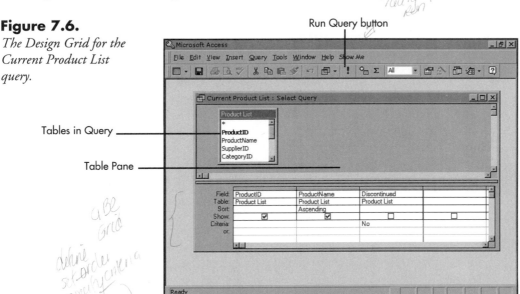

The top of the Design Grid window is referred to as the *table pane* because it displays the Field List table for each of the tables involved in the query. For the Current Product List query, only the Product List table is shown.

The grid at the bottom of the window is the actual QBE Design Grid. This is where you define the fields returned by the query, set the sort order, and specify any criteria.

SQL View

Using the SQL view is an advanced way of examining the query. This view provides you with the actual SQL code that will be executed when the query runs. Figure 7.7 shows the SQL view for the Current Product List query. The information provided by this view says exactly what is represented in the QBE Grid Design view, but in the language that Access 97 uses to execute the query.

Figure 7.7.

The SQL Design view for the Current Product List query.

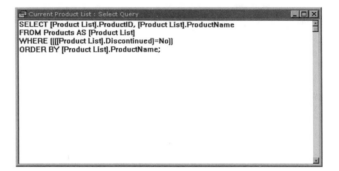

```
Current Product List : Select Query                                    _ □ ×
SELECT [Product List].ProductID, [Product List].ProductName
FROM Products AS [Product List]
WHERE [[([Product List].Discontinued]=No]]
ORDER BY [Product List].ProductName;
```

Looking at the Basic Structure of Queries

The previous section showed you how to use the two different query design view windows and in this section you'll learn how a query is constructed. This section concentrates on the QBE Design Grid View window. You'll learn all about fields, how the sorting is specified, how the record criteria is determined, and how to view the properties for the query and its fields. This section uses the Current Product List query shown in Figure 7.6 as the sample query for this section.

Fields

Every select query returns at least one field. The fields that appear in the grid of the Design Grid window are the fields that will be displayed when the query is executed or that will be used in the sorting or criteria settings for the query. (Refer to Figure 7.6.)

7

Action queries do not return fields, but their fields are shown in the Design Grid. The fields that appear in an action query's Design Grid are the fields that are being acted upon by the query or that are used in the sorting or criteria settings for the query.

NEW TERM   An *action query* modifies many records in a single execution. Action queries are used to update, insert, and delete records, or to populate a new table from data in existing tables.

In the Design Grid, the Show check box determines whether the field is displayed in the query's datasheet. In the Current Product List query, the `Discontinued` field is not shown in the Datasheet view; only the `ProductID` and `ProductName` fields appear.

Sorting

Let's say you wanted to present the results of a query in a specific order. Perhaps you have a query that returns a list of all of your customers whose birthdays occur in the current month. You would want to sort this list by date so you could easily see whose birthday cards need to be sent first. Access 97 provides a Sort row in the Design Grid view to accomplish this.

The Sort row of the Design Grid is where the sort order for the query is specified. This determines the order in which records appear in the datasheet or in any reports or forms that use the query as their source of data. If a query is sorted in ascending order on a Birthday field, for example, the birthdays that occur earliest will appear first when the query is executed.

You can set the sort order to Ascending (from A to Z, for example), Descending (from Z to A), or Not Sorted. You also can use the sort order on numeric data returned by the query. If a Numeric field is sorted in ascending order, the smallest values appear first. In descending order, the largest numbers appear first.

The Current Product List query is sorted by the `ProductName` field.

Criteria

Each field that appears in the Design Grid can be used to determine which records are returned by the query. Only records with data matching the specified criteria are returned by the query when it's executed or used in a form or report.

For each field, you can specify criteria by using the rows below the first criteria row. These extra criteria values are used in an OR fashion with the other criteria specified for this field. This means that records are returned when the values in the field match any of the rows in the Criteria area.

If the Criteria rows are used for multiple fields, the criteria information is combined in an AND fashion. This means that the data must meet all the criteria entries in order to be included in the resulting set of data.

For the Current Product List query, the third column specifies that the query should return only rows from the Product List table that have their Discontinued field set to No.

Let's return to the customer birthday example. Because we want to list only customers whose birthdays occur in the current month, we would specify the criteria on the birthday field. The criteria would be defined using the expression Month([Birthday]) = Month(Now()). This specifies that a customer's record will be returned if the month in the Birthday field is the same as the current month. (The Now() function returns the current date and time.)

Query Properties

Like every other object in an Access database, queries have properties. To view the properties specific to the query as a whole, click in the blank area of the Design Grid's table pane. Then choose **V**iew | **P**roperties or right-click and choose **P**roperties from the shortcut menu that appears. Figure 7.8 shows the Query Properties window. In this hour, you'll review some of the properties. You'll get a more in-depth analysis in Hours 11, "Modifying and Using Existing Queries," and 18, "Creating Queries."

Figure 7.8.

The Query Properties window for the Current Product List query.

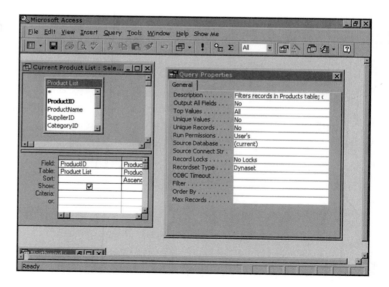

The Query Properties window can be resized, so if some of the property settings are cut off (such as the Description property), you can resize the window and see more of the information.

The Description property is a string that describes the query. This is the same description you see on the Database window's Queries tab when in Details view or after you choose **P**roperties from the shortcut menu.

The Output All Fields property specifies whether all fields in the grid are shown in the query's datasheet. Setting this property to Yes is identical to enabling the Show check box for each field in the grid.

The Unique Values and Unique Records properties are used to remove duplicate field values or duplicate records from the query's resulting data.

The Filter property shows any filter that was created when the query was being viewed in Datasheet view. The Order By property is similar; it shows any sorting information used when the query was viewed in Datasheet view.

Field Properties

Just like tables, fields shown in queries also have individual properties. Properties affect how the field appears in the Datasheet view. Fields that are used in the query but are not shown in the result set (that is, they don't have the Show box checked) do not have properties that can be set.

Fields inherit their properties from the table in which they reside. This means that after a property is set in the table's design, the value of the property is used whenever the field appears in a query. The ProductName field in the Current Product List field inherits the Caption property value Product Name, for example.

To view the properties for a field, select the field in the grid at the bottom of the Grid Design view and choose View | Properties. Table 7.2 lists the available properties.

Table 7.2. Grid Design view properties.

Property	Function
Description	Specifies a description of the field in the query.
Format	Specifies the formatting string used to display the data in the field.
Input Mask	Specifies the mask used when editing data in the field. This property is available only for fields that you can edit. The ProductID field is an AutoNumber field, which Access automatically fills with data. Therefore, you cannot edit the data, and it has no Input Mask property.
Caption	Specifies the label caption (for forms and reports) or column heading (for Datasheet views) that will be displayed for the field.
Decimal Places	Specifies the number of digits to display to the right of the decimal point (for numeric fields that aren't integers).

You'll notice that all the properties for the fields in the Current Product List query are empty. That's because the values set in the Product List table design are sufficient for this query. You can override the table's property settings by specifying values for the query fields' properties. You would want to do this, for example, if you wanted a date to appear in a specific format in the query's datasheet view. You would enter a format expression in the field's Format property.

The Lookup tab also is available on the Query Properties window. This is useful for fields that can look up values in other tables. See Hour 17, "Creating Tables," for more information on creating lookup fields.

Using Toolbars

Queries have two standard toolbars: one for the two design views and one for the Datasheet view. The Design View toolbar has the same buttons for both Design Grid and SQL view, but some are disabled in SQL view. This section will cover only the buttons specific to query design. Common functions such as Save, Cut, and Paste will not be covered here.

The Design View Toolbar

Figure 7.9 shows the Design View toolbar. In this hour, you won't use all these buttons, but in the upcoming hours, when you modify and create queries, this toolbar will become very familiar to you. Several buttons are not available on the toolbar and are grayed out. These won't be covered in this section.

Figure 7.9.

The Design View toolbar.

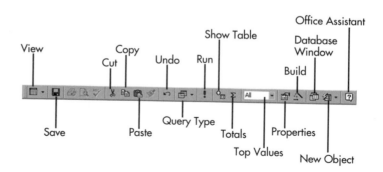

Table 7.3 describes each of the buttons on the Design View toolbar.

Table 7.3. Design View toolbar buttons.

Icon	Button Name	Description
	Query Type	Displays a drop-down list that enables you to change the query type among the select, crosstab, or various action queries.
	Run	Executes the query. If the query is a select or crosstab query, Datasheet view displays the resulting records. If the query is an action query, you receive a message box informing you of the results.
	Show Table	Displays the Show Table dialog box, which enables you to add tables to the QBE Grid's table pane. This button is disabled in SQL view.
Σ	Totals	Displays the Totals row in the QBE Grid's field grid. Used for creating summations such as Sum, Min, and Max.
All ▼	Top Values	Provides an edit box that enables you to limit the query's results to only the top (or bottom) portion of a certain number of records. You can set this to an integer number of records (display the five most expensive products, for example) or to a percentage of the total number of records (display the top 10 percent of the orders for a year, for example). You can click the down arrow button to display a drop-down list of common choices for the Top Values.

continues

7

Table 7.3. continued

Icon	Button Name	Description
	Properties	Displays the Properties dialog box for the currently selected object. You can use this dialog box to edit the properties for the selected object.
	Build	When an appropriate item or property is selected, displays the builder for that object. If the cursor is in the Criteria row of the QBE Grid, for example, clicking Build displays the Expression Builder. Hour 10, "Modifying an Existing Table," discusses the Expression Builder in more detail.
	Database Window	Causes the Database window to become the active window. Provides a quick way to return to the Database window.
	New Object	Displays a drop-down menu that provides a quick way to create an AutoForm or AutoReport based on the current query or to create a new object in the database. AutoForms and AutoReports are wizards provided by Access to quickly create forms and reports having a predefined format.
	Office Assistant	If you installed the Office Assistants, displays the current assistant.

7

The Datasheet View Toolbar

datasheet

Figure 7.10 shows the Datasheet View toolbar.

Figure 7.10.

The Datasheet View toolbar.

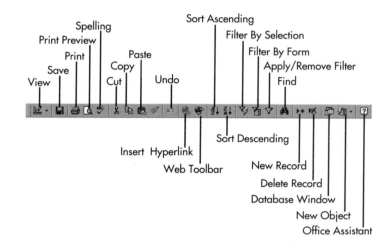

Table 7.4 describes the buttons on the Datasheet View toolbar that are specific to the query datasheet.

Table 7.4. Datasheet View toolbar buttons.

Icon	Button Name	Description
	Insert Hyperlink	If the current column is a hyperlink column, displays the Insert Hyperlink dialog box.
	Web Toolbar	Displays the Web toolbar, which is useful when browsing the World Wide Web from Access 97.
	Sort Ascending	Using the current column or the selected columns, sorts the data in the datasheet in ascending order.

becomes active if column is hyperlink

browsing www

ascend

continues

7

Table 7.4. continued

Icon	Button Name	Description
	Sort Descending	Using the current column or the selected columns, sorts the data in the datasheet in descending order.
	Filter by Selection	Uses the data in the current cell to create a filter. Only data that is the same as the currently selected cell or currently selected text in a cell is displayed in the datasheet. In the Current Product List query's Datasheet view, for example, highlight the letter C in the Product Name column for the Camembert Pierrot product. Then click Filter By Selection. Only those products beginning with the letter C are displayed.
	Filter by Form	Displays a form with all the fields in the query and enables you to create a filter by using a filter-by-example methodology. You enter data into the form that defines the records that will appear in the resulting datasheet.
	Apply/Remove Filter	If a filter is not active, applies the last used filter. If a filter is active, removes the filter criteria to display all the data returned by the query.
	Find	Displays the Find in Field dialog box, which searches the current column for text you enter into the dialog box. This is useful for locating specific records in a query's returned data.

7

Icon	Button Name	Description
▶✳	New Record	Inserts a new record into the underlying table (if the query can be updated). This button is not as useful in a query datasheet as it is in a table datasheet, but it is available.
▶✗	Delete Record	Deletes the current record from the underlying table (if a query can be updated).
🗗	Database Window	Causes the Database window to become the active window. Provides a quick way to return to the Database window.
🗐	New Object	Displays a drop-down list, which provides a quick way to create an AutoForm or AutoReport based on the current query or to create a new object in the database.
?	Office Assistant	If you installed the Office Assistants, displays the current assistant.

Closing Queries

When you finish working with a query, click the box with the X in the top-right corner. If you made any changes to the query's fields or properties, you are prompted to save those changes. Because, for now, you're only looking at queries and how they are defined, click No to avoid changing the Northwind database. You also can close a query window by pressing Ctrl+F4.

Summary

This hour showed you how an existing query is structured and how to view, sort, and filter the data returned by the query. In the next hour, you'll learn all about finding and editing data by using Access 97 forms.

You'll learn more about queries in Hours 11 and 18.

Workshop

The Workshop is designed to help you anticipate possible questions, review what you've learned, and begin thinking ahead to putting your knowledge into practice. The answers to the quiz are in Appendix A, "Quiz Answers."

Q&A

Union query not updatable

Q When I open the Customers and Suppliers By City query in Datasheet View, all of the cells are grayed out and I cannot type in them. Why is this?

A This query is a *union query*. Union queries are not updatable. You should update the tables that make up the query instead. Also, union queries cannot be opened in Grid Design View.

Parameters

Q When I attempt to open the Employee Sales By Country query, I am prompted to enter a Beginning Date and an Ending Date. What causes this to happen?

A This query uses two parameters in its query definition: [Beginning Date] and [Ending Date]. Access requires values for these parameters before the query's datasheet can be constructed. See Hour 18 for more information on parameters in queries.

Quiz

1. Which field property can be used to specify how data is entered into a field in an updatable query?

N no

2. How can you, in one step, cause all fields involved in a query to be shown in the query's datasheet?

C?

3. While in Datasheet view, when is the Insert Hyperlink toolbar button active?

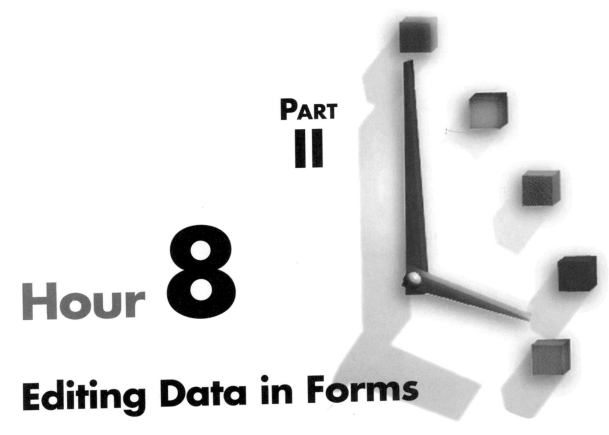

PART II

Hour 8

Editing Data in Forms

by Timothy Buchanan

This hour gives you an introduction to forms. Forms are the most flexible way to view, add, and delete your raw data. Some topics covered in this hour include the following:

- ☐ Looking at the basics of forms
- ☐ Working with forms versus datasheets
- ☐ Using different views of a form
- ☐ Entering data in a form
- ☐ Printing data from forms
- ☐ Using Form toolbars

Understanding Forms

All the raw data you will use in your database is stored in tables. Although you can view and edit your data in a table, forms provide a much easier and flexible interface to view and edit data. Forms display data from an underlying table or query. Forms enable you to view all or just a few records at once while also viewing all the fields. Table datasheets enable you to view several records at once, but you are limited to the number of fields you can view. Forms also provide an easy way to enter, change, and delete records.

All the information a form displays is contained in controls. *Controls* are the objects that display data, perform certain actions, and create special effects on the form. You'll learn more about controls in Hour 12, "Modifying an Existing Form Design."

Opening a Form

Now take a look at forms by opening a form in the Northwind database. Make sure that you have the Northwind database open. If you forget how to open a database or do not know how, refer to Hour 2, "A Quick Tour of Access 97." When you have the Northwind database open, select the Forms tab. Figure 8.1 shows what your screen should look like at this point.

Figure 8.1.

The database window with the Forms tab selected, showing all the forms in the Northwind database.

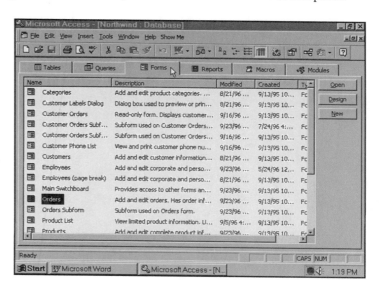

Start with a simple, basic form. Double-click the form name Customers to display the Customers form. This form should be similar to Figure 8.2; it displays the contents of the Customers table. Go ahead and close the Customers form, and double-click on the

8

Customers table. You can see that this is the same information you just viewed in the Customers form but, although you can see many records onscreen at once, you can see only a few fields. Now close the table and open the Customers form again. The globe picture behind the form is a graphic that is displayed only in this form. Graphics and other special effects tools help you design good-looking, easy-to-use forms. How to add special effects to your forms will be discussed in Hour 12.

Figure 8.2.

The Customers form in the Northwind database.

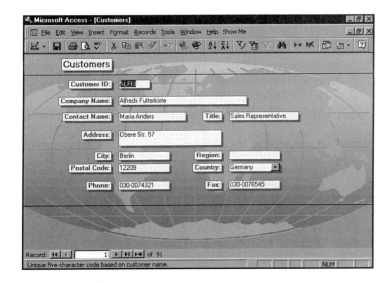

JUST A MINUTE

Microsoft made the forms in the Northwind database very fancy to show off all the power and possibilities of Access 97. You do not have to create forms that display pictures behind your data, special text, or formatting. When you are ready to use special effects such as shadows, three-dimensional effects, and graphics, Access 97 makes it easy to create these forms. For now, just concentrate on learning the basics of forms.

Looking at the Types of Forms

Six basic types of forms are available:

- ☐ Single-column
- ☐ Datasheets
- ☐ Tabular

☐ Subforms

☐ Pivot table

☐ Graphs

In this hour, you'll look at single-column and tabular forms.

Single-Column Forms

The Customers form has a single-column or columnar format. (Refer to Figure 8.2.) Single-column forms show the fields from the table on which they are based in columns. Forms can be more or less than one full screen, depending on your screen resolution. The Customers form should fit on one screen. Single-column forms are a good example of a data-entry screen. Although you can enter all your raw data into tables from the table's Datasheet view, entering data in a form can be easier, much more reliable, and more productive.

Tabular Forms

The Product List form in the Northwind database is an example of a tabular database. To open this form, click the Forms tab, and double-click the Product List form. The form appears, as shown in Figure 8.3.

Figure 8.3.

Looking at the Product List tabular form in the Northwind database.

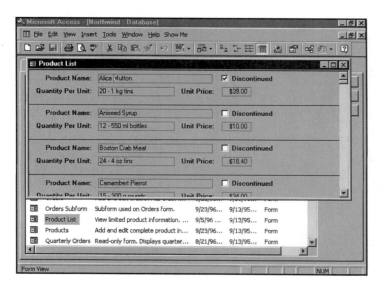

You can use the tabular form to see several records at one time, along with all the fields for those records. This type of form is useful for viewing or printing all the records and fields in a table.

JUST A MINUTE

Most information on a form comes from an underlying table or query, but information completely independent of a table or query also can be on your form. You can display data such as a company name or logo on the form. More about forms will be discussed in Hours 12, "Modifying an Existing Form Design," and 19, "Creating Forms."

Using Forms Versus Using Datasheets

Datasheets enable you to view only limited information about your data. You have little control over the appearance of your information. With forms, however, you can place information on your screen exactly where you want it to be displayed. You also can format each field differently and use several types of special effects. Forms also give you much greater flexibility. Forms provide data validation and the capability to add calculated fields. In addition, you can add pictures such as the globe picture in the Product List form. These graphics or pictures are called *OLE objects*.

NEW TERM

OLE stands for *object linking and embedding*. OLE is a Windows method for inserting and embedding objects in Windows applications.

Now you'll take a look at the different ways to view a form.

Viewing Forms

When you open the Product List form in the Northwind database, you are using Form view. This is the view you use to enter or change data. If you choose **V**iew | **D**atasheet, you are in Datasheet view, as shown in Figure 8.4. This is the same view as the table Datasheet view; the form displays raw data. Choose **V**iew | **D**esign View. Now you are in Design view, as shown in Figure 8.5. Here, you can design the different fields and controls to tell Access how you want to view your data. The last view of a form is Print Preview, as you can see in Figure 8.6. This view shows how a form looks when printed.

JUST A MINUTE

You can print or preview a form from any of the other three views, as well as from the main Database window.

Figure 8.4.

Using the Datasheet view of the Product List form.

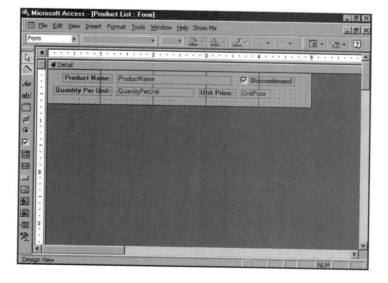

Figure 8.5.

Using the Design view of the Product List form.

Figure 8.6.

Using the Print Preview view of the Product List form.

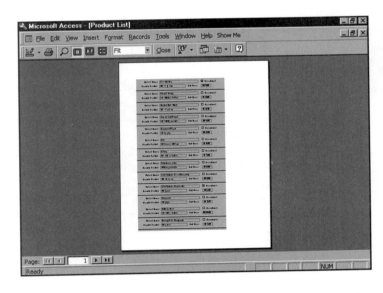

The Design view is where all the work is done to tell Access what data you want to display and in what format. You can open a form in Design view by clicking it in the main Database window and clicking the **Design** button on the right-hand side of the screen. The form Design view consists of three sections:

☐ **Detail section:** Contains the form's main body. All controls are displayed in this section. You cannot delete or remove the Detail section.

☐ **Form Header/Footer sections:** Contain information such as title, date, or other information you want to display only at the top or bottom of a form. You can add or remove these sections by choosing **View | Form Header/Footer**. The data is displayed when you print the form, as well as when you view it onscreen.

☐ **Page Header/Footer sections:** Contain information such as date, form name, page number, or other information you want to display at the top or bottom of each page, but only in the printed form. These sections do not appear onscreen. You can add or remove these sections by choosing **View | Page Header/Footer**.

Working with Data in Forms

As mentioned earlier in this hour, the best reason to use a form to enter data is that it is the easiest, most flexible, and most reliable way to enter data. Now you'll see how to enter or change data using a form.

Navigating in a Form

Open the Customers form from the Northwind database in Form view. The form in Figure 8.2 appears. Except for the actual information and graphics on the screen, you should notice that the rest of the screen looks familiar. The top of the screen has a title bar, menu bar, and toolbar, just like the datasheet. The line at the bottom of the screen is the status bar. The status bar displays the information you entered in the table design for each field. If no information is stored in the table design for that field, Access displays FORM VIEW in the status bar. Directly above the status bar are the form-navigation buttons. You use these buttons to navigate quickly between records. Figure 8.7 shows these various screen elements.

Figure 8.7.

Identifying the various elements in Form view.

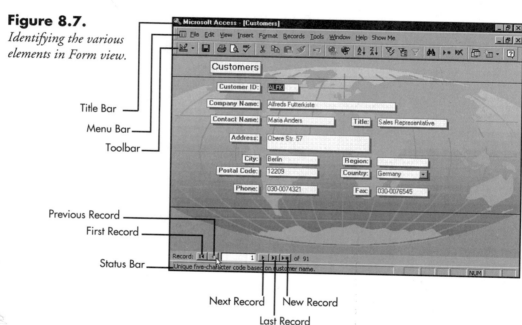

You also can move around the fields on a form. This is very similar to using a datasheet. You can click any field and make changes or additions, and you can press Tab to move around the fields.

Adding and Editing Records in a Form

Adding and editing records in a form is similar to adding and editing records in a datasheet. If you want to add a new record, click the New Record button at the bottom of the screen. You also can press Ctrl++ (hold down Ctrl and press the plus sign key) to move to the end of the records in the datasheet and display an empty record on your form. To edit any of the fields, you can click a field with your mouse pointer and type new information. As you press Tab to move around the form, you can edit the information simply by typing. To select the entire field, press F2 or double-click the field.

> You can lock fields so that no one can change the information stored there. This is a good idea for important information that rarely changes or should be changed only by certain individuals, such as salary information.

Deleting Records in a Form

Deleting records is very easy. Some forms automatically display a button to add or delete records. If your form doesn't display these buttons, simply select a field in the record you want to delete and press Ctrl+– (hold down Ctrl while pressing the minus sign key).

CAUTION

> Make sure that you really want to delete a record before you actually delete it. It is not always possible to undo deletions.

You can delete information in fields by tabbing to that field or selecting that field with your mouse pointer and then pressing Delete, or choosing Del from the main menu.

Copying Records

Sometimes you will enter repetitive data or change several records to a new value. To copy information from the same field in the preceding record, select the field and press Ctrl+' (hold down Ctrl and press the apostrophe key). This copies the information stored in the preceding field into the current field. If the field has a default value, you can replace the current value with the default value by pressing Ctrl+Alt+Spacebar. You also can insert common information into fields, such as the current date or time. To insert the current date, press Ctrl+; (hold down Ctrl and press the semicolon key). To insert the current time, press Ctrl+: (hold down Ctrl and press the colon key).

Finding Records Using Forms

You can search for certain records by using forms. To understand how Access finds records, you will search for information using the Customers form in the Northwind database. Open

the Customers form in Form view, click the `Contact Name` field, and choose **E**dit | **F**ind from the main menu. A dialog box appears, as shown in Figure 8.8.

Figure 8.8.

Using the Find dialog box.

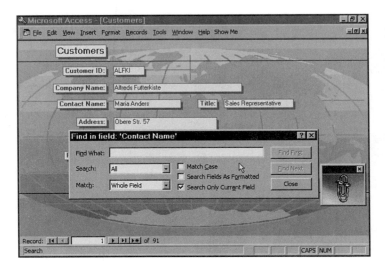

You will search for any customers named Simpson. Type the name you are searching for in the Fi**n**d What text box. Several options are available to you in the Find dialog box. Enable the Search Only Curr**e**nt Field check box, because you know that the information you are searching for is located in the `Name` field. If you were looking for customers from a certain state, you would select the `State` field before running Find and then select the Search Only Current Field check box. Because you know only the last name of the customer for whom you are searching, in the Where section of the Find dialog box, you select Any Part of Field. This gives you all records where Simpson is in any part of the field name. If you know the customer's first and last names, you type both and select Whole Field from the Matc**h** drop-down list. Now click the Find Fir**s**t button. Access takes you to the first record where Simpson is located in the `Name` field, as shown in Figure 8.9.

TIME SAVER

> You can use the Find function with the Replace function to replace numerous instances of the same data. If you need to change all the customers named Smith to Smythe, for example, you can use Find and Replace together to accomplish that feat easily.

Figure 8.9.

Using the Find function with the Northwind database Customers form.

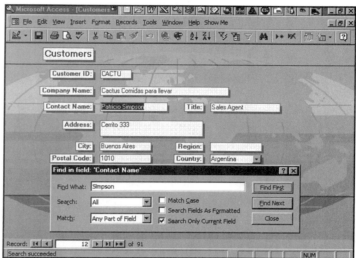

Using Filters and Sorts in Forms

In Hour 5, "Using the Datasheet View," you learned how to filter and sort records. The techniques you learned there are the same techniques you will use to filter and sort records in a form. The only difference is that you will display a single record instead of positioning on a specific field.

Printing Data from Forms

It is easy to print one or more records contained on your form. The printed version looks exactly as it does onscreen. The easiest way to print a form is to choose **File | Print** or to click Print on the toolbar. The Print dialog box appears. If the dialog box shows the correct printer you want to print to, click **OK**, and the form is printed, using the font you selected for the form. The printed form displays any formatting or special effects you designed in the form. To display what the printed version of the form will look like, choose **File | Print Preview** or click Print Preview on the toolbar. You can print the form from the Print Preview screen by clicking the Print button on the toolbar, or you can click the **C**lose button to return to Form view.

Closing and Saving Forms

Access automatically saves each record as you move off the record. You can force Access to save the record before you move off it by pressing Shift+Enter (hold down the Shift key while pressing the Enter key). Choose **R**ecords | Save Rec**o**rd to save your design changes and keep the form open. To close the form and return to the Database window, choose **F**ile | **C**lose or click the close box in the upper-right corner of your screen. If you have not saved your design changes, Access asks whether you want to save the changes.

Summary

This hour provided a quick tour of the basics of forms and how they work in Access 97. You learned how to open a form, as well as how to identify the basic parts of a form. The different views of a form were discussed, as well as how to enter, add, delete, find, filter, and sort records. You now should know how to print information from your form, as well as how to save your changes and close your form.

Workshop

The Workshop is designed to help you anticipate possible questions, review what you've learned, and begin thinking ahead to putting your knowledge into practice. The answers to the quiz are in Appendix A, "Quiz Answers."

Q&A

Q What are some uses of forms other than data entry?

A Forms can be used to display pictures, such as graphs or other graphical information. They can also be used as menus to navigate around your database application.

Q How can you print the underlying data in a form?

A When you use the print function from the Form view, you print the form as you see it. To print the data only, either select the Datasheet view and then print or print the data from the table or query that the form is based on.

Q What happens if I shut off my PC without saving the changes on a form? Does Access save them automatically?

A No, Access saves data that has been entered into a form or table but does not automatically save any design changes to a form unless you specifically ask to do it.

Quiz

1. What are the six types of forms in Access?
2. Why should you use forms instead of tables?
3. Where is the underlying information in forms stored?

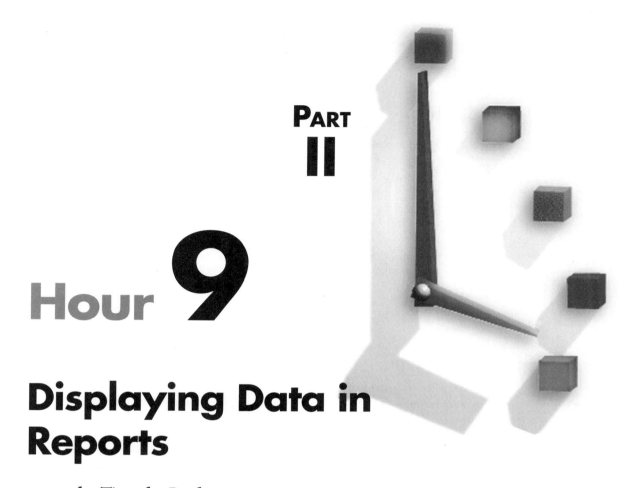

Hour 9

Displaying Data in Reports

by Timothy Buchanan

In this hour, you'll learn how to preview and print reports. Opening reports, printing reports, understanding the basics of reports, and saving reports will be covered. Reports have many uses, and this hour will introduce their basic functions and capabilities.

Topics that will be covered in this hour follow:

- ☐ Understanding the fundamentals of reports
- ☐ Looking at the types of reports
- ☐ Looking at the differences between forms and reports
- ☐ More on opening and previewing reports
- ☐ Printing reports
- ☐ Saving reports
- ☐ Closing reports

Examining Report Fundamentals

Reports are the most powerful and flexible way to view and print the information in your database. You can print only the information that is important to any specific request or task, and you can view or print this information in any format or style. You can add other information, such as totals, comparisons, graphics, and pictures. You will begin your understanding of reports by taking a look at how to open them and view them.

customized view

JUST A MINUTE

Reports present a customized view of the information in the underlying table or query. Although reports can be viewed onscreen, it usually is better to print them. If you can imagine a way that you want to view your data, Access probably will be able to generate a report to match.

Using Reports

using reports — analysis of different styles / perform calc / from ? / add graphics / can group

Reports provide the best way to print information to be distributed, and they provide greater control and flexibility in the overall design. Some major advantages of using reports to print data follow:

- ☐ You easily can control font styles and sizes.
- ☐ You easily can perform calculations on the underlying data.
- ☐ You can format data to fit forms already designed and printed, such as purchase orders, invoices, and mailing labels.
- ☐ You can add graphics, such as pictures, graphs, and other elements.
- ☐ You can group and organize data to make a report easier to read.

Opening and Viewing Reports

You open a report much like you open a form or table. Select the Report tab in the Database window and then select the report you want to open. You can double-click the report to open it, or you can click on the report and then click Open. Figure 9.1 shows the Products by Category report from the Northwind database. This view is called the Print Preview view of the report. The default preview view of your report is to show it at 100 percent. This setting enables only a small percentage of the actual report to fit onscreen. Later this hour we will discuss more ways to open and view reports.

9

Looking at the Types of Reports

Access offers four basic types of reports:

- ☐ **Tabular reports**: Print data in rows and columns
- ☐ **Single-column reports**: Print data as a form
- ☐ **Mail-merge reports**: Print form letters
- ☐ **Mailing-label reports**: Print multicolumn labels

Tabular reports display data in rows and columns, similar to a table. Tabular reports are different from tables, though, because they group their data by one or more field values. Tabular reports also can have other elements, such as page totals, dates, and subtotals. They are usually used to calculate and display subtotals for the numeric fields for groups in the report. Figure 9.1 shows the Print Preview screen of the Products by Category tabular report.

Figure 9.1.

The Products by Category report is a tabular report.

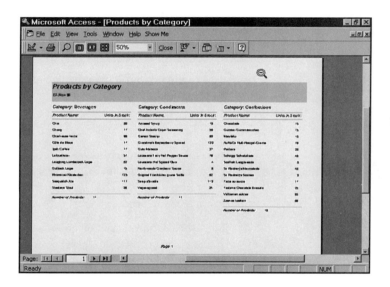

Single-column reports display data vertically, with one or more records per page. These reports display data much like data-entry forms, but they are for viewing and printing only—not for entering data. The Northwind database uses a single-column report to print invoices. Figure 9.2 shows the Print Preview screen of the Invoice report.

Figure 9.2.

*The Invoice report is a
single-column report.*

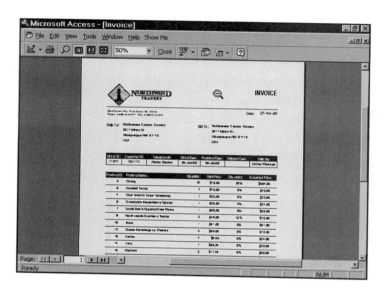

The Invoice report has many other examples of report capabilities. The
form uses graphics, grouping, and totals to create a good-looking,
multifunctional report.

JUST A MINUTE

You use mail-merge reports to print form letters using data from your database. These reports
are linked to Microsoft Word to sort and print the mail-merge documents. You can find more
details about these kinds of forms in Access's Help feature. Look in Help under Mail Merge
for a complete walk-through of the procedures.

You can use the Mailing Label Report to create labels from several different sizes of Avery
brand labels. You generate this report by using the Mailing Label Report Wizard. Figure 9.3
shows the Print Preview screen of the Customer Labels report, which is a mailing-label report
from the Northwind database. The quality and ease of printing mailing labels will depend
on your printer. A good laser or ink-jet printer is recommended for best results.

Looking at Forms Versus Reports

Forms and reports are similar in many ways, but they serve two very different purposes. The
main difference is the reason for the output. Forms generally are used for data entry, whereas
reports are used to view data onscreen or on paper. You can display anything onscreen with
a report that you can display with a form. Both forms and reports are based on the data from
underlying tables or queries, but only forms can add or change the original data.

Figure 9.3.
The Customer Labels report is a mailing-label report.

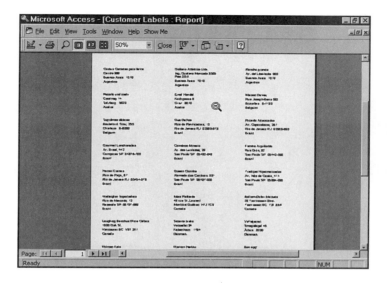

Access enables you to save a form as a report. This capability is helpful when you want to base a new report on a form that you already have created. After you save the form as a report, you can customize the report.

More Ways to Open and View Reports

Now that you know how to open and view a report, what a report is, and what its function is, here are some additional ways to open and view reports. Again, the Print Preview option shows only a small percentage of the report. To see more of the report, move your mouse over the report. The mouse pointer changes to a magnifying glass with a minus sign inside it. After you click the report with this icon displayed, the report zooms out so that the whole report is displayed onscreen. This is called the *Page Preview view*. (See Figure 9.4.) You also can select the Zoom drop-down list from the toolbar. This list gives you several percentage options to view the report. When you move the mouse over the report now, the magnifying glass icon has a plus sign inside it. Clicking the report returns the original 100 percent view. You can view the entire report by dragging the elevator boxes in the vertical and horizontal scrollbars. Also, you can use the page controls at the bottom left corner of the screen to move around between pages.

Figure 9.4.

Using Page Preview to show the entire Products by Category report onscreen.

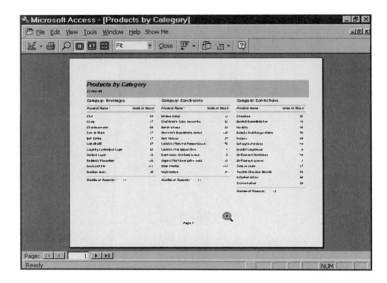

The Preview screen offers several options. The first button on the toolbar (on the far left) is the View button. You click this button to toggle between the Design and Preview views of the form. You can use other buttons on the toolbar to print, close, and export the form to other Office products. You will learn how to export reports in Hour 20, "Creating Reports."

You also can open a report in Design view by selecting the report from the Report tab in the main database window and clicking Design. Figure 9.5 shows the Products by Category report in Design view.

Figure 9.5.

Viewing the Products by Category report in Design view.

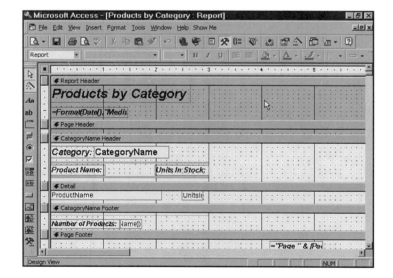

9

JUST A MINUTE

Notice how the report Design view looks very similar to the form Design view. Many of the functions of a form are the same as a report. The only difference is the actual output. The main difference in the Design view is the different sections that make up the report. Forms and reports both contain a Detail section, but reports also provide several different headers and footers that you can use to better display data.

Printing Reports

You can print your reports in several ways:

- ☐ Click the Print button in the Print Preview screen.
- ☐ Choose **File | P**rint in the report Design screen.
- ☐ Highlight the report from the Report tab in the main database window and then choose **File | P**rint from the Database window.
- ☐ Highlight the report from the Report tab in the main database window and then click the Print button in the Database window.

When you use any of the **File | P**rint methods, the standard Windows 95 Print dialog box appears, as shown in Figure 9.6. You use the Print dialog box to choose the printer that will print the report, which pages to print, what range of pages to print, how many copies, and other printer properties.

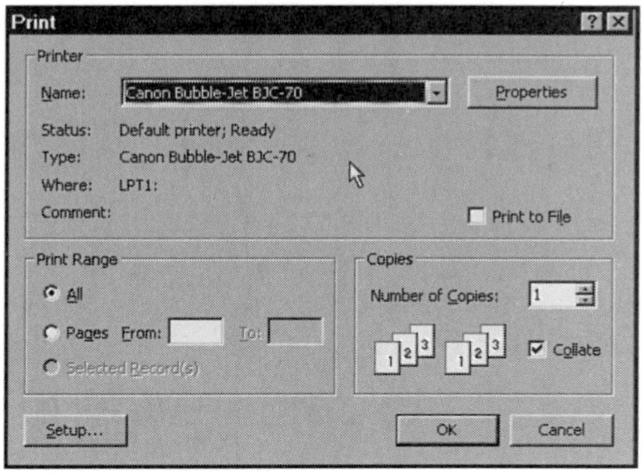

Figure 9.6.

The Windows 95 standard Print dialog box gives you several options to choose from when printing a report.

port/landscape
are saved

After you click the Print icon, the report prints from the default Windows 95 printer; a dialog box is not displayed.

JUST A MINUTE

You use the Page Orientation option in the Print dialog box to print your report in portrait or landscape orientation. This option is saved with the report, so you only need to set it once.

You use the Print Range option to choose which pages of the report to print. You select All to print the entire report. You choose Selection to specify what range of pages to print, and you select Pages to print only the pages you specify in the From and To boxes.

margins does
exceed paper

Sometimes, extra blank pages are printed when you print your report. This usually happens because the dimensions of the report are larger than the size of the paper. Make sure that the width of the report plus the width of the margins does not exceed the width of the paper.

TIME SAVER

resize the
selections to better
fit

Another common problem is too many blank areas surrounding sections of data on the report. To remove this blank area, resize the sections to better fit the information being displayed. You can resize any controls on the report by moving the mouse over the lines of the box in Design view, and clicking and dragging the lines to resize them to fit the data being displayed.

TIME SAVER

Closing and Saving Reports

File
save

You can save reports at any time by choosing **File** | **Save**. Or, you can choose **File** | **Save As/Export** if you want to change the name of the report. When you save a report for the first time, or exit a report the first time without saving it, a dialog box appears and asks you to name the report. The text box gives the report a default name, such as Report1, if you do not want to change it.

Summary

This hour was devoted to studying reports and how they display data. You learned what kinds of reports Access offers, and you learned about the differences between forms and reports. You also looked at the many ways to print and preview reports. You will take another look at reports and learn how to create and modify them in Hours 13, "Modifying an Existing Report," and 20, "Creating Reports."

Workshop

The Workshop is designed to help you anticipate possible questions, review what you've learned, and begin thinking ahead to putting your knowledge into practice. The answers to the quiz are in Appendix A, "Quiz Answers."

Q&A

Q What else can be added to reports?

A Graphics, images, graphs, different fonts, colors, and lines. Just about anything you want to add to make your report look better can be added.

Q Can reports be saved in other formats? My boss wants to see my report onscreen, but he does not have Access.

A Yes, you can save reports in Word or Excel format. The Save As function has this feature.

Quiz

1. What are reports?
2. Why should I use reports?
3. What are the four basic types of reports?
4. What is the difference between forms and reports?

PART
III

Modifying an Existing Database

Hour

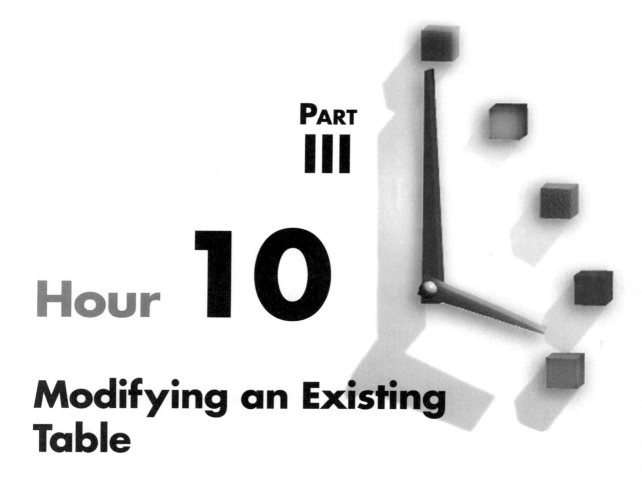

Hour 10

Modifying an Existing Table

by Craig Eddy

In the first section of this book you learned all about viewing and using existing database objects. With that knowledge safely in hand, this section of the book will help you learn all about modifying tables, queries, forms, and reports that already exist in a database.

In this hour, you'll learn how to modify existing tables. You'll learn how to modify table properties and fields, and add and delete fields from the table. Also, you'll learn more about primary keys, indexes, and table relationships.

The highlights of this hour follow:

- ☐ Changing the table design
- ☐ Modifying, adding, and deleting fields
- ☐ Understanding primary keys and indexes

☐ Editing table relationships
☐ Using the Field Builder
☐ Using the Expression Builder

Changing the Table Design

The bulk of this hour will be spent discussing how to modify an existing table's structure. You'll learn how to modify a table's properties, change the fields available in a table, and modify the properties of the fields in a table.

Looking at Table Properties

Each table in the database has a few properties of its own. Figure 10.1 shows the Tables tab of the Database window for the Northwind database.

Figure 10.1.

The Tables tab of the Northwind Database window.

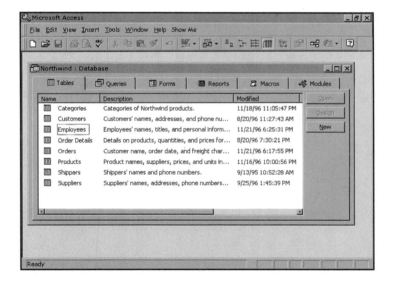

In Figure 10.1, the Tables tab is displaying the list of tables in Details view. To modify the properties for a given table, select the table by clicking its name in the list. Then right-click and choose **P**roperties from the shortcut menu. Alternatively, you can select the table and choose **V**iew | **P**roperties. The Table Properties dialog box then appears, as shown in Figure 10.2. The title bar of the dialog box changes to show the name of the table whose properties you're editing.

10

Figure 10.2.

The Employees Properties dialog box for the Northwind database.

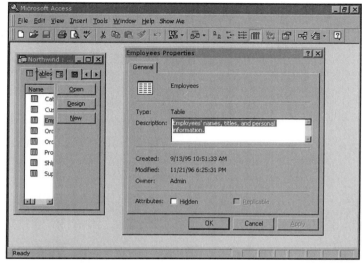

In the Table Properties dialog box, you can change the description of the table, hide the table, and—if the database is the design master of a replicated database—specify whether the table is replicated to other databases.

> synch.

NEW TERM A *replicated database* is a database that has been specially set up to be copied to one or more other databases. The copies can than be synchronized, copying data changes to all copies of the replicated database.

The Table Properties dialog box also shows the dates and times the table was created and last modified. The Owner field specifies the user who created the table and is useful only if you're using Access 97's security features. The security features are discussed in Hour 23, "Database Administration."

owner
specify
the user
who created

If you change the table's description, the change is reflected when you return to the Database window. If you enable the Hidden check box, the table disappears from the Database window. You might want to hide a table, for instance, if it contains data that other users should not have direct access to. Hiding the table does not necessarily prevent such access, but it does make it more difficult to get to the table.

record
level.

Tables also have record-level validation rules and can be provided with a default filter and sort order that are applied when the table is opened in a data view (Datasheet, Form, or Report). To set these properties, make sure that the table Design View window is active. Then choose **View | Properties** or press Alt+Enter.

Modifying, Adding, and Deleting Fields

Just because you have a database design that works for today's needs doesn't mean that you won't need to make modifications to the table's structure in the future. It often becomes necessary to add and modify fields in tables as new needs are discovered. It also might be necessary to delete fields from a table, but this should be done only with careful consideration. Chances are that if a field already contains data, you won't want to delete the field altogether; instead, you simply might want to move the field to another table.

All these changes are performed in the table Design view. Open the Northwind database and select the Tables tab on the Database window. Select the Employees table and click Design. The Employees table Design view appears, as shown in Figure 10.3.

Figure 10.3.

The Employees table in Design view.

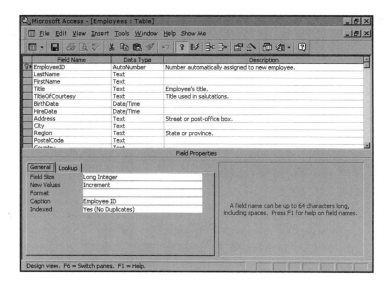

Modifying Fields

When modifying an existing field, you may change several attributes. In general, you'll be modifying the field's properties. You'll learn more about field properties a little later in this hour.

In addition to the field's properties, you can modify the field's name, data type, and description. You modify all these items by using the top portion of the Design View window. To change the field's name, for example, click in the Field Name column for the field you want to change. The cell containing the field's name works like a standard Windows 95 edit box: You can highlight text; cut, copy, and paste; and use the arrow keys to move back and forth in the text that makes up the field's name. You can modify the field's description in a similar manner.

To modify the field's data type, click in the Data Type column and then click the down arrow on the button that appears at the right side of the cell. Select the new data type to be used.

If you change a field's data type and the field already contains data, Access attempts to convert that existing data to the new data type. If you have a field that contains text data and you attempt to change the field to the Number data type, Access attempts to convert the text data to numeric form. This works just fine, as long as the field contains nothing but numerals. If records with any non-numeric data exist in the field, Access displays a warning message. If you allow Access to continue, the contents of the field are cleared for these records.

Suppose that you want to select the PostalCode field and change its data type to Number. Choose **File** | **S**ave to save the table. A message box appears when Access attempts to update the data type. If you choose Yes, the contents of those fields are cleared. If you choose No, the table design is not saved and you are returned to the table Design view. You then should change the field's data type back to Text, or simply close the Design View window and choose No when Access prompts you to save the table's design.

Adding Fields

Usually when you're modifying a table's design, you are adding fields to the table. Fortunately, Access 97 makes adding fields a simple process. This section describes how to add fields to your existing tables.

You add fields to a table by using the table Design view. You can add a field to the bottom of the Field list by clicking in the row below the last field. In Figure 10.4, I have clicked in the row below the ReportsTo field. Access 97 now is ready to accept the new field's name, data type, and other properties. Simply type the name for the field. Then press Tab or click in the Data Type column to set the new field's data type. You then can press Tab or click in the Description column to enter the description.

If you press Tab while the cursor is in the Description column, you wind up in the Field Name column of the next row. If you want to change the new field's properties from their default values, you must click in the Field Properties section at the bottom of the Design View window.

If you want to insert a field between existing fields in the table, select the field you want to appear after the new field. Choose **Insert** | **R**ows to insert a blank row into the grid. Then add the field by following the steps outlined earlier in this section.

Figure 10.4.

*Adding a field to the
Employees table.*

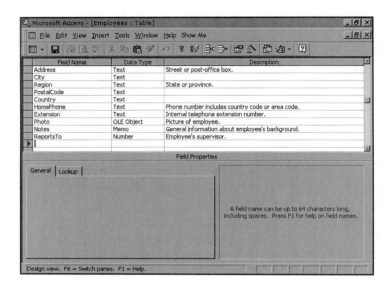

Deleting Fields

Access 97 enables you to delete fields as well. You should be careful when deleting fields that
have data in them, however. Make sure that you really want to delete the fields.

To delete a field, simply select it in the top of the table Design View window and choose **E**dit
| Delete **R**ows. You also can delete multiple fields at once by pressing Ctrl while clicking in
the row-selector column (the leftmost column of the grid) for each field you want to delete.
Then choose **E**dit | Delete **R**ows. If you saved the table's design after the fields to be deleted
were added, Access asks you to confirm that you really want to delete the fields. Choosing
Yes causes Access to delete the fields and any data they contain.

If the field has a relationship with another table, you will be unable to delete the field until
the relationship is dissolved. You will learn more about this subject later in this hour in the
section titled "Editing Table Relationships."

Using the Field Builder

You can add a field manually, but Access 97 also provides a Field Builder feature. You can
use the Field Builder to choose from a wide range of predefined fields that can be added
instantly to your table. This is by far the easiest way to add fields to a table.

To use the Field Builder, click in the grid at the top of the table Design View window. Right-
click and choose Build from the shortcut menu. The Field Builder then appears, as shown
in Figure 10.5.

10

Figure 10.5.

Using the Field Builder to add a field.

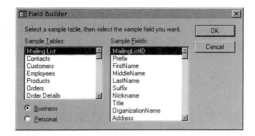

You can select from business or personal tables by selecting the radio buttons at the bottom of the Field Builder dialog box. Select a table and field combination in the Sample Tables and Sample Fields list boxes. Then click OK to add the new field—properties and all—to the table.

Because you're working with the Employees table, select `Employees` in the Sample Tables list box. The Sample Fields list box changes to show fields related to employee data. Select `SocialSecurityNumber` in the Sample Fields list box and click OK. The new field is added to the Employees table and even has an input mask (which defines how data can be entered into the field) and a caption specified.

Field Descriptions

To edit the description of a field, simply press Tab or click to place your cursor in the Description column. The text in the Description column is used as default status bar text whenever the field has *focus* (whenever the edit cursor is in the field) when the field is displayed in a Datasheet view or a form.

Field Properties

To change any of a field's properties, you first select the field in the top of the Design View window. Then click in the Field Properties section at the bottom of the window. Select the property you want to modify.

The Property edit box comes in three control types. There's a standard edit box, a drop-down list box, and an edit box that sports a button with an ellipsis. The first two boxes are standard Windows 95 edit controls. The third control is used to invoke the Expression Builder shown in Figure 10.6 or, in the case of the `Input Mask` property, an Access wizard. The valid property values determine which control type is used for the edit box.

Figure 10.6.

The Expression Builder.

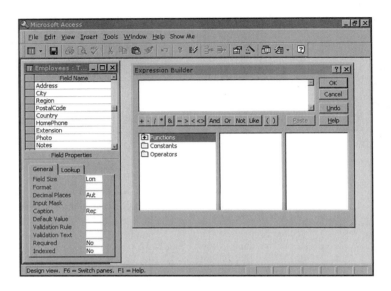

JUST A MINUTE

The Input Mask Wizard is an advanced wizard that is available only if you installed the advanced wizards when you installed Access 97. If you did not install the advanced wizards, you can use the Control Panel Add/Remove Program applet to add the advanced wizards to your Access 97 setup. See Hour 2, "A Quick Tour of Access 97," for information on installing Access 97.

To change a property that has the standard edit box, simply click in the box and make your changes. To change the field size of the Employees table's LastName field to 30, for example, double-click in the Field Size property text box and type 30.

To change a property that has the drop-down list box control, select the field and then click the down-arrow button. Select an item in the list to change the property's value. To change the format Access uses to display the BirthDate field, for example, select BirthDate in the field list at the top of the Design View window. Then click in the Format column, click the down-arrow button, and select a new format. There are several properties that have Yes/No values. These also use the drop-down list box.

To change a property using an Expression Builder, select a property such as Validation Rule. Click the ellipsis button that is at the right-hand side of the property's edit box to invoke the Expression Builder. The Expression Builder makes it easy to create complex expressions by using a point-and-click method. Select one of the items in the leftmost list box, and the other two list boxes display items you can use in your expression. With the Functions folder in the

10

leftmost list, you must double-click to expose subfolders that contain expression items. You also can type directly into the text box at the top of the dialog box, as well as use the many buttons located between the Expression text box and the list boxes. These buttons enable you to insert common operators (such as add, subtract, multiply, and divide) and expressions by pointing and clicking.

Understanding Primary Keys and Indexes

In the relational database model on which Access 97 is built, primary keys uniquely identify records. Indexes help the database engine search and sort records in your tables. Both primary keys and indexes are very important to any good database design. In this section, you'll learn how to view and modify the primary keys and indexes for a table.

10

 NEW TERM A *relational database model* is a database model that groups the underlying data into one or more discrete tables that can be related to one another by using fields common to each related table.

The Primary Key

The *primary key* is a field or a set of fields that uniquely identifies each record stored in the table. Although primary keys are not required, they are necessary if you want to relate the table to any other table in the database.

Refer to Figure 10.3, which shows the Employees table in Design view. The primary key for the Employees table is the `EmployeeID` field. This is represented in the Design View window by a key icon in the row-selector column (the leftmost column) of any fields that make up the primary key. To change the primary key fields, simply select the fields that should make up the primary key by pressing Ctrl while clicking the row-selector column of each field. Then choose **Edit | Primary K**ey or click the Primary Key button on the toolbar. (Its picture is identical to the key icon that appears in the Design View window.)

JUST A MINUTE

If the table has certain relationships with other tables, you will not be able to modify the primary key. You first must dissolve any relationships involving the table's primary key before modifying the primary key's fields.

Indexes

Indexes are used to optimize searching and sorting by the database engine. If certain fields will be used more often than others for searching the table, they probably should be indexed. You can create an index on a single field or on multiple fields. You use a multi-field index in cases where the first field may have duplicate values in the table. Indexes can cause some operations to take longer, so you should be careful not to over-index your tables.

To view and modify the indexes 'r a table, choose **View** | **I**ndexes while the table Design view is active. This opens the Indexes window for the current table. Figure 10.7 shows the Indexes window for the Employees table.

Figure 10.7.

The Indexes window for the Employees table.

In the Indexes window, you specify the name for the index, the fields that make up the index, and the sort order for each field in the index. To create an index made up of more than one field, enter the index name, a field name, and a sort order on the first available row. In the next row, leave the index name empty, and specify the next field name and sort order. Do this for each additional field in the index.

In Figure 10.7, you can see that the Employees table has three indexes: LastName, PostalCode, and PrimaryKey. As you can see, the table's primary key also is used to create an index on the table. You can give an index any valid object name, as long as you don't use the same name twice in a given table.

By using the row-selector column, you can insert and delete rows into the grid. To delete an index, select its row by using the row selector and press Del. To insert rows, select the row that will appear below the new row and press Ins.

CAUTION

If you attempt to use the Edit and Insert menus, your actions are applied to the Design View window rather than the Indexes window.

10

Saving the Table Design

After you make all the necessary changes to the table's design, you must save the design. Click the Save button on the toolbar, choose **File** | **Save**, or press Ctrl+S. Access 97 attempts to save the table design.

If you made any changes that affect validation rules, Access asks whether you want to check any existing data against these new validation rules. Figure 10.8 shows the message box that asks this question.

Figure 10.8.

A message informing you that the data integrity rules have changed and asking whether you want to test the existing data with the new rules.

If you choose Yes, Access tests the existing data against the new rules. If any data fails to meet the validation rules, Access displays the dialog box shown in Figure 10.9.

Figure 10.9.

A message box telling you that the data integrity rules have been violated.

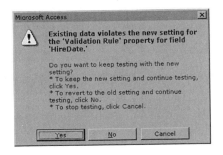

If you want to keep the new validation rule even though some data doesn't meet the requirement (not a good idea), choose Yes. If you want to change the validation rule back to the old setting, choose No. To cancel the operation, choose Cancel. You should (in most cases) choose No from this message box, save your table using the reverted-to validation rule, adjust the data accordingly, and attempt to change the validation rule again (if you still want to use the new rule).

If you have made changes to any field's data type, Access attempts to convert any existing data in that field to the new data type. If it cannot convert the data, the message box shown in Figure 10.10 appears.

Figure 10.10.

A message box informing you that a data conversion error has occurred.

If you choose Yes from this message box, the existing data that could not be converted is cleared from the field. If you choose No, you should change the data type back to its old value, save the table, and adjust the data accordingly. You also should consider whether you really want to change the data type given the fact that data of an incompatible type already exists in your table.

Editing Table Relationships

As I've mentioned several times in this hour, it is possible for tables in a relational database to be related to one another. That's where the term *relational* comes from, after all. For example, in the Northwind database are a Customers and an Orders table. The two tables are related to each other by a common field: CustomerID. In the Customers table, CustomerID is the primary key which uniquely identifies each customer. In the Orders table, CustomerID specifies which customer placed the order. This relates an order (which is represented by a record in the Orders table) to a specific customer (which is represented by a record in the Customers table).

To edit relationships in an existing database, use the Relationships window shown in Figure 10.11. You open the Relationships window by choosing **T**ools | **R**elationships.

JUST A MINUTE

> You cannot edit a table's relationships if that table is opened in Design view. Be sure to close any Design View windows for a table whose relationships you wish to modify.

To edit a relationship, double-click the thinner portion of the line joining the two tables that have the relationship you're modifying. The Relationships dialog box shown in Figure 10.12 appears. From here, you can modify the properties pertinent to a relationship in Access 97. These properties are discussed in greater detail in Hour 17, "Creating Tables."

10

Figure 10.11.

The Relationships window for the Northwind database.

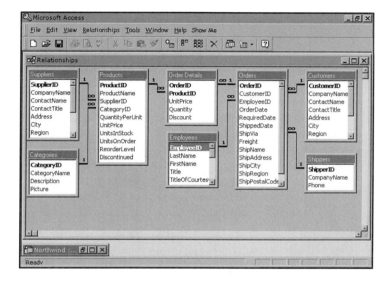

Figure 10.12.

The Relationships dialog box.

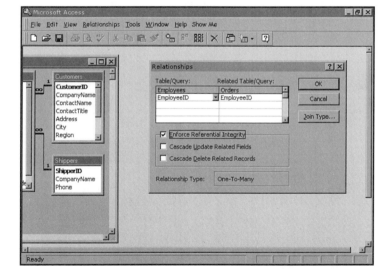

To dissolve a relationship, click the line joining the two tables and press Del. To create a new relationship, select the field in the master table and drag it to the related field in the other table. To try these activities, select the line that joins the Employees and Orders tables. Press Del. Access asks you to confirm that you really want to remove the relationship; choose Yes.

The term *join* is used to denote a relationship between two tables. The tables are said to be *joined* if there is a relationship between them.

 The *master table* in a relationship is the table in which the field or fields used to join the tables is the primary key.

Now it's time to replace the relationship. Click and hold down the mouse button while the pointer is over the `EmployeeID` field in the Employees table. While keeping the mouse button pressed, drag the field name over the `EmployeeID` field in the Orders table. Release the mouse button to drop the field name onto the Orders table's `EmployeeID` field. The Relationships dialog box appears. Enable the **Enforce Referential Integrity** check box. This causes Access to ensure that any data entered in the `EmployeeID` field in the Orders table has a corresponding `EmployeeID` value in the Employees table. It does not mean, though, that every employee must have a corresponding order. Click Create to finish creating the new relationship.

 Referential integrity consists of rules used to ensure that data contained in fields involved in a relationship with another table is valid in that table. Referential integrity is checked when data in such fields is updated, added, or deleted.

After you finish modifying the relationships, you must save the Relationships window's layout before you can close the window. You can choose **File | Save**, click the Save toolbar button, or press Ctrl+S.

Summary

In this hour, you learned about the process of editing an existing table. You will use most of what you learned here again in Hour 17. By now, you should be able to view and modify all the pertinent pieces of a table's structure: field names, data types and properties, primary keys and indexes, and table relationships. You also should be adept at adding and removing fields from an existing table.

The next hour delves into modifying existing queries. This is when you'll learn how to really make Access 97 give you the answers to your data-related questions.

Workshop

The Workshop is designed to help you anticipate possible questions, review what you've learned, and begin thinking ahead to putting your knowledge into practice. The answers to the quiz are in Appendix A, "Quiz Answers."

Q&A

Q **Some of the tables have disappeared from the Tables list. What happened to them?**

A One of two things: You deleted the table or you changed the table properties and marked the table as hidden. To view hidden tables, choose **Tools** | **O**ptions to display the Options dialog box. Select the View tab and enable the Hidden Objects check box in the Show section. Click OK and return to the Database window's Tables tab. If the tables still do not appear, you probably have deleted them. Otherwise, the hidden tables now should be listed, and you can modify their properties to make them not hidden (see "Looking at Table Properties," earlier in this hour).

Q **Whenever I attempt to edit or delete a relationship, I get a message box informing me that one of the tables is in use by another person or process. How do I resolve this problem?**

A More than likely, the table specified in the message box is opened in Design view. Use the **W**indow menu to see if the table has an open window. If it does, click its entry in the **W**indow menu and close its window.

Quiz

1. What types of controls are available for editing field properties?
2. How can you view and modify the indexes defined for a table?
3. Can you change a field's data type if it already contains data?

PART III

Hour 11

Modifying and Using Existing Queries

by Craig Eddy

In this hour, you'll learn how to take an existing query and modify it to better suit your current needs. This is probably the easiest way to learn about defining and using queries. You can take advantage of the work someone else has done in setting up the query and build on that foundation.

You might want to modify a query to add additional fields to its output recordset, or you might need to modify the criteria that a query uses to determine which records to include in its output. For either of these needs and many others, the material in this hour provides you with the information you need to make a query work your way.

The topics covered in this hour follow:

- ☐ Using the Field list
- ☐ Using the Design Grid

☐ Specifying criteria
☐ Querying multiple tables
☐ Using properties

This hour uses queries from the Northwind sample database that ships with Access 97. If you have not installed the sample, return to Hour 2, "A Quick Tour of Access 97," for instructions on installing the sample databases.

Using the Field List

As you saw in Hour 7, "Using Existing Queries," queries have two design views. The SQL view enables you to examine and edit the actual SQL coding that generates the query. You'll learn about the Design Grid view throughout most of this hour.

Figure 11.1 shows the Design Grid view for the Current Product List query. To get to the Design Grid view, select the Current Product List query in the database window and click the **D**esign button.

This section discusses the Field List pane, which is the top half of the Design Grid view.

Figure 11.1.

The Design Grid view for the Current Product List query.

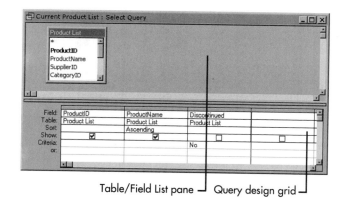

Table/Field List pane ⏌ Query design grid ⏌

The Field list for the Current Product List query contains fields from the Products table. This table is represented by the list box with the caption Product List (as you'll see later in this hour, this caption is set by the Alias query table property). This list box is the Field list for the Products table.

The Field list has an entry for each field in the table. It also has an entry containing only an asterisk (*). This entry represents all the fields in the table; when used, it will cause all fields in the table to be included in the query. It also is used in the SQL view to represent all the fields in the SQL statement SELECT * FROM Products.

11

Also, notice that the ProductID field is in bold type. This signifies that the field is part of the Products table's primary key. The primary key field is used to link this table to other related tables that may be added to the query as needs dictate.

It's a simple matter to add a field from the Field list to the query design grid at the bottom of the window. You can use several methods. First, you can double-click the field's name to place the field in the first available column at the right-hand side of the QBE grid. This means that this field appears as the last column in the Datasheet view when the query is executed.

Second, you can add a field to the grid by clicking the field name and dragging it onto the grid. You can control which column the field is displayed in by using this method as well. The column onto which you drop the field shifts to the right, and the new field is placed in front of the other fields. You also can select multiple fields from the Field list and drag and drop them to add them to the QBE grid.

CAUTION

> The drag-and-drop action cannot be undone and produces no confirmation message, so the only way to revert to the old query is to close the query without saving. Use this menu item with caution!

The Field list's list box also has a shortcut menu, which you access by right-clicking while the pointer is over the Field list. The shortcut menu contains two items. The first item is Remove Table, which removes the selected table and all its fields from the query. The second item is Properties, which displays the Table Properties window discussed in the section "Working with Properties," later in this hour.

To add tables to the Field List pane, you first must display the Show Table dialog box. (See Figure 11.2.) Just choose **Query | Show Table**.

As you can see, the Show Table dialog box has three tabs: Tables, Queries, and Both. The Tables tab displays a list of all the tables in the database. The Queries tab displays a list of all the queries saved in the database. The Both tab displays a list of both the tables and the queries.

To add a table or query to the query's Field List pane, you can double-click the item's name or select the item and click Add. You also can make multiple selections by clicking Add. When a table is added that is related to an existing table in the query, a line is drawn between the related tables to show the fields that *join* the two tables. Suppose that you add the Categories table to the Current Product List query. A line is drawn between the CategoryID fields in the two tables, as shown in Figure 11.3.

11

Figure 11.2.

*The Show Table dia-
log box.*

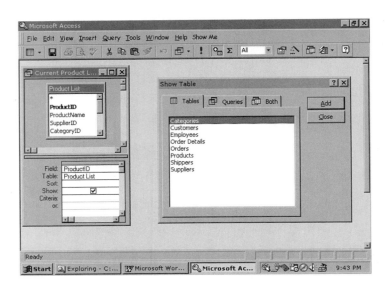

> **NEW TERM**   A *join* describes the relationship between two tables in a relational database. The
> tables are *joined* because a field or group of fields is common to both tables. This join
> forms the relationship between the two tables.

Figure 11.3.

*The Current Product List
query with the Categories
table added.*

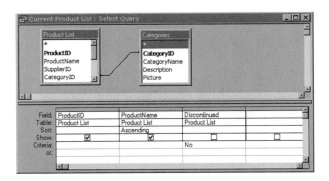

Using the Design Grid

The area at the bottom of the Design Grid view is the QBE grid. This is where the various
field-specific attributes of the query are defined. Each field added to the query has its own
column in the QBE grid. The rows in the grid represent different attributes for the field.
There are rows for field name, table name, sort order, and visibility of the field in the result
set; there also are rows for setting result set criteria based on the field.

The Field Name and Table Name rows contain drop-down list boxes that enable you to change the field represented by the column or to add new fields to the query. Simply select the desired table and field from the drop-down lists. To add a field, select an empty column in the grid and choose the table name and field name. If the required table does not appear in the list, you must add it to the Field List pane using the earlier instructions in the section"Using the Field List."

To remove a field from the query, move the pointer over the top of the field's column until the pointer changes to a down arrow. Then click on the column to select it. Press Delete to remove the field. You also can remove a field by clicking in any row in the field's column and choosing **E**dit | Delete Columns.

CAUTION

> This field-removal action cannot be undone, so use it with caution.

To move a field to a different column position (and change the field's display column in Datasheet view), select the column. Then click the column's header and drag-and-drop it at the desired location.

Specifying the Sort Order and Showing Fields

For each field in the query, you also can specify the sort order and whether the field is included in the query's result set. Each of these attributes has its own row in the QBE grid.

The sort order determines how records are ordered when the query executes. You specify the sort order by using the Sort row's edit box. Just open the drop-down list box and choose Ascending, Descending, or Not Sorted, which is equivalent to having no entry in the Sort row.

Refer back to Figure 11.1, or if you're following along in Access 97, look at the QBE Grid Design view for the Current Product List query. The ProductName field is sorted in ascending order. This means that the products are listed in alphabetical order (from A to Z). If you execute the query by choosing **Q**uery | **R**un (or clicking the Run toolbar button), you'll see that the products are indeed listed in alphabetical order. Return to the QBE Grid by choosing View | **D**esign View and change the sort entry for the ProductName field to Descending. Run the query again, and observe carefully that the products now are listed in reverse alphabetical order. Amazing, isn't it?

11

To review some important considerations to keep in mind when setting the sort order, search the Access 97 Help file for the phrase "sorting data, overview" and review the tips.

In Figure 11.1, the Show row contains a checkbox for each field in the query. If the box is checked, the field appears in the query's result set. If the box is not checked, the field does not appear. This option is available because you might want to use a field as part of the sort order or criteria but not display it to the user.

In the Current Product List query, the Discontinued field is not shown. It specifies the criterion for being a current product: The Discontinued field must be set to No. Because all records returned have their Discontinued field set to No, there's really no need to display the field; its value is implied by the fact that the product is included in the query's result set.

Just for fun, enable the Show checkbox for the Discontinued field and execute the query. You see that none of the products has its Discontinued field checked, as shown in Figure 11.4. This is because all the records have their Discontinued field set to No.

Figure 11.4.

The Current Product List query with the Discontinued field visible.

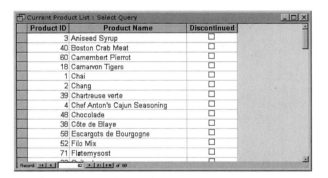

Specifying Criteria

Part of the reason queries exist is to draw from the database records that match a specific criterion. The list of current products consists of all those products that are not discontinued, for example. The products that *are* discontinued are not included in the current product list.

The rows that start with the Criteria row in the QBE grid are where you specify the data that must be present in a field in order for that record to be included in the query's result set. You can specify multiple criteria in an OR fashion by entering the different values on separate rows in the field's column. This means that if the field's value in a record matches a condition on any row, that record will be included in the query's output.

11

The entries made in the Criteria rows must be valid Access expressions. The Criteria edit boxes have an Expression Builder Wizard that can help you quickly build a valid expression. (Figure 11.5 shows the Expression Builder.) You access the Expression Builder by clicking the Build button on the toolbar (the Magic Wand icon) or by right-clicking the Criteria edit box and choosing Build from the shortcut menu. The Expression Builder was covered in Hour 10, "Modifying an Existing Table," and isn't covered in detail here.

Figure 11.5.

The Expression Builder dialog box.

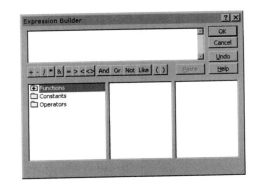

Now you'll look at a few common examples of using criteria to change a query's result set. These examples use the Current Product List query, so open that query in Design view if you're following along in Access 97.

In the first example, you will modify the query so that only the current products on order are returned when the query is executed. The Products table has a UnitsOnOrder field, which shows the number of units ordered for a product. Add that field to the grid by double-clicking its name in the Field list. The grid now should appear as shown in Figure 11.6.

Click in the Criteria row for the UnitsOnOrder field. To see which products are currently on order, type >0 in the edit box. Then execute the query by choosing **Query** | **Run** or by clicking the Run toolbar button. Figure 11.7 shows the results. Instead of 69 records, as you saw in earlier executions of this query, now there are only 17.

Now suppose that you want to return only the products that cost between $10 and $50. First, remove the UnitsOnOrder field by clicking its column in the grid and choosing **Edit** | **Delete Columns**. Add the UnitPrice field by double-clicking its name in the Field list. Click in the field's Criteria edit box and type >=10 and <=50. Now when the query is executed (assuming that you haven't modified any of the information in the Products table), you should see 54 rows—all with prices between $10 and $50.

Figure 11.6.

The QBE Grid view for the Current Product List query with the UnitsOnOrder field added.

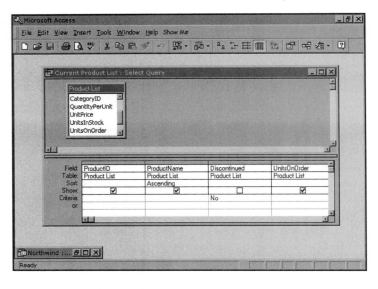

Figure 11.7.

Viewing the Current Product list.

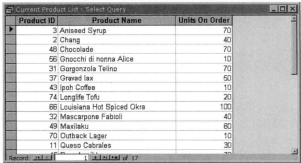

Querying Multiple Tables

Because Access 97 is built on the relational database model, you can create a query that combines information from multiple, related tables. You'll continue to use the Current Product List query in this section, so if you're following along in Access 97, open the QBE Grid Design view for that query.

The first step in querying multiple tables is to add a reference to the necessary tables to the query's Field List pane. Choose **Q**uery | Show **T**able. The Show Table dialog box appears, as shown in Figure 11.8. To add a reference to a table or an existing query to the current query, simply double-click the item's name in the list box.

11

Figure 11.8.

The Show Table dia-
log box.

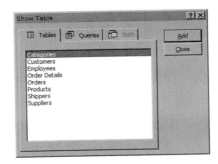

For this example, double-click the Suppliers and Categories tables. As you add each table, a line appears between the Product List Field list and the new table's Field list. This line represents the join between the two fields. The Product List and Suppliers lists are joined using the SupplierID field present in both tables. For the Categories table, the CategoryID field is used. After both tables are added, click Close.

For the supplier information, you're currently interested in the company's name. Double-click the CompanyName field in the Suppliers table Field list. The field is added to the QBE grid. For the category information, you're interested in the category name, so double-click CategoryName in the Categories table.

The Design View window now appears, as shown in Figure 11.9. When you execute this query, the results appear as shown in Figure 11.10.

Figure 11.9.

The Design View
window for the modified
Current Product List
query.

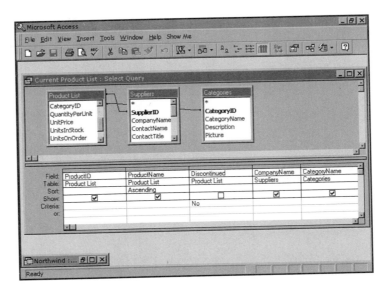

Figure 11.10.

*The Datasheet View
window for the modified
Current Product List
query.*

Product ID	Product Name	Company Name	Category Name
3	Aniseed Syrup	Exotic Liquids	Condiments
40	Boston Crab Meat	New England Seafood Cannery	Seafood
60	Camembert Pierrot	Gai pâturage	Dairy Products
18	Carnarvon Tigers	Pavlova, Ltd.	Seafood
1	Chai	Exotic Liquids	Beverages
2	Chang	Exotic Liquids	Beverages
39	Chartreuse verte	Aux joyeux ecclésiastiques	Beverages
4	Chef Anton's Cajun Seasoning	New Orleans Cajun Delights	Condiments
48	Chocolade	Zaanse Snoepfabriek	Confections
38	Côte de Blaye	Aux joyeux ecclésiastiques	Beverages
58	Escargots de Bourgogne	Escargots Nouveaux	Seafood
52	Filo Mix	G'day, Mate	Grains/Cereals
71	Fløtemysost	Norske Meierier	Dairy Products

Record: ◄◄ ◄ | 1 | ► ►► ►* | of 69

Setting Join Properties

As you learned earlier in the section "Using the Field List," when two or more related tables are included in a query, a line appears between the two tables. This line represents the join that exists between the tables.

There is a property you should adjust to match the way in which data is stored in the database. To access this property, double-click the line that joins the two tables or click the line and choose **View** | **J**oin Properties. The Join Properties dialog box appears, as shown in Figure 11.11.

Figure 11.11.

*The Join Properties
dialog box.*

Join Properties

○ 1: Only include rows where the joined fields from both tables are equal.

○ 2: Include ALL records from 'Product List' and only those records from 'Suppliers' where the joined fields are equal.

○ 3: Include ALL records from 'Suppliers' and only those records from 'Product List' where the joined fields are equal.

[OK]   [Cancel]

As you can see in Figure 11.11, there are three settings for the join. The default setting is 1: Only include rows where the joined fields from both tables are equal. This means that the only records that are returned have matching values in the field or fields used to join the two tables. In the modified Current Product List query you created earlier, the only records from the Products table that appear are those in which CategoryID and SupplierID match a CategoryID and SupplierID in the Categories and Suppliers tables. For the data included with the Northwind database, this setting is fine.

In the Products table, however, neither the SupplierID nor the CategoryID field is required to have values. Leaving the joined properties set to the default values causes any records that have no SupplierID or CategoryID specified to be excluded from the query's result set. Instead, set the join property for both joins to 3. Include all records from Product List and only those records from Categories where the joined fields are equal. This setting specifies that all records from the Products table appear when the query is executed.

Changing the join property causes an arrowhead to be added to the join line, as shown in Figure 11.12. This arrow indicates the direction of the join—from the Products table to the Categories table, for example.

Figure 11.12.

The modified Current Product List query with its joins modified.

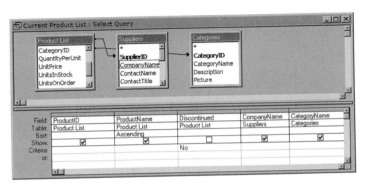

Working with Properties

Queries and the objects that are used in defining a query, like most objects in Access 97, have properties that affect their behavior in the query. This section deals with how you can modify these properties.

Query Properties

The properties for the query itself are the most interesting. You can modify the query properties by clicking in the Field List pane at the top of the QBE grid and choosing **V**iew | **P**roperties. You also can right-click with the pointer over the Field List pane and then choose Properties from the shortcut menu. The Query Properties dialog box appears, as shown in Figure 11.13.

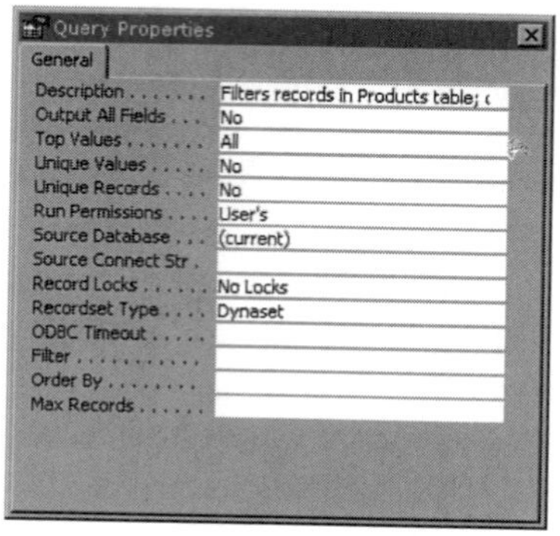

Figure 11.13.

*The Query Properties
dialog box.*

Some of the more common properties you can modify in the Query Properties dialog box
are

- [ ] Description: Specifies a string to describe the query. This is the same description
  you'll see on the Database window's Query tab when in Details view or after you
  choose Properties from the shortcut menu. If you change a query, you should make
  sure that the description still matches the query's function and results.

- [ ] Output All Fields: Specifies whether all fields in the grid are shown in the query's
  datasheet. Setting this property to Yes is identical to enabling the Show checkbox
  for each field in the grid. This property is useful when you want a quick way to
  display every field in a query with many fields that currently aren't being displayed.

- [ ] Unique Values: Excludes records with duplicate values in the query's resulting data.
  This means that only one row with the same values in all the query's fields is
  displayed in the output. Setting this property to Yes enables you to see unique data
  in each row of the query's result set.

- [ ] Unique Records: Similar to the Unique Values property, except that the uniqueness
  is extended to *all* fields in the table on which the query is based—not just the fields
  included in the query. In other words, a record is considered a duplicate (and
  therefore is excluded from the result set) if the value of all fields in the record is a
  duplicate of another record in the query's result set.

- [ ] Filter: Shows any filter that was created when the query was being viewed in
  Datasheet view. You create such filters in Datasheet view by choosing **Records** |
  Filter. When a filter is applied in this manner, the definition of the filter appears in
  the Filter property in the QBE Grid Design view.

- [ ] Order By: Similar to the Filter property because it shows any sorting information
  used when the query is viewed in Datasheet view.

11

Field Properties

Fields that are displayed in the query's result set (their Show checkbox is enabled) also have properties that affect how the data is displayed and edited by the user who executes the query.

To view the properties for a field, select the field in the QBE grid and choose View | Properties. The Field Properties dialog appears, as shown in Figure 11.14.

Figure 11.14.

The Field Properties dialog box.

The properties you can modify in the Field Properties dialog box follow:

JUST A MINUTE

Not all the fields discussed below appear in Figure 11.14. The available properties change, depending on the datatype of the field.

☐ Description: Provides a description of the field in the query. Again, this should describe the field's purpose in the query.

☐ Format: Specifies the formatting string used to display the data in the field. The edit box has a drop-down list that offers predefined format strings for the data type of the field. If the field is a Numeric field, for example, the Format list box offers numeric format strings; if the field is a Date/Time field, the list box offers date/time-specific format strings.

☐ Input Mask: Specifies the mask used when editing data in the field. This is useful for entering information such as phone numbers or social security numbers. The mask defines the format used for these numbers, such as *xxx-xx-xxxx*. This property is available only for fields you can edit. The ProductID field is an AutoNumber field that Access automatically fills with data. Therefore, you cannot edit the data in that case, and it has no Input Mask property. The Input Mask property has a builder that you can invoke by clicking the button that appears to the right of the edit box when it has focus or by clicking the Build button on the toolbar when the edit box has focus.

- ☐ Caption: Specifies the label caption (for forms and reports) or column heading (for Datasheet views) displayed for the field.
- ☐ Decimal Places: Specifies the number of digits to display to the right of the decimal point (for Numeric fields that aren't integers).

You can use the Lookup tab in the Field Properties dialog box to create a lookup column for displaying and editing the field's data. See Hour 17, "Creating Tables," for more information on creating lookup fields.

Table Properties

Each table represented in the Field List pane also has two properties. You access these properties by clicking in the Field list and choosing **View | Properties**. The properties you can change in the Table Properties dialog box follow:

- ☐ Alias: Specifies a user-friendly name for the table or uses the table many times in the same query. You can set the Alias property to any name not currently used in the database. The Current Product List query has an Alias property value of Product List for the Products table. This causes the heading of the Field list box to read Product List instead of Products.
- ☐ Source: Used when the table is attached from an external data source. It specifies the source database and connection string required to access the external data.

Saving Queries

After you make any modifications you want to keep, you must save the query definition. Click the Save button on the toolbar, choose **File | Save**, or press Ctrl+S.

If you attempt to close the query window without saving your changes, Access asks whether you want to save the modified query. Choose Yes if you want to keep the changes, choose No if you want to discard the changes, and choose Cancel if you want to return to the query window instead of closing it.

Summary

In this hour, you learned a great deal about working with existing queries. You saw how to use the Field list and QBE grid, modify the sort order for the query, and change the criteria used to select the records returned by the query. You also learned about querying multiple tables and setting various properties for the query and its underlying objects.

In the next hour, you'll learn about modifying an existing form.

Workshop

The Workshop is designed to help you anticipate possible questions, review what you've learned, and begin thinking ahead to putting your knowledge into practice. The answers to the quiz are in Appendix A, "Quiz Answers."

Q&A

Q When I open the Customers and Suppliers By City fields, using the Design button on the Database window, I'm taken to the SQL View, and the Design Grid View toolbar button is unavailable. Why is this?

A This query is a union query. Union queries cannot be displayed in the Design Grid view.

Q Sometimes the Lookup tab on the Field Properties dialog box is empty. What causes this?

A If you are searching the field properties for a primary key field of a table used in the query, there will be nothing on the Lookup tab because there is no natural way to look up the values for this field as it is being used by the query.

Quiz

1. Which query property specifies how data is displayed when a query is executed?
2. In the Design Grid view, what do the lines that sometimes appear between tables in the table pane represent?
3. What are the two ways to limit the results returned when the query is executed?

Hour 12

Modifying an Existing Form Design

by Timothy Buchanan

This hour goes into more detail on forms. Form controls, properties, text boxes, and labels are discussed in this hour. Now that you have a better understanding of forms and their functions, you'll learn how to modify forms that already have been designed. The topics covered in this hour include the following:

- ☐ Control types
- ☐ Text boxes
- ☐ Labels
- ☐ Advanced controls
- ☐ Properties
- ☐ The toolbox
- ☐ Customizing forms
- ☐ Subforms

Controls and properties are the fundamental building blocks of forms and reports. You must understand these concepts before you begin to design and develop forms and reports.

Using Form Controls

A control has several definitions in Access 97. When I refer to a *control* in this hour, I mean any object on a form, such as text boxes and labels. Controls provide a way for you to enter values, and the controls display the values. These types of controls are linked to an underlying table or query, but other objects, such as lines or boxes, are also controls. You will learn about controls in Hour 13, "Modifying an Existing Report"; for now, I'll discuss form-specific controls.

Control Types

Many types of controls exist on a form. Some of the most common controls you will create have easy-to-use buttons to create them on the Form toolbox toolbar. You can see this toolbar in Figure 12.1.

Figure 12.1.

Using the Form toolbar.

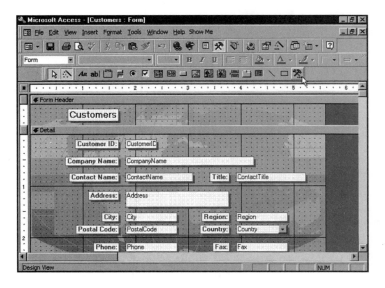

12

JUST A MINUTE

The basic controls I discuss this hour are labels and text boxes. I briefly discuss a few more advanced controls this hour, including option groups, toggle buttons, check boxes, combo boxes, list boxes, subforms, and graphics controls. You will get into more detail on these advanced controls in Hour 19, "Creating Forms."

Three basic types of controls exist:

☐ **Bound controls:** Controls for which the source of data is a field in a table or query. After you enter a value into a bound control, that value is updated to the bound table's current record. Most controls that allow information to be input can be bound controls.

☐ **Unbound controls:** Controls that do not have a source of data. These controls retain any values you enter but do not update any field in the table. You can use these controls to display text, or you can use them as graphics or special effects on the form itself.

☐ **Calculated controls:** Controls for which the source is an expression instead of a field in a table or query. These controls are based on expressions or calculations. Calculated controls do not update any table fields, so they are also types of un-bound controls. A calculated control can take a purchase price and multiply it by the local tax to get a final total, for example.

Open the Northwind database and double-click the Orders form. This form shows an example of all three types of controls, as shown in Figure 12.2.

Figure 12.2.

Looking at all three basic controls in the Orders form in the Northwind database.

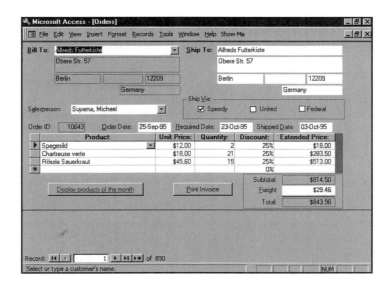

12

Label Controls

Label controls display descriptive text, such as titles, on forms. Labels can be separate controls, such as when they are used for titles, or they can be linked to the control they are describing. Labels do not accept any input; they are unbound controls. They are like any text, because you can format them with any font or point size. You can display labels on single lines or across multiple lines.

Text Box Controls

Text box controls display data or enable the user to enter information. These controls enable you to accept the current data or to edit or delete it. Text boxes accept many kinds of data and can be bound, unbound, or even calculated controls. You will use text box controls more than any other type of control. They are the most powerful and flexible control for forms. Figure 12.3 shows the Customers form from the Northwind database. Here, you can see several examples of text boxes.

Figure 12.3.

Viewing label and text box controls in the Customers form of the Northwind database.

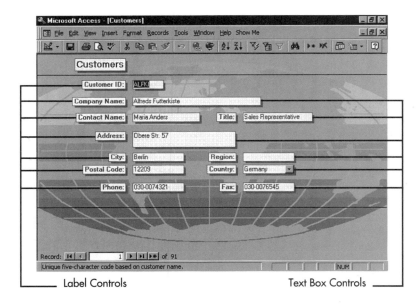

Label Controls   Text Box Controls

Each text box should have a label associated with it to describe its purpose. Like labels, text boxes can contain many lines of data or just one line of data. Text boxes have an automatic *word wrap* feature—any words that are too long to fit in the box automatically wrap to the next line within the field if the text box is big enough to handle extra lines of data. If not, the words scroll to the left as you enter or view them.

12

Using Advanced Control Types

You can use several other types of controls in forms. This hour briefly explains the advanced types of controls and their basic functions. Hour 19 will go into more detail on these controls.

Buttons and Boxes

Fields that have Yes/No data types can use different kinds of controls, known as toggle buttons, option buttons (or radio buttons), and check boxes. Toggle buttons have a sunken or raised button to signify whether a value is True or False. Selected option buttons have a circle with a dot inside, and enabled check boxes are squares with an x in the middle. All three controls provide a way to select one of the Yes/No options, but are visually very different. These controls return a -1 value to the bound field if the button value is Yes and return a 0 value if the button value is No. When you design the button, you can select a default value. If no value is entered, the button is displayed as a null value, which is the same visual appearance as a No.

JUST A MINUTE

You can place Yes/No fields in a text box, but the actual contents of that field—a -1 or 0—are displayed. It makes more sense and looks better to use a button control.

Option Groups

Option groups contain several toggle buttons, option buttons, or check boxes. These controls work together instead of separately when they are combined inside an option group. Instead of being used with Yes/No data types only, they can be used to select one option from a selection. Only one option in the group can be selected at one time. Try not to exceed more than four option buttons. If you need more options, it is best to use a list box, which is covered later this hour. Option groups usually are bound to one field or expression. Each button has a different value that it passes back to the bound field if it is selected.

JUST A MINUTE

You also can have a group of controls contained in a box, but this box is not an option group. By listing several check boxes—all of which are bound to Yes/No fields—and surrounding them with a box, you allow the user to select more than one option from the list.

12

List Boxes

List box controls display a list of data similar to a pull-down menu, but the list box always stays open. You can select any of the options by moving the cursor to the desired item and pressing Enter or clicking the item. The value of the item selected then is passed back to the bound field. List boxes have no limit on how many fields or records can be displayed. If more records are available than can be displayed, a vertical scrollbar enables you to browse up and down the list. You usually will use list boxes when you have more than four choices or want the user to be able to view all the choices available.

JUST A MINUTE

Combo boxes are another control available to use in forms. Combo boxes initially display a single choice with an arrow next to it that shows all the options available when selected. Combo boxes also enable users to enter information that is not in the list.

Using Control Properties

You use properties to determine the characteristics of the controls or fields on a form or report. Some common properties are Color, Font, Size, or Name. You also can use properties to modify certain behaviors of controls, such as whether a control is visible or whether it has a default value. Each control on a form has a list of properties. These properties are used heavily in forms and reports to change certain characteristics of the controls. Even the form itself has its own properties. Figure 12.4 shows the property sheet for the Products form in the Northwind database. To display this sheet, open the Products form. Select the form and click the Properties button on the toolbar, or double-click the control.

Figure 12.4.

The property sheet for the Products form in the Northwind database.

12

The first column of the property sheet displays the property names. The second column is used to enter the actual properties. The property sheet has numerous properties listed on it. To see all the properties, you must scroll up and down or resize the property sheet. Four tabs on the property sheet enable you to view only certain sections of the property sheet. You can select the tab with the properties that are needed most often, or you can leave the default tab All selected. More about form property sheets will be covered in Hour 19.

You can change any of the properties displayed in the property sheet in various ways. You can enter the desired property directly into the property sheet. You can choose from a list of properties by clicking the down arrow in the property field, if one is available. A button with three dots in it (called the Builder button) might appear next to the property field. You can use the Builder button to build that property. Most properties already have default properties entered.

Customizing Forms

Now that you understand what controls are and what they do in a form, you can learn how to add or change these controls in the form Design view. In Hour 19 you will learn how to create forms from scratch. For now, though, you will just concentrate on adding to or changing forms that already exist.

Creating New Controls

If it is not already open, open the Northwind database. Click on the Customers form to open it in Form view. Then choose **View** | **Design** View to switch to Design view.

You can create a control in one of two ways:

- ☐ Drag a field from the field List window to the form Design window. This creates a bound control.

- ☐ Click the toolbox button for the control you want to create and click on the form Design window. This creates an unbound control.

JUST A MINUTE

The toolbox is displayed by default when you are in the Design view of a form. Figure 12.5 shows a toolbox. The toolbox is a quick and easy way to add controls to a form or report. To add a control, click the toolbox icon to select the tool to add it. You can click on the form to add an unbound control, or you can click-and-drag a field from the field list to create a bound control. You can move the toolbox to a different location and modify it to display different toolbar buttons.

Figure 12.5.

*The Access form toolbox,
which contains all the
tools you need to create
and edit forms.*

Figure 12.6 shows the Field List window. To view this window, click the Field List button
on the toolbar or choose **View** | Field **List**. The field list shows all the fields in the table or query
to which the form is bound. You can move or resize this window.

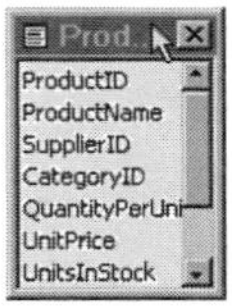

Figure 12.6.

*The Field List window,
with the fields for the
Customers database
displayed.*

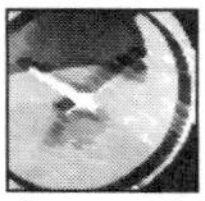

JUST A MINUTE

If you drag fields from the field box windows, the control you create is
placed where you click with the mouse button. Make sure that you have
room to the left of the control to display the labels.

Working with Controls

After you have the control on the Form Design window, you can begin to manipulate it. After
you click a control, between four and eight handles appear around the Products control box,
as shown in Figure 12.7. You use the handle in the upper-left corner to move the control. You
use the other handles to size the control.

You can select a single control by clicking anywhere on the control. You know that a control
has been selected when the handles appear on the control box. The label also is selected, if
there is one. To select multiple controls, hold down the Shift key while clicking all the
controls you want to select. You also can drag the mouse pointer around all the controls you
want to select.

Figure 12.7.

The eight handles displayed for a control, which enable you to move and resize controls.

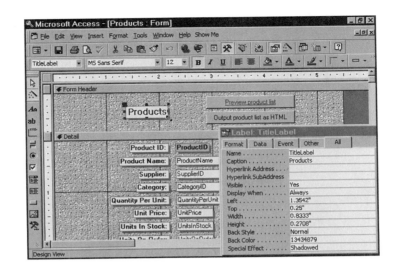

Aligning and Sizing Controls

If you have several controls on one form, you might want to move some of them to align them. After you select the controls you want to align, choose Format | **A**lign to see several options on how to align your controls. (See Figure 12.8.)

Figure 12.8.

Using the menu options for aligning controls.

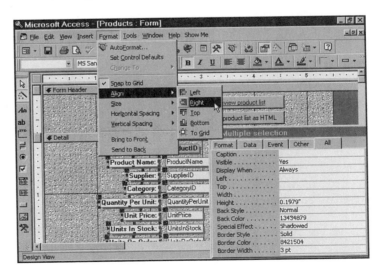

12

After you choose one of the options in the menu, Access uses the control that is the closest to the selection as the model for the alignment change. You must perform each type of alignment separately.

JUST A MINUTE

> To help when you are adding and manually aligning controls, make sure that the Grid is displayed by choosing **V**iew | **G**rid. You can choose Fo**r**mat | S**n**ap to Grid to align all new controls to the grid when you create them. After you turn on this function, you will be able to align controls only to a grid point.

You can size controls in several ways. Select the controls you want to size, and then choose Fo**r**mat | **S**ize to view the options available. (See Figure 12.9.)

Figure 12.9.

The Format | Size menu gives you many options for sizing your controls.

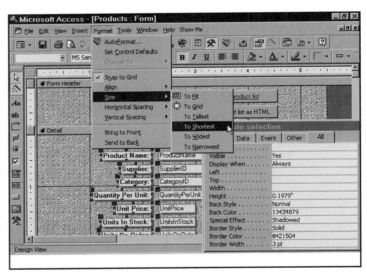

The options you can choose include the following:

- [ ] **To Fit:** Adjusts the height and width of the control to fit the font you have selected for the text
- [ ] **To Grid:** Moves the control box sides to meet the nearest grid points
- [ ] **To Tallest:** Adjusts controls to the same height as the tallest control
- [ ] **To Shortest:** Adjusts controls to same height as the shortest control
- [ ] **To Widest:** Adjusts controls to the same width as the widest control
- [ ] **To Narrowest:** Adjusts controls to the same width as the narrowest control

12

If you no longer need a control on your form, you can delete it by selecting the control and pressing Delete. You also can choose **E**dit | **D**elete.

Using Subforms

A *subform* is a form within another form. You can use a subform to display and enter data from multiple tables. A regular form enables you to edit multiple tables, but you need to use a subform if you want to display data from multiple queries or tables at once. Figure 12.10 shows the Orders form from the Northwind database. Notice how the subform enables you to display data from different tables in various formats.

Figure 12.10.

The Orders form in the Northwind database with a subform to allow data from different tables to be displayed.

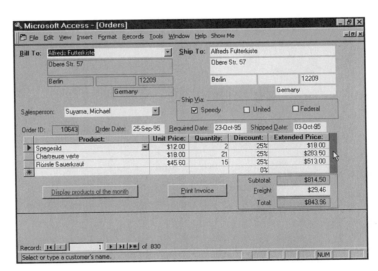

The most important feature of subforms is the capability to display one-to-many relationships. The main form is the one side of the relationship, and the subform is the many side.

Subforms are discussed later in the book. For now, take a look at the form in Figure 12.10. Notice that the tables and relationships are linked in this form.

Summary

This hour, you learned more about forms and how to edit some of the controls on a form. The basic control types were explained, and some more advanced control types were covered as well. You also learned how to understand properties and customize some aspects of forms. Subforms and their relationship to main forms is an advanced topic, and Hour 19 will explain more about them. You should be able to open any form you come across and change the appearance to your satisfaction now.

Workshop

The Workshop is designed to help you anticipate possible questions, review what you've learned, and begin thinking ahead to putting your knowledge into practice. The answers to the quiz are in Appendix A, "Quiz Answers."

Q&A

Q What other controls can be used in a form?

A More advanced controls, such as command buttons, scroll bars, and spin buttons, among many others can be added to a form.

Q What other uses does a form have?

A Forms make wonderful main menus, as well as provide security by restricting users from your underlying data.

Quiz

1. What is a control?
2. What do controls do?
3. What is an option group?

12

Hour **13**

Modifying an Existing Report

by Timothy Buchanan

This hour explains the properties and controls of a report, and ways to modify their design. After this hour, you will know how to modify existing reports and design future reports.

The topics covered in this hour are the following:

- ☐ Report window
- ☐ Report components
- ☐ Report properties
- ☐ Report controls
- ☐ Using expressions in reports
- ☐ Special effects in reports

JUST A MINUTE

Many of the controls and properties of reports are similar to the controls and properties of a form. Make sure you understand the basics of these elements before completing this hour. You can review the form controls and properties in the previous hour.

The Report Window

Hour 9, "Displaying Data in Reports," discussed the basic fundamentals of reports. As you remember, there are two main views of reports: Design view and Print Preview. In this hour, you will take a closer look at these different views.

Design View

The Design view has several areas. The two main components are the Field list and the Property sheet. These two components work with the report exactly like the Field list and Property sheet work with forms. The Field list contains the fields of the table or query on which the report is based. The Property sheet is where the various report properties can be set and changed. The Toolbox is another important component and is used as an easy way to add various controls and design elements to the report. The report Toolbox has the same tools as the form Toolbox. Figure 13.1 shows the Design view of the Products by Category report from the Northwind database, with the Field list box and Property sheet displayed.

Figure 13.1.

The Products by Category report from the North-wind database, with the Field list box and Property sheet open.

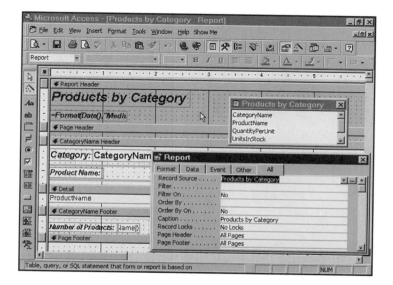

13

Print Preview and Layout Preview

When you select the Print Preview view, the query that the report is bound to is run (if one exists) and up-to-date information is displayed. If the report is based on a table, the latest information from the table is used. The report is displayed exactly as it will appear when it is printed. A third view, called the Layout Preview, can be selected by clicking the View button on the Design toolbar and selecting Layout Preview. The Layout Preview button can be used only from the Design view. It provides a fast view of the basic layout of the report using sample data. It might not include all of the data from the report. This view is useful when the underlying query is large and takes a long time to preview the report in the normal way. The Layout Preview of the Products by Category report is shown in Figure 13.2.

Figure 13.2.

The Products by Category report from the North-wind database is shown in Layout Preview.

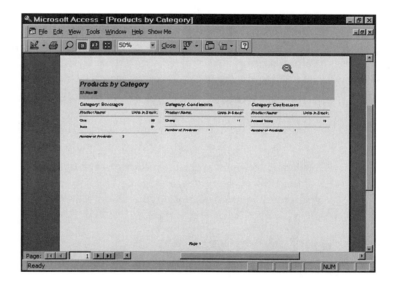

The Report Components

Reports consist of different sections:

☐ The report header is the main header of the report. It is printed only once, at the beginning of the report. It is usually used as the title of the report. The Products by Category report uses the report header to show the title of the report and the current date.

☐ The page header contains information (such as page numbers or column titles) that is printed at the top of every page. The Products by Category report does not use the page header. Other reports use the page header for graphics such as lines or boxes to be printed at the top of every page.

13

☐ Group headers (not used by all reports) contain data that is printed at the beginning of each new group of data on a report. This option can be set up by changing the Group Header property in the Grouping dialog box to Yes. On the design screen, this header will be named after the Field name that is being grouped. In the Products by Category report, the report is being grouped by the `CategoryName` field, and the name of the group header is CategoryName Header.

☐ The detail section is the main section of the report. The data contained in the detail section is printed for each record in the underlying table. The Products by Category report contains the product name and the number of units.

☐ Group footers (not used in every report) contain data that is printed at the end of each new group of data on your report. Usually the information in this section will be summary information, such as subtotals. This option can be set up by changing the Group Footer property in the Grouping dialog box to Yes. On the design screen, this footer will be named after the Field name that is being grouped. In the Products by Category report, the report is being grouped by the `CategoryName` field, and the name of the Group footer is CategoryName header.

☐ The page footer contains information that is printed at the top of every page. This usually is page numbers or page totals or current date. The Products by Category report does not use the page header. Other reports use the page header for graphics, such as lines or boxes to be printed at the top of every page.

☐ The report footer is the main footer of the report. It is printed only once, at the end of the report and is usually used for summary information. The Products by Category report does not use the report footer.

Report Properties

Reports, similar to forms, have certain properties that determine elements of the report. Each section of the report has properties, as does the report as a whole. Figure 13.3 shows the property sheet displayed for the Products by Category report. To display the property sheet, either click the Properties button on the toolbar or right-click the mouse anywhere on the screen and select the Properties icon.

To display the property sheet for a certain section, double-click the section itself, and the property sheet for that section automatically opens. If the property sheet is already open, it will display the properties for the currently active section. To display the property sheet for the whole report, double-click the gray area outside of any report section or the box where the rulers meet in the upper-left corner and the property sheet will be displayed.

13

Figure 13.3.

The Products by Category report from the North-wind database, with the Property Sheet displayed.

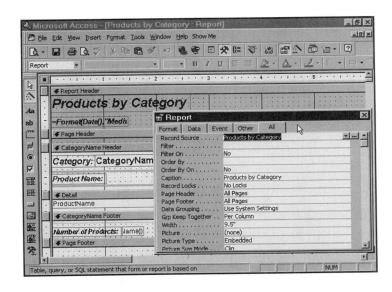

Changing any of the properties is as easy as clicking the property you want to change and typing in a new value. When you click the property you want to change, a down arrow sometimes appears. This indicates that you have options listed for that property to choose from. Otherwise, you can type in any value. The properties are divided into five categories and are listed under five tabs in the property sheet:

☐ Format properties determine the appearance characteristics of the report, such as height, width, color, and whether any pictures or graphics are included. This is shown in Figure 13.4.

☐ Data properties determine the characteristics of the data displayed in the report, such as the control source, input mask, and order of data. This is shown in Figure 13.5.

Event properties determine the characteristics of what macros or event procedures happen when certain events occur, such as when certain keys are pressed or when certain areas of the report are clicked. This is shown in Figure 13.6. Macros help automate repetitive tasks, without you having to write complex code or learn a programming language. You will be introduced to macros in Hour 21, "Creating Macros."

☐ Other properties display characteristics of the report, such as names and date grouping. This is shown in Figure 13.7.

☐ All properties display all the properties of the section or report. This is shown in Figure 13.8.

13

Figure 13.4.

The Products by Category report from the North-wind database, with the Property Sheet displayed and the Format proper-ties tab selected.

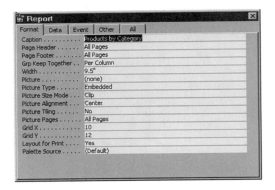

Figure 13.5.

The Products by Category report from the North-wind database, with the Property Sheet displayed and the Data properties tab selected.

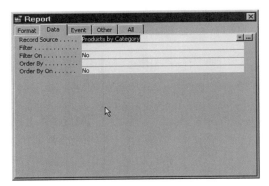

Figure 13.6.

The Products by Category report from the North-wind database, with the Property Sheet displayed and the Event properties tab selected.

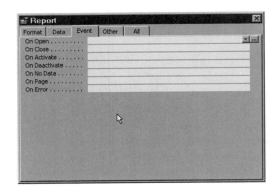

Figure 13.7.

The Products by Category report from the North-wind database, with the Property Sheet displayed and the Other properties tab selected.

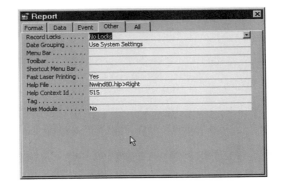

Figure 13.8.

The Products by Category report from the North-wind database, with the Property Sheet displayed and the All properties tab selected.

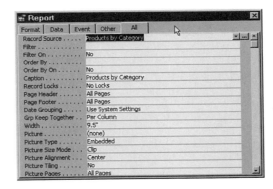

Common Report Properties

Many of the report properties are never changed. Some of the more important ones are the following:

- [ ] The record source property specifies the default table or query on which the report is based. This property is already set up for you when you use a wizard to create your report; you can set it yourself when creating reports from scratch.

- [ ] The caption property is listed in the Report's property sheet. It specifies the name that appears in the title bar when you view the report in Print Preview.

- [ ] The picture property determines whether any picture or graphic is displayed in the report, or in any of the sections.

- [ ] The format property, when used on controls involving numbers, determines what format the number is displayed. Some of the formats are currency, time, date, integer, standard, and percent.

13

JUST A MINUTE

Changing a control's format property does not change the data in the underlying table. For instance, if the number in the table is 12,972.4556, it could be displayed as $12,972 if the format is set to currency. The number is still 12972.4556 in the table, but is displayed as $12,972 in the report.

Using Expressions in Reports

Expressions are used to calculate values for certain fields on a report, and to calculate mathematical and statistical values. Expressions can calculate numerical values as well as text values. Text values from multiple text fields can be combined to form one text field on a report. Expressions in reports are used the same way as on forms. Expressions in forms are covered in Hour 12, "Modifying an Existing Form Design." Some additional expressions are covered in this hour.

Date Expressions

Access provides an easy way to get the date of when a report was printed. Access has two ways to display dates, the Now function and the Date function. Now displays the current time and date stored on your computer. Date displays the current date. These values can be formatted to any of the time and date formats available in the property sheet. The Products by Category report has the current date in the report header, which is shown in Figure 13.9. To add the current date to a control on your report, add an unbound text box to your report. In the Control source section of the report's property sheet or in the text box, type in the value =date().

JUST A MINUTE

The Products by Category report has a more complex version of the Date function. The date is displayed with the Format function, which tells Access to display the current date as well what format to use to display the date. (See Figure 13.10). You can add =date() to the control source and then change the Format property to the desired date format.

Page Numbers

Page numbers help organize printed reports. Use the Page function to add the page numbers. The Page function automatically adds the page numbers when you preview or print the report. The Products by Category report displays the page number at the bottom of each page. (See Figure 13.11.) Add the Page function to an unbound text box, similar to the way you add a date. Usually you have the page number in the page header or page footer of the report. In an unbound text box, add =[Page] to the Control Source property. This will print only the actual page number. To add the word Page before the page number, you must add to the function. ="Page " &[Page] prints the word Page, a space, and then the page number. This is the format that the Products by Category report uses. Figure 13.12 shows the property sheet used to display the page number.

Figure 13.9.

The Products by Category form from the North-wind database displays the current date in the report header.

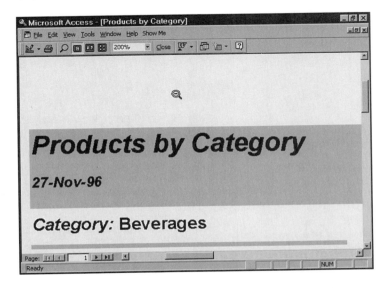

Figure 13.10.

The Products by Category form from the North-wind database uses the Format and Date functions to display the current date in the Report Header.

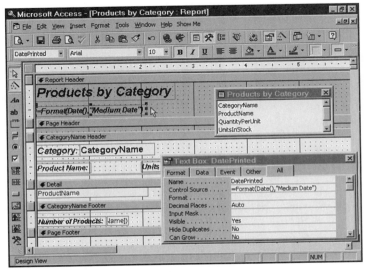

Figure 13.11.

The Products by Category form in the Northwind database displays the page number at the bottom of each page.

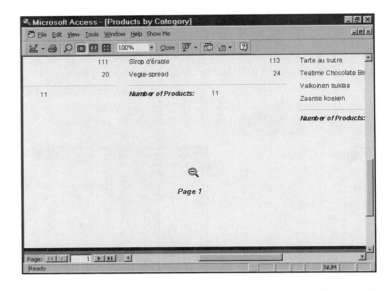

Figure 13.12.

The Products by Category form in the Northwind database uses the Page function in an unbound text box to display the page number at the bottom of each page.

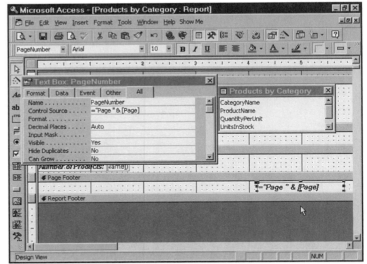

Special Effects in Reports

You can add graphics to reports. Open the Catalog report in the Northwind database, in Preview. The first screen you see has the Northwind logo displayed, as shown in Figure 13.13. If you take a look at the design view of the Catalog report, you see that the logo is added to the report in the report header. Most image formats are usable by Access.

13

Figure 13.13.

The Catalog report from the Northwind database uses an image of a logo on the report.

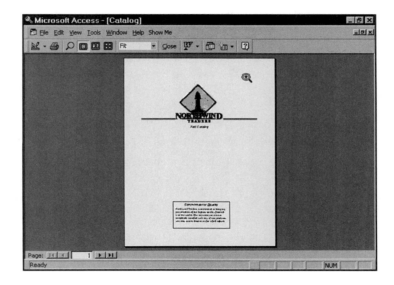

Summary

This hour explained the properties and controls of a report and ways to modify their designs. It discussed the report window and report components, as well as the report properties and report controls and their similarities to form properties and controls. Finally, you saw how to use expressions and some special effects.

Workshop

The Workshop is designed to help you anticipate possible questions, review what you've learned, and begin thinking ahead to putting your knowledge into practice. The answers to the quiz are in Appendix A, "Quiz Answers."

Q&A

Q What other types of properties does a report have that can be changed to make the report look better?

A Some other important properties that you can use are the Views Allowed property (which lets you choose what views the user will be able to use to view the report), Allow Edits (which lets you choose whether the user will be allowed to change the report), and Navigation Buttons (which lets you choose to add the regular navigation buttons to the report—or leave them out). There are many more properties that you can use to perfect your report.

Q What other types of expressions can I add to my reports?

A There are dozens of different expressions and functions, but a couple that are helpful return the current month, hour, minute, and even the current second or the current user. You can also use expressions to display a message to the user.

Quiz

1. What are the two main views of reports?
2. What database objects do reports get the information to display?
3. What sections make up a report?

PART
IV

Creating a Database Using Wizards

Hour

14

Hour

Creating a Database Using Wizards

by Craig Eddy

In the previous section of this book you learned all about using the components of an existing Access database. Now it's time to create your own databases. The two hours you'll spend in this section discuss using Access 97's Wizard feature to build and extend a new database.

This hour covers creating a new database using the Database Wizard and the Table Wizard. The Database Wizard creates an entire database for you. It can even populate the new database with sample data if you'd like. The Table Wizard aids you in adding tables to an existing database and, possibly, relating those tables to other existing tables in the database. Before you create a new database, however, you should do some up-front planning, which is the next topic.

Planning a Simple Database

The first step in creating a database is to plan your work. This involves deciding which of the components of an Access database will be included in your new database. That is, will it have tables, queries, forms, or reports? After you have decided which components you'll use, you must then decide the specifics of these components. How many tables will you require? What will the forms be used for? And so on.

The most important of these is deciding what the tables in your new database will look like. You should create a simple database model to map out your tables before you begin to do any other work with your new Access database. Even a very simple model will go a long way toward making sure that nothing falls through the cracks. It is much harder to add components to your database at a later date and keep everything working properly than it is to get your database's structure right the first time around.

NEW TERM A *database model* is a design document that describes the tables in a database. The model specifies which tables (also called entities) are included in the database, what the properties (sometimes referred to as attributes) of those tables are, and what relationships exist between the tables.

For now, a simple database model done with pen and paper will suffice. First, decide what data you are going to store in the database. Break this data into an organized fashion by grouping the different attributes of the data. For example, if you're creating a home inventory database, you'd want to have a table that contains the rooms in the home. Each room stored in the table has specific attributes: Name, Floor, and so on. You'd also want a table to store the Items found in each room. The attributes for an item might include Description, Room, Cost, Replacement Value, Insurance Coverage, Place of Purchase, and so on. Each of these attributes would become attributes of the tables. You would also define a primary key field for each table. This is simply an identifier field that allows Access to uniquely identify an individual room or item regardless of the other data stored about the room or item.

You would also note that there is a relationship between Rooms and Items: Each item has a reference to a specific room. This relationship should be noted on your database model by drawing a line between the primary key of the Rooms table and the Room field in the Items table.

After your simple model is completed, you may proceed to create your database. You may use the Database Wizard described in the next section or you might create a blank database and then use the Table Wizard described later in this hour to add your tables to the empty database. More details about database design are left for an hour by themselves. You'll find that in Hour 16, "Planning and Designing Your Access Database."

14

Using the Database Wizard

Now that you know the basics of planning your new database, it's time to actually create one. The simplest and quickest way to create a database in Access 97 is to use the Database Wizard. This will create within the new database the tables, forms, queries, reports, and even data for a database style that you choose. You can then, of course, add to the database other elements which your data model included but the wizard did not create. Or, you can remove those items that the wizard did create but which aren't in your data model.

You can launch the Database Wizard in one of two ways. First, in the initial dialog that appears when you launch Access 97 you can select the Database Wizard option button. Second, if you've already opened an Access database you can use the **File** | **New** menu item. On the New Database dialog that appears, select the Databases tab. Either way, the initial dialog of the Database Wizard will be displayed.

To use the Database Wizard, follow these steps:

1. Figure 14.1 shows the initial dialog of the Database Wizard. It is in this dialog that you choose the template to use for your database. Using the data model you created in the previous section, choose the database template that seems to most closely match your data model.

Figure 14.1.

The initial dialog of the Database Wizard.

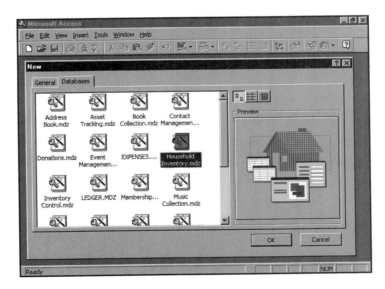

14

The dialog shown in Figure 14.1 includes the filename extensions for the database templates. The extensions appear because on my system I have turned off the "Hide MS-DOS file extensions for file types that are registered" option in Windows Explorer. If you want to see the extensions on your system, launch Windows Explorer and use the **V**iew | Options menu item. Remove the check from the hide extensions check box that appears near the bottom of the dialog. You will now start to see filename extensions everywhere filenames are displayed.

The Preview control in the Database Wizard will show you whether Access 97 considers the selected database template to be a business or a personal database. If the Preview shows a chart in the background of some reports and forms, it's a business template. If the Preview shows a house in the background, it's a personal template. After you've chosen the appropriate template, click the OK button to move on.

2. The next dialog, which is shown in Figure 14.2, is where you will choose a location and filename for the new database. Use the dialog box just like the typical Save As dialog box you'll find throughout the Office 97 suite. Select the folder in which to create the database and give it an appropriate name. Click the Create button to continue.

Figure 14.2.

The File New Database dialog.

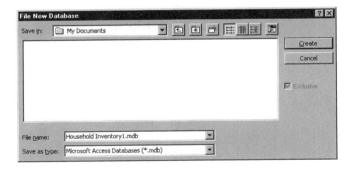

3. The next dialog provides you with some information about the purpose of the database being created. Click the **N**ext button to move on.

4. The dialog shown in Figure 14.3 is where you have the chance to add some suggested fields to the database. These additional fields are not required, but the Database Wizard provides them to allow you to customize the new database to more closely match your data model. This dialog is also where you instruct the Database Wizard to include sample data with the new database. Including the sample data will give you the opportunity to quickly test the queries, forms, and

reports that will be created in the database. Choose whether or not to include the sample data and click **N**ext to continue.

Figure 14.3.

The additional fields/ sample data dialog.

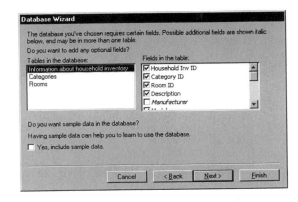

5. The next dialog, shown in Figure 14.4, allows you to pick a style for the display elements of the new database. The style even includes such things as background graphics for forms. The picture box on the left side of the dialog displays a sample of how the style will appear. Select a style from the list and click **N**ext.

Figure 14.4.

The screen displays style dialog.

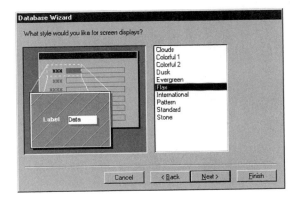

6. Similar to the screen displays style dialog, this dialog allows you to choose a style for the reports. Choose a style and click **N**ext.

7. The next dialog, shown in Figure 14.5, allows you to specify a title for the database. There is also a check box for choosing whether to display a graphic on the printed reports. If you check this box, the Picture button will be enabled. This button opens a File Open dialog where you'll locate the graphic file to be displayed on the reports.

14

Figure 14.5.

*The database title and
report graphic dialog.*

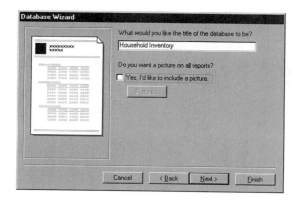

8. Click **N**ext to move to the final dialog. Here you choose whether or not to start the
new database when you're finished, as well as whether to display some extended
help on using a database. If you leave the Yes, start the database check box checked,
the database's main form will load when you click **F**inish. Otherwise, you'll be
taken straight to the Database window. Choose accordingly and click **F**inish.

The Database Wizard displays a progress dialog showing you what elements it's
currently creating. This dialog also contains two progress bars, one for the entire
database and one for the current element being created. This allows you to gauge
the progress of the database creation. When the wizard finishes, you'll have a
complete, working database.

Congratulations! You've just created an entire database!

Using the Table Wizard

Access 97 contains a wizard more useful than the Database Wizard—the Table Wizard. This
wizard assists you in creating a new table for an existing Access database. You'll pick and
choose from a variety of templates to create a table that can exactly model the data you're
going to be adding to the database. In my examples, I'm adding a table to the Household
Inventory database I created in the previous section. This table will contain information
about the insurance agencies with which I have policies.

To use the Table Wizard, follow these steps:

1. Either start a new blank database or open an existing database. Select the Tables tab
on the Database window and click New. The New Table dialog, shown in Figure
14.6, appears.

14

Figure 14.6.

The New Table dialog.

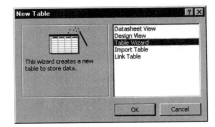

2. In the list box on this dialog, select Table Wizard and click OK.

3. The first screen of the Table Wizard appears, as show in Figure 14.7. Here you select the type of table to be created, either business or personal, by using the radio buttons at the bottom left of the dialog. Then choose a sample table in the list box at the far left. Choosing a different table will cause the list of sample fields to change.

Figure 14.7.

The Table Wizard's initial dialog.

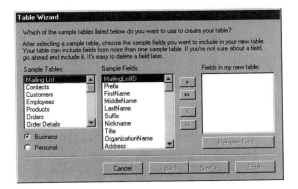

4. From the list of sample fields, select the fields you'll need in your new table and click the > button. You can add fields from different sample tables by choosing the desired fields from one sample table and then selecting a different table and choosing fields from that one. The Fields in my new table list stays populated even if you change to a different sample table. To remove a field from this list, select the field and click the < button. You can remove all fields by clicking the << button.

You can also rename a field if you want. To do so, select the field in the Fields in my new table list box and click the Rename Field button. An input box will appear where you can edit the field's name.

14

Figure 14.8 shows the wizard after I've chosen the fields I want to add to my Agencies table. Note that I used the Customers sample table. I changed the CustomerID field name to AgencyID, the CompanyName field to AgencyName, and the ContactFirstName and ContactLastName fields to AgentFirstName and AgentLastName.

Figure 14.8.

The Table Wizard's initial dialog for the Agencies table.

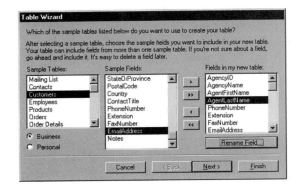

When you've chosen the necessary fields, click the **N**ext button to move on.

5. The next dialog is where you'll specify the name for the new table as well as tell the wizard whether to choose a primary key for the table. I'm naming the new table Agencies, so I'll change the name. Also, it's a good idea to let Access choose a primary key, and because I've included the AgencyID field, Access will probably choose that one. Click **N**ext to move on when you've modified this screen appropriately.

6. The next dialog, shown in Figure 14.9, is where you define any relationships that exist between the new table and existing tables. Although I could have created a field in the Household Inventory table (which stores the items in my house) to hold the AgencyID of the insurance company which is insuring the item, I decided against this for now. It's a simple matter to add such a field at a later time. For now, there are no relationships between this table and existing ones, so I'll leave the dialog as is.

If you want to change a particular relationship, select its entry in the list box and click the Relationships button. The Relationships dialog shown in Figure 14.10 appears. Here you can specify the type of relationship that exists between these two tables. Hour 16 describes table relationships in more detail. Click **N**ext to continue.

Figure 14.9.

The table relationship dialog.

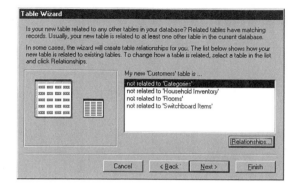

Figure 14.10.

The Relationships dialog.

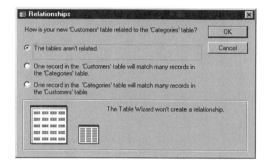

7. The final dialog of the Table Wizard has three option buttons: Modify the table design, Enter data directly into the table, and Enter data into the table using a form the wizard creates for me. Choose which option you'd like to pursue and click Finish.

Congratulations! You've added a whole new table to your database!

Summary

In this hour you learned the basics of creating and adding tables to a database. With just this one hour you have enough knowledge to create and extend usable Access 97 databases in a short period of time. The next hour, "Adding to a Database Using Wizards," will discuss more wizards that Access 97 provides for adding forms, queries, and reports to your database.

14

Workshop

This section contains a questions and answers section as well as a quiz to test your knowledge of queries. The quiz answers are contained in Appendix A, "Quiz Answers."

Q&A

Q Can I create my own wizards?

A Yes. Using Access 97's Visual Basic for Applications, you can create wizards to be included and distributed with your Access database. A good reference on this topic is Sams Publishing's *Access 97 Unleashed.*

Q Is a data model really necessary? Can't I just start adding tables to my database until I've completed it?

A In my opinion, yes, a data model is necessary before you begin. It will serve as a road map, guiding your path as you create your database. Without it, you might get lost or sidetracked. At the very least, create a simple model of the major elements in your database.

Quiz

1. What is a data model?
2. For which elements can you specify a style when creating a database using the Database Wizard?
3. When creating a table using the Table Wizard, are you stuck with the field names in the wizard's template?

Hour 15

Adding to a Database Using Wizards

by Timothy Buchanan

In this hour, you'll learn about wizards. All the objects in an Access database can be created from scratch. This can be time consuming and repetitive, though, so Access 97 includes several wizards that make it easy to create many objects. You can create most of the objects in Access using wizards. You even can create complete, ready-to-run databases by using a Database Wizard.

The topics covered in this hour follow:

- ☐ Using the Table Wizard
- ☐ Using the Table Analyzer Wizard
- ☐ Using the Form Wizard
- ☐ Using Query Wizards
- ☐ Using Report Wizards
- ☐ Using Database Wizards

Using the Table Wizard

You use the Table Wizard to create a new table. After you click New in the Database window with the Table tab selected, Access displays the New Table dialog box, as shown in Figure 15.1. You select the Table Wizard and click OK to load the Table Wizard and display the Table Wizard dialog box, as shown in Figure 15.2. The first Table Wizard dialog box has three sections. You use the first section to choose from a selection of sample tables. There are different tables for business use and for personal use. After you select the sample table on which you will base your new table, you can choose from a number of sample fields for that particular table. Each sample table has different sample fields. By clicking the arrow buttons on the dialog box, you can select the sample fields you want to include in your table. You can rename the fields now, or you can rename them later in Design view. After you select the fields you want to use in your table, click Next.

Figure 15.1.

The New Table dialog box.

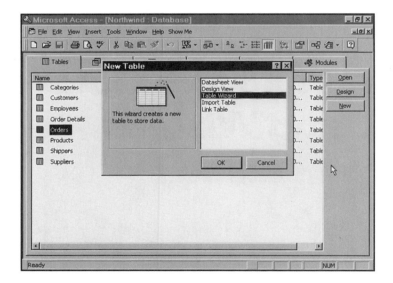

The next dialog box asks you what you want to name your new table. (See Figure 15.3.) You also can have the Table Wizard set the primary key, or you can set it yourself. After you name your table, decide on the primary key, and click Next, the Table Wizard displays the dialog box shown in Figure 15.4. Here, you are asked about the relationships between your table and any other tables in your database. You can make changes to the relationships in this box, or you can change them later. Click Next when you are through with this screen, and the Table Wizard tells you that it has all the information it needs to create your table.

15

Figure 15.2.

Deciding to base your new table on one of many business and personal tables.

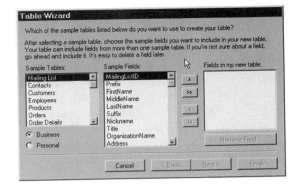

Figure 15.3.

Naming your table.

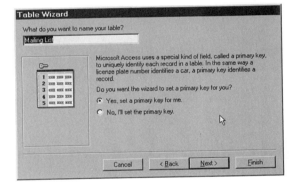

Figure 15.4.

Defining table relationships.

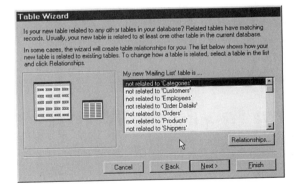

Now the wizard creates your table and then gives you a choice of what you want to do, as shown in Figure 15.5. The default choice is to open the table in Datasheet view and enter data directly into the table. You also can choose to open the table in Design view and modify the design, or the wizard can create a form to use for data entry and will enter data into the table using this new form. Click Finish to continue after you make your choice. Your new table then opens in the view you selected. After you make any changes, save the table. It then is listed on the Tables list on the main database screen with the other tables in the database.

Figure 15.5.

Deciding to modify your table design, enter your data directly, or enter the data using a table created by the wizard.

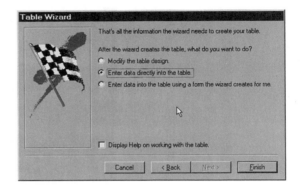

Using the Table Analyzer Wizard

The Table Analyzer Wizard is a tool that splits a table containing a lot of duplicate data into related tables. These separate but related tables store each type of information only once. This method results in more efficient storage, making the database easier to update and more efficient, as well as reducing the size of the database. After the tables are split, you still can view the data in one place by using a query to combine the tables. Only tables—not queries—can be analyzed.

Using the Form Wizard

You use the Form Wizard to simplify the layout process of a new form. Using the Form Wizard is a quick and easy way to create a new form that is bound to a table. The Form Wizard visually walks you through the form-creation process, asking you questions about the form you want to create. These questions include what type of form you want and where the data will be located in your database. The Form Wizard then creates the form. You can use the form immediately, or you can make any changes to get the form to look exactly the way you want.

15

To create a new form by using the Form Wizard, select the Forms tab in the Database window and click New. The New Form dialog box appears, as shown in Figure 15.6. Select the Form Wizard from the list, and choose the table or query that has the information you want to display on the form. Click OK to continue.

Figure 15.6.

The New Form dialog box.

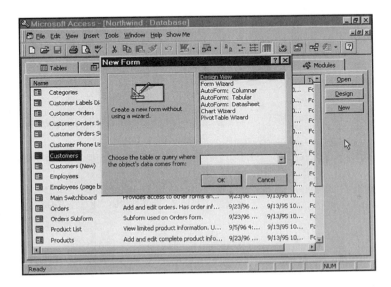

The first Form Wizard dialog box asks you to select which fields from the table or query you want to place on the form. Figure 15.7 shows this dialog box with the Customers table selected and all the fields added to the new form. By clicking the arrow buttons, you can add one field at a time, or you can click the double-arrow button to select and move all the fields. After you select the fields, click Next to continue.

The next Form Wizard dialog box asks you to choose which layout you want for your new form. The default form is a single-column form, as Figure 15.8 shows. Your other choices are Tabular, Datasheet, and Justified. After you select each option, the left half of the box shows a sample of that layout. Choose your layout and click Next to continue.

The Form Wizard next displays a dialog box that enables you to choose what style to use for the form. The style controls the color and font used to display the data, as well as other formatting options, such as a background picture. The default choice is Clouds. (See Figure 15.9.) Choose your style option and click Next to continue.

Figure 15.7.

Specifying which fields to display on the form.

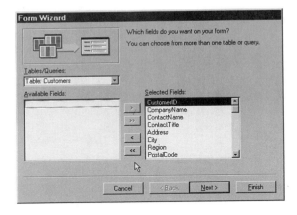

Figure 15.8.

Specifying which layout the form uses to display data.

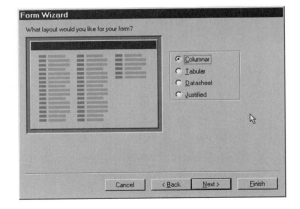

Figure 15.9.

Specifying the style the form uses to format the data it displays.

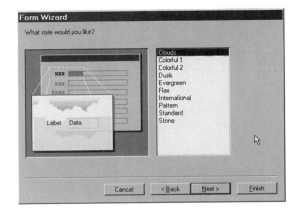

15

15

Figure 15.10 shows the last Form Wizard dialog box. Here, you can choose a name for your new form. You also can choose what to do after the form is created. You can open the form in View mode and begin entering data, or you can open the form in Design mode and make any changes you need. You can change any of the options you chose in the Form Wizard dialog boxes. Name your form, choose to open the form to view or enter information or to modify the form's design, and click Finish. The Form Wizard creates the form for you and opens it in the view you selected. You can also select the Help button from many of the wizard menus. These help options give you help on other ways to work with your data.

Figure 15.10.

Naming the form and choosing the view in which to open the form.

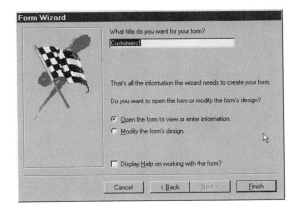

Figure 15.11 shows the completed form. You could have created this form from scratch, but using the Form Wizard is much easier and quicker.

Figure 15.11.

The form created using the Form Wizard is based on the Customers table.

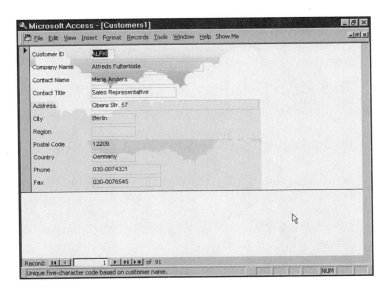

Using AutoForm to Create a Form

You can create a simple form instantly by using the AutoForm feature. AutoForm creates a new form that displays all the fields and records from the selected table or query. Each field from the table appears on the form on a separate line with a label to its left. You can use AutoForm by clicking the New Object button on the toolbar and choosing the AutoForm icon. AutoForm creates single-column, tabular, and datasheet forms.

Using Query Wizards

Query Wizards are a little different from some other wizards in Access. Access has four Query Wizards to help you easily create a query: the Simple Query Wizard, the Cross Tab Query Wizard, the Find Duplicates Query Wizard, and the Find Unmatched Query Wizard.

The Simple Query Wizard

You use the Simple Query Wizard to create a simple query. This wizard is very easy to use. The queries created by using this wizard are not as powerful as queries created in Design view using QBE, however. This type of wizard is fine for queries that use only one table because it simply enables you to choose which fields are included in the resulting query.

The Cross Tab Query Wizard

You use the Cross Tab Query Wizard to create a crosstab query quickly and easily. Crosstab queries display summary data in cross-tabular form, similar to a spreadsheet. The row and column headings are based on fields in the table. The individual cells in the dynaset created by this query are tabular—in other words, computed or calculated.

The Find Duplicates Query Wizard

You use the Find Duplicates Query Wizard to create a Find Duplicates query. Find Duplicates queries show any duplicate records in a single table, using fields in the table as a basis. This wizard asks which field or fields you want to use to check for duplication and then asks you what other fields you want to view in the query. This type of query helps you find duplicate data in your database, such as duplicate-key violations. Finding duplicate-key violations is helpful if you have an existing table without a unique primary key field and you want to designate one field as the unique primary key but are not sure whether any duplicates exist. Using this type of query, you can check the field to make sure that no duplicates exist that could cause problems.

15

15

The Find Unmatched Query Wizard

You use the Find Unmatched Query Wizard to create a Find Unmatched query. This type of query shows all records in a table that do not have a corresponding record in another table. Some of these records, called *orphan records*, are records on the many side of a relationship, and they have no records on the corresponding one side. Other records, called *window records*, are records on the one side of a one-to-many or one-to-one side of a relationship that do not have corresponding records in another table. This type of query helps you find records that have no corresponding records in other tables. You easily can find records that may be causing errors when you try to set relationships and enforce referential integrity.

Using Report Wizards

Access provides many kinds of reports you can use in your database. Some reports are very easy to create, whereas others can be tedious and time consuming. Report Wizards supply a very easy way to create any kind of report, and they are great tools for those more complicated reports. You can use Report Wizards for these types of reports: single-column, group/totals, mailing label, summary, tabular, auto, and Microsoft Word mail merge. To create a report using the Report Wizards, select the Report tab from the main database screen and click the **New** button. Select the Report Wizard from the selections on the first menu and select what table or query to base the report on. The Report Wizards help you lay out the fields by asking you questions about the type of report you want to create and other information needed for the report. The wizard then creates the report for you.

Using AutoReport to Create a Report

You can create a simple new report instantly by using the AutoReport feature. AutoReport creates a new report that displays all the fields and records from the selected table or query. Each field from the table appears on the form on a separate line with a label to its left. You can use AutoReport by clicking the New Object button on the toolbar and clicking the AutoReport icon. AutoReport creates single-column or tabular reports. Although AutoReport is the easiest and quickest way to create a report, you usually want more control over the design of your report. You can use AutoReport to add all the fields to a report and then customize it to your specifications.

Using Database Wizards

Database Wizards provide an easy way to create new databases based on pre-programmed database templates. Access 97 actually combines the features of the other wizards with a tool that creates complete applications, or an application generator. When you run the Database Wizard, it creates a complete, customizable database application. You choose which fields you require from the table definitions for the database you selected, and Access creates a ready-to-run application for you. To run the Database Wizard, choose **F**ile | **N**ew Database. A New dialog box similar to the one shown in Figure 15.12 appears. Each icon represents a different application that the Database Wizard can create. You can choose from more than 22 applications, including the following:

Address Book	Music Collection	Asset Tracking
Order Entry	Book Collection	Picture Library
Contact Management	Recipes	Donations
Resource Scheduling	Event Management	Service Call Management
Expenses	Students and Classes	Household Inventory
Time and Billing	Inventory Control	Video
Ledger	Wine List	Membership
Workout Log		

Figure 15.12.

The New dialog box has more than 22 database templates.

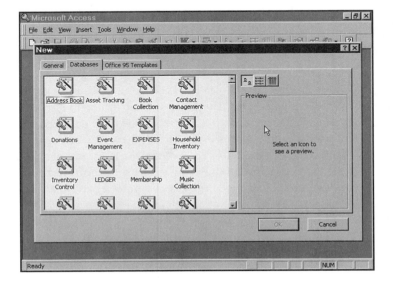

15

After you choose which application is similar to the one you want to create, double-click its icon to begin defining your new application. The Database Wizard first displays the File New Database dialog box, as shown in Figure 15.13. Here, you name your new database and specify where you want to store it.

Figure 15.13.

The File New Database dialog box asks you to name the new database and specify where to save the database file.

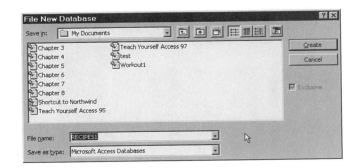

JUST A MINUTE

The different database templates you can use are not only very easy and quick ways to create powerful and useful databases, but they can be great learning tools as well. Create a few of these databases and take a look at how they are designed and what features they use to create great-looking, user-friendly databases.

Summary

This hour went into more detail about wizards. Access 97 includes several wizards that make it easy to create many different objects. You learned about Table, Form, Query, Report, and Database Wizards in this hour. You looked at many examples of the wizards. You can create many different database objects using wizards.

Workshop

The Workshop is designed to help you anticipate possible questions, review what you've learned, and begin thinking ahead to putting your knowledge into practice. The answers to the quiz are in Appendix A, "Quiz Answers."

Q&A

Q Can you create your own wizards?

A Yes, Access 97 gives you the tools to create your own wizards.

Q Can you change any of the wizards?

A Yes, you can change the existing wizards, but that is something best left to an expert programmer.

Quiz

1. Why should you use wizards?
2. Why should you use the Table Analyzer Wizard?
3. What Query Wizards are available?
4. How many Database Wizards are there that create complete, new databases?

PART
V

Creating a Database from Scratch

Hour

Hour 16

Planning and Designing Your Access Database

by Craig Eddy

Up until the previous section you dealt with databases that already existed. The previous section discussed creating and extending databases using Access 97's many wizards. This section explains how to manually create a database from scratch.

The first step in creating any database is to plan the database carefully. This is especially important when you're using a relational database such as Access 97. In fact, a good database design is the single most important factor in creating an effective database. The design must be flexible, logical, and methodical. By the time you finish this hour, you'll have learned how to design such a database.

Some of the key points that define an effective relational database are

☐ It is easily adapted to meet future changes in design requirements.

☐ Its table layout and relationships are easily understood.

☐ It provides acceptable performance and disk space utilization.

Relational Databases

There is no single definition of a relational database. A relational database can best be described as a set of data tables, each modeling a single entity and having certain "key" fields in common with other tables. These key fields establish the relational links between the data tables. The relational database model excels at providing the ability to collect, organize, and report on data that may be of a different nature but is in some way related. This section discusses relational databases in detail by providing definitions for the database terms used when discussing relational databases.

The Northwind sample database is shown in Figure 16.1. This screen shot is of the Relationships window for the database and shows the relational nature of the Northwind database. The lines connecting the tables illustrate the joins between the key fields in the tables.

Figure 16.1.

The Northwind database's Relationships window.

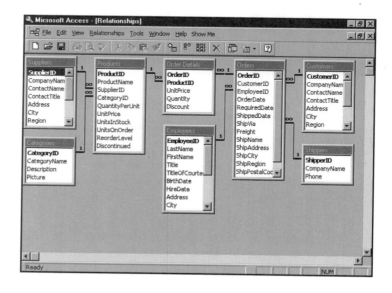

16

Review of Relational Database Terms

Most objects used in a relational database closely parallel objects used in spreadsheet applications and flat-file databases; therefore, the terms are not difficult to visualize or understand. Although this section will not serve as a complete dictionary of relational database terms, it will go a long way toward helping you create effective relational databases.

16

Field

The term *field* refers to the basic building block of any database, relational or not. A field is the database's way of representing a single piece of information or an attribute of an object. Fields should always be atomic, meaning that they cannot be broken into multiple pieces of information. Fields are given a data type that defines the kind of data that can be stored in the field.

Table

A table is a collection of fields. The data contained in a table is stored as a record. Each table in a database should represent a different entity. For example, the Northwind database contains separate tables for customers, suppliers, employees, products, and orders. Although these are all related in some way, they are all completely different entities. The fact that a table can only represent a single entity should not be overlooked—it is one of the keys to creating an effective relational database. Figure 16.2 shows the Customers table in Datasheet view.

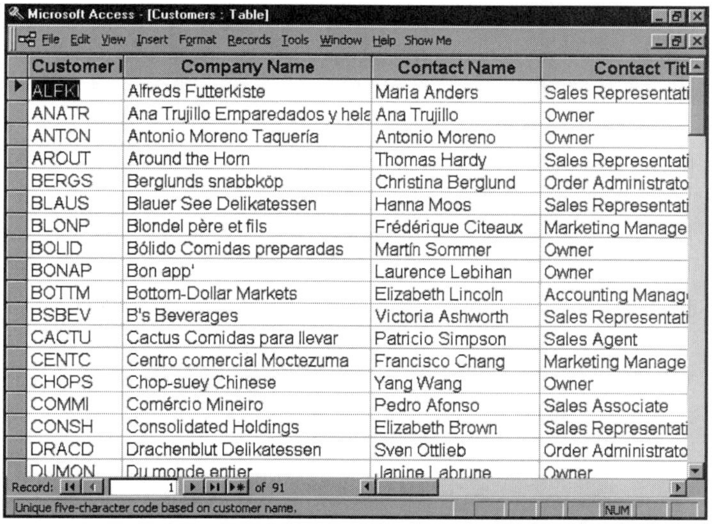

Customer I	Company Name	Contact Name	Contact Titl
ALFKI	Alfreds Futterkiste	Maria Anders	Sales Representati
ANATR	Ana Trujillo Emparedados y hela	Ana Trujillo	Owner
ANTON	Antonio Moreno Taquería	Antonio Moreno	Owner
AROUT	Around the Horn	Thomas Hardy	Sales Representati
BERGS	Berglunds snabbköp	Christina Berglund	Order Administrato
BLAUS	Blauer See Delikatessen	Hanna Moos	Sales Representati
BLONP	Blondel père et fils	Frédérique Citeaux	Marketing Manage
BOLID	Bólido Comidas preparadas	Martín Sommer	Owner
BONAP	Bon app'	Laurence Lebihan	Owner
BOTTM	Bottom-Dollar Markets	Elizabeth Lincoln	Accounting Manag
BSBEV	B's Beverages	Victoria Ashworth	Sales Representati
CACTU	Cactus Comidas para llevar	Patricio Simpson	Sales Agent
CENTC	Centro comercial Moctezuma	Francisco Chang	Marketing Manage
CHOPS	Chop-suey Chinese	Yang Wang	Owner
COMMI	Comércio Mineiro	Pedro Afonso	Sales Associate
CONSH	Consolidated Holdings	Elizabeth Brown	Sales Representati
DRACD	Drachenblut Delikatessen	Sven Ottlieb	Order Administrato
DUMON	Du monde entier	Janine Labrune	Owner

Figure 16.2.
The Northwind database's Customers table.

Record

A record is a collection of data for a specific object or table. In the Northwind database, a customer record is the row of data stored for each customer. Each record in the database should contain a unique piece of information. In the Customers table, each record should represent one and only one customer.

Because a relational database does not store or retrieve records in any set way, there is no physical order to the records. In other words, there is no concept of a record number as there is in many other database systems.

Key Field

A field is said to be a key field when it is used to relate two or more tables to each other. The keys are fields that these related tables have in common. The values stored in key fields are duplicated among the related tables. For example, in the Orders table, CustomerID and EmployeeID are fields that relate a specific order to a customer and an employee, respectively. Therefore, if an order record is created for Around the Horn (a customer in the Northwind database), the CustomerID field in the Orders record will contain the data AROUT. This just happens to be the CustomerID for Around the Horn.

Keys are classified as either primary, foreign, or composite, depending on their use and the fields that comprise them. The different types of keys are discussed in the upcoming section, "The Three Types of Keys."

Relationships and Joins

A relationship is what a key field establishes between two or more tables. The order discussed in the preceding section is related to a customer. The fact that the order has a value in its CustomerID field establishes a relationship between this particular order and Around the Horn's Customers table record.

A join is a sort of virtual table created when the user requests information from different tables that participate in a relationship. The key fields are used to find the matching records in the different tables participating in the join. Figure 16.3 illustrates a join created to return the customer name and phone number along with some details about orders they've placed.

A more advanced form of a join is called the self-join. This is a join in which a table is joined to itself based on a field or combination of fields that have duplicate data in different records. This can be used in the Northwind Employees table, for example, to create a join among the employees using the ReportsTo and EmployeeID fields. The ReportsTo field may contain the EmployeeID of another employee in the table. This EmployeeID would be the EmployeeID of the employee the current employee reports to.

16

Figure 16.3.

Using a join to return information from multiple tables.

Company Name	Phone	Order Date	Employee
Bon app'	91.24.45.40	05-Jun-96	Peacock, Margaret
Richter Supermarkt	0897-034214	05-Jun-96	Callahan, Laura
Simons bistro	31 12 34 56	05-Jun-96	King, Robert
Rattlesnake Canyon Grocery	(505) 555-5939	05-Jun-96	Davolio, Nancy
Ernst Handel	7675-3425	04-Jun-96	Peacock, Margaret
LILA-Supermercado	(9) 331-6954	04-Jun-96	Davolio, Nancy
Lehmanns Marktstand	069-0245984	04-Jun-96	Fuller, Andrew
Pericles Comidas clásicas	(5) 552-3745	04-Jun-96	Fuller, Andrew
Tortuga Restaurante	(5) 555-2933	03-Jun-96	Davolio, Nancy
Drachenblut Delikatessen	0241-039123	03-Jun-96	Davolio, Nancy
Queen Cozinha	(11) 555-1189	03-Jun-96	Callahan, Laura
LILA-Supermercado	(9) 331-6954	31-May-96	Callahan, Laura
White Clover Markets	(206) 555-4112	31-May-96	King, Robert
Save-a-lot Markets	(208) 555-8097	31-May-96	Davolio, Nancy
Hungry Owl All-Night Grocers	2967 542	30-May-96	Leverling, Janet

Record: 1 of 830

16

The Three Types of Keys

As mentioned previously, there are three different types of keys. A database's keys really do unlock the relationships contained within the database, but only if they're correctly implemented. Each table in a relational database must have a unique identifier that consists of one or more fields. Without this unique identifier, there is no way to retrieve a unique record from the related tables to create the joined table.

TIME SAVER

Give each key field the same field name throughout the database. This makes creating joins between the tables easier. It also aids in understanding the database design. For example, the customer identifier should be called `CustomerID` in all tables in which it appears.

Primary Keys

The field or group of fields that is the unique identifier for a table is called the table's primary key. The selection of which field or fields to use as the primary key is one of the most important decisions made when designing a database.

The primary key must uniquely identify each record in the table and must never have duplicated values. For this reason, I recommend that you use the `AutoNumber` data type when creating a primary key field. The `AutoNumber` field guarantees that a duplicated value is never inserted into the primary key field. Access automatically inserts a unique value in the field when a record is inserted into the database. Access also prevents you from modifying or deleting the values in this field after they are inserted.

If you look back at Figure 16.1, you'll see that the primary key fields of each table are displayed in a bold typeface.

Composite Keys

There are often cases in which a record cannot be uniquely identified by a single field. In these cases, a composite key is used. A composite key is a group of fields that uniquely identify a record. A composite key is also the primary key for that table. While duplicate values are allowed within any of the fields of a composite key, there cannot be duplicated values across all the fields that make up the composite key.

An example explains this concept in a clearer way. The OrderDetails table is used to relate a record in the Orders table to a record in the Products table. Each line item of an order references a specific product. The OrderDetails table has a composite key consisting of its OrderID and ProductID fields. Using this table and its composite key, you can create relationships between many orders and many products. A specific OrderID can appear many times in the OrderDetails table, as can a specific ProductID. However, the same values for both OrderID and ProductID in a record cannot be repeated within the table. Each order can have only one OrderDetail for each product on the order.

Foreign Keys

If you understand the concepts of primary and composite keys, you will easily grasp the concept of foreign keys. Essentially, a foreign key is a field (or group of fields) in one table that has duplicate values in the primary key of a related table. For example, the Orders table has a CustomerID and an EmployeeID field. These fields are foreign keys in the Orders table but are the primary keys of the Customers and Employees tables, respectively. The Relationships window shown in Figure 16.3 graphically shows the relationship between foreign and primary keys. It is this relationship that actually allows Access to join data between the tables.

Referential Integrity

The term *referential integrity* refers to the ability to maintain links among tables. Basically, maintaining referential integrity means that every foreign key value stored in a table must map to a corresponding record in the table that has this foreign key as its primary key.

For example, if an order were created and an invalid value were placed in the CustomerID field, there would be no corresponding record in the Customers table. This Orders record would be called an "orphan" record because it has no "parent" record in the Customers table.

16

Allowing this condition would violate the rules of referential integrity and would render your data practically useless.

Access can be made to enforce referential integrity and thus avoid this situation. This mechanism is part of the Relationships window (select Relationships from the **T**ools menu). To change the referential integrity settings for a relationship, select the relationship by clicking the line that joins the two tables and then use the **R**elationships | Edit **R**elationship menu.

16

The Three Types of Relationships

The real power of a relational database is the ability to combine primary and foreign keys to establish relationships between data tables. There are three types of relationships that can be created using the relational database model. Essentially, the type of relationship created between tables determines the format of the data retrieved when the tables are joined.

One-to-One

The simplest (and least used) type of relationship is the one-to-one relationship. This means that for every record in one of the tables in the relationship there is a single corresponding record in the other table that takes part in the relationship. Because these tables could easily be combined into a single table (thus avoiding having to join the two tables), this relationship is used only in special circumstances.

One instance where this type of join is useful involves the use of secure data. You might want certain users to have access to some fields but not to others. For example, in a human resources database you might want to give everyone access to common information in the Employees table. You would not want everyone to view the employees' salary, however. This is a prime example of when using a one-to-one relationship is a necessity.

One-to-Many

A one-to-many relationship is a relationship in which a record in one table has one or more related records in another table. The one-to-many relationship is by far the most common relationship used in a relational database. Strictly speaking, the Northwind database contains nothing but one-to-many relationships.

In the Northwind database there is a one-to-many relationship between the Customers table and the Orders table. Each customer can have more than one order related to it. The key field CustomerID is used to join the tables.

Many-to-Many

A many-to-many relationship is a relationship in which many records in one table may have many records in another table. The strict definition of relational databases does not allow for many-to-many relationships. Instead, an intermediate table is created that holds the primary keys from the two original tables as foreign keys. This creates two one-to-many relationships for the intermediary table—one for each table in the many-to-many relationship.

In the Northwind database, each product can be used on multiple orders and each order can contain multiple products. Therefore, a many-to-many relationship exists between these two tables. The OrderDetails table is used as the intermediary table in this relationship. A one-to-many relationship exists between Orders and OrderDetails (a record in the Orders table can relate to multiple records in the OrderDetails table) and a one-to-many relationship exists between Products and OrderDetails (a record in the Products table can relate to multiple records in the OrderDetails table).

Steps to Creating a Relational Database

This section describes the methods used in creating a database from scratch. The process of creating a database structure is known as data modeling. The term modeling is used because databases are used to actually model a real-world system or collection. This section presents a methodical means of modeling data and creating an effective database.

Identifying Required Data

The first step in creating a database is to determine exactly what information needs to be tracked and what the objective for tracking this information is.

The questions to answer in this stage should deal with how the data will be used. It is important to answer as fully as possible these high-level questions up front because the answers will determine how best to structure the data within the database. By studying the current forms and reports used to track the data, you can get a good feel for the amount and types of data being tracked. You'll also need to analyze the business process to gain some insight into how data is collected. This insight will help you in organizing the data into logical tables and also tell you how your database's forms should be designed.

Collecting the Identified Fields into Tables

The next step of the process is to arrange the fields you identified in the preceding step into logical tables. One of the requirements of a table is that it model one and only one entity. Thus, fields containing contact information should be stored in a separate table from fields containing company information. Also, the collection of fields used should describe the entity in question as fully as possible.

Along the way, watch for fields that are candidates for lookup tables. If the data being modeled has a field that consistently has repeated values, this field is a good candidate for a lookup table. The lookup table will most likely consist of two fields: a primary key field (the `AutoNumber` data type is recommended) and a description field that contains the values being repeated. The main table's field would then be replaced with a foreign key field that matches the primary key of the lookup table. In the Northwind database, the Shippers and Categories tables are the best examples of lookup tables.

NEW TERM A *lookup table* is a table that holds a list of possible values for a field in another table.

The use of lookup tables prevents data inconsistencies that can occur when free-form text is entered into fields. However, lookup tables may not always be warranted. The drawback to using lookup tables is that a join must be created between the base table and the lookup table in order to retrieve a meaningful description of the data stored in the lookup table. This can sometimes degrade performance if too many joins are attempted in a single query. A balance must be struck between the desire for consistent data and performance.

Identifying Primary Key Fields

Every table must have a unique identifier for each record. This can be one field or a set of fields. Attempt to identify candidates for the primary key at this stage. I recommend that an `AutoNumber` field be added to the table to serve as the primary key if the table in question is not an intermediate table for a many-to-many relationship.

Drawing a Simple Data Diagram

Now comes the task of creating a diagram (similar to the one shown in Figure 16.1) for the new database. Draw each entity in its own box and be sure to include the primary key fields. After each entity (table) is drawn, draw the links between the tables by connecting primary (and composite) keys to foreign keys.

While these links are being drawn, check for links that would benefit from intermediate tables. These links are usually present when there are links in different directions between two tables.

16

Normalizing the Data

The process of modifying a database's structure so that it fully conforms to the relational model is known as normalization. The basic goal of normalization is to remove redundant data from the database. In the process, the final database is made more flexible and better able to absorb the inevitable changes to its structure. Now is the best time to make sure the new tables follow these recommendations!

Normalization involves the following processes:

☐ Ensure that each table's fields are uniquely identified by the table's primary key.

☐ Ensure that each field represents a single piece of information. Do not store both city and state in the same field, for instance.

☐ Remove redundant data from the tables. Each record of the database should contain unique data. Each unique piece of information should be stored in one place (except for key fields, which have duplicated values throughout the database).

☐ Remove repeating group fields if there is a possibility that more fields will be added to the group. For example, if a table holding contact information stores a home phone number, a business phone number, and a fax number, it might be wise to create a table to hold the number and a description of its type, along with a foreign key to the contact belonging to each phone number. That way, if you want to track additional types of phone numbers in the future you merely add the new phone number type to the list of available phone numbers. This becomes a data issue because you won't need to change the structure of the database to accomplish this task.

Identifying Field-Specific Information

After the complete structure has been created, it is time to start defining the physical layout of the tables. Here's the recommended process:

1. Create sensible field and table names. These should describe the data but not be excessively long.

2. Identify the data type for the fields: text, numeric, currency, and so on. For text fields, determine the maximum length that will be allowed. For numeric fields, determine the range of numbers that will be stored.

3. Determine whether there are any validation rules, defaults (a value that will be inserted automatically when a new record is added), or input formatting that should be applied to the field.

16

Creating the Physical Tables

The last step of the design process is to use Access to create the physical database tables. As you saw in the previous two hours, Access has several wizards that aid in the creation of new or linked tables. I recommend that you create some tables using the wizards and then experiment in the Design view of the tables. The upcoming hours discuss manually creating components of an Access 97 database.

16

Summary

During this hour you learned how to design effective databases. However, all the reading in the world is no substitute for on-the-job training. The best way to learn the ins and outs of database design is to design and work with a lot of different databases. Fortunately, Access 97 makes database design and construction nearly painless and very efficient.

Always remember these two key points:

- ☐ An effective database design is flexible, logical, and methodical by nature.
- ☐ The power of relational databases lies in the relationships that can be created between diverse tables.

Workshop

The Workshop is designed to help you anticipate possible questions, review what you've learned, and begin thinking ahead to putting your knowledge into practice. The answers to the quiz are in Appendix A, "Quiz Answers."

Q&A

Q Does Access require that every table have a primary key?

A No. There is no such requirement imposed by Access itself. However, if the table is going to be used in conjunction with another table (that is, in a join), there must be a unique identifier in order to create the joined data.

Q Does Access have any built-in features for assisting in the use of joins?

A Yes. When a relationship is defined between two tables, you can specify the type of join to use when querying on both of the tables in the same query. This is done by opening the Join Properties dialog in the Relationships window. You access the Join Properties dialog by double-clicking the line representing the join in question.

Quiz

1. Name the three types of keys.
2. What is the main difference between a primary and a foreign key?
3. Name the three types of joins.
4. Briefly define normalization.
5. Having multiple fields in a single table to represent different types of phone numbers is an example of what?

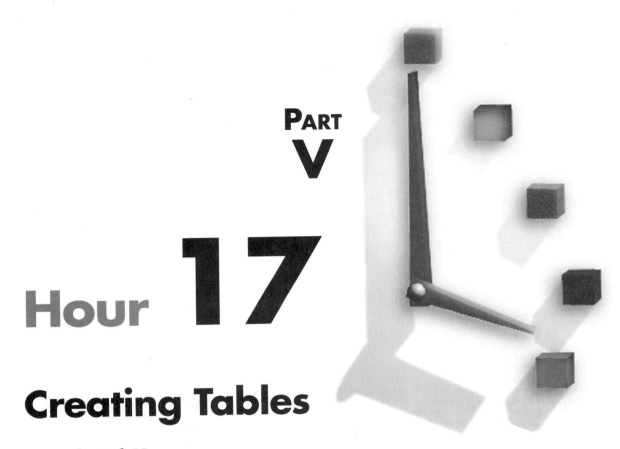

Hour 17

Creating Tables

by Rob Newman

Before you start creating a new table, take a look at the different methods Access provides for creating tables. Access 97 provides five ways to create a table. You use the first three, Datasheet View, Design View, and Table Wizard, to create a new blank table. You use the last two methods, Import Table and Link Table (called Attach Table in versions prior to Access 97), to create a table from an external data source. Examine each method with its advantages and disadvantages:

Datasheet View	Datasheet View presents you with a free-form, spreadsheet-style way to create your table. With this method, you start with an empty sheet where you enter data. Its advantages are that you can select this method and start typing data immediately without defining the structure of the table first. Access 97 even determines the correct data type for each field that has data in it when you save the table. The main disadvantage is you can't set parameters such as field size, default values, and so on, so you will probably modify the table in Design View sooner or later.
Design View	Design View is the more traditional way of designing a table. You see a grid with multiple rows of three columns where you enter the name, data type, and description of each field. Below the grid are a couple of tabs for assigning specific attributes and properties to each field you create. The advantage to this method is that it gives you the most control over how your table is defined. It does require that you understand a little more about table design and relationships between tables in a multitable system.
Table Wizard	This method is the shortcut way to create a table. In Hour 14 you learned how simple it is to create a new table using the Table Wizard. This method is useful if you want to pump out a quick table and you are content to use one of the template tables. However, if you want to create a custom table or one that relates to others, it is best to use either of the first two methods.
Import Table	With this method, you literally import data from an external database or file. You can then edit and print this data just as you do with any other Access table. The new table is only a copy of the data, so any changes you make to the data affect only the table.
Link Table	This method is similar to the Import Table in that you specify an existing data source. The difference with this method is that you create a live link to the database where the original data is stored. Any changes you make to the data in a linked table are also updated to the data in its main source (in an SQL Server database, for example).

17

Creating a New Table

Now that you know how to use the various methods for creating a new table, walk through the steps required to design a new table. First you'll build a table using the Datasheet View method, and then you'll create one using the Design View method so you can get an idea of how each method is used.

JUST A MINUTE

> Make sure to save the tables from the exercises because you will be working with them throughout the hour.

Building a Table Using Datasheet View

First, ensure you have a database open. You can use any of the sample databases that Access provides or use the one you created in previous hours. Perform the following steps:

1. Select the New button while on the Table tab of the database container window. (You can also select **Insert | Table** from the main menu.) You see the New Table dialog.

2. Select the first option, Datasheet View. The grid you see is waiting for you to input some sample data.

TIME SAVER

> Notice that the columns (or fields, as Access calls them) are named Field1, Field2, Field3, and so on. You can change these names while in Datasheet View by double-clicking the column name.

3. Enter the following data in the first row across the top of the grid:

Field1	1
Field2	Jumping Java
Field3	1901 Auburn Way
Field4	Auburn
Field5	WA
Field6	12/22/96
Field7	$1509
Field8	%6

4. Click the Save button on the toolbar. You are prompted for a name for your new table. Type CustomerTable and click OK to finish.

5. What's this? Access says you do not have a primary key defined. This is Access's polite way of indicating that you forgot something essential in the table, a primary key. A primary key is nothing more than a field that contains unique, non-repeating values. For now, select No.

That's all there is to it. Make sure that what you have looks something like Figure 17.1.

Figure 17.1.

Building a table using Datasheet View.

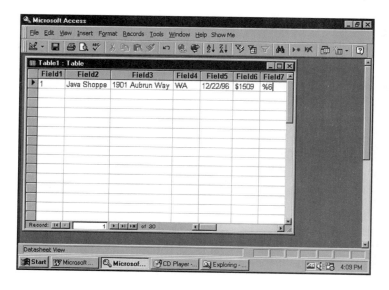

Take a moment to look at how Access defined the table. Open the table you just created in Design View. Notice how Access chose the number data type for Field1 and Field7. Field2 through Field5 were created as text. Field6 was defined as currency because for that field, you entered the dollar symbol followed by a number. Also, do you remember Field7 where you entered a percent symbol followed by a number? Click Field7 and notice on the General tab that Access selected percent for the format type.

Now that you've seen how Access uses the Datasheet View to create tables, move on to the next method.

Building a Table Using Design View

This time, you'll build a simple Orders table. Making sure you have an open database, click the New button. You are prompted to select a method. Follow these steps:

1. Select the second option, Design View. This time, you see a grid that has only three columns across the top.

17

2. In the first row and under the Field Name column, type `CustomerID`.

3. Move to the Data Type column and select AutoNumber for the data type (a special kind of data type I'll explain later in the section on Data Types). Continue to add the remaining fields as follows:

Field Name	Data Type
CustomerName	`Text`
OrderDate	`DateTime`
Amount	`Number`

Before you save this table, customize it to make it better suited for your needs.

4. Click CustomerName. Below the grid on the General tab, click Field Size and change it from 50 to 30.

5. Click OrderDate. On the General tab, click Input Mask and enter the following: `!##/##/####`.

6. Click Amount. On the General tab, click Format and select Currency.

7. Finally, click CustomerID and click the Primary Key button on the toolbar to assign this field as the primary key.

8. Click the Save button on the toolbar and type `OrdersTable`. Click OK to finish.

Make sure that what you have looks something like Figure 17.2.

Figure 17.2.

Building a table using Design View.

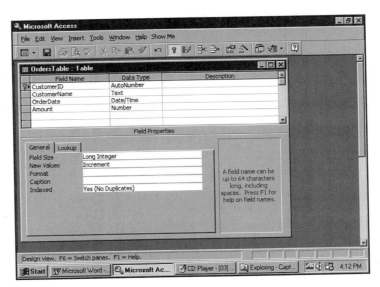

Great! Now that you've walked through how to create tables using the Datasheet View and Design View methods, take a more in-depth look at what you did and how you used some of Access's powerful features to create these tables.

Data Types

In the preceding exercise, you covered a couple of interesting data types that Access provides to make creating and managing a database a breeze. One of these is the AutoNumber type, which is a special data type. When you assign this type to a field, Access ensures that a unique number is assigned to each and every record that you enter into your table. By using AutoNumber, you are not required to produce a unique number because Access always provides it.

When considering which data type to use in your table, it's important to know the capabilities and limitations of the various data types. It is also important to know what data will be used in each field. For example, if you create a table to contain employee data, you might have a field to track the marital status of each employee. You could use a Yes/No data type field that allows you to signify whether the person is married. Suppose that later, you want to track whether the person's status is married, never married, divorced, or widowed. You now have four options rather than two, and a number or text data type might be better suited for this.

Field Properties

When you created the table in Design View mode, you customized a few of the properties on the General tab below the fields grid in the Design View window. These properties give you a powerful edge in creating the table to fit your design needs. The following sections describe some of these properties and how you can use them.

Field Size

The Field Size property allows you to determine the amount of data that can be entered in Text, Number, or AutoNumber fields. In general, set this to more than you think you need. Access uses variable-length record storage, so it only stores the information you actually enter into a field. In other words, if you set a Name field to a length of 50 and you enter Bob, Access stores only three characters for the field, not all 50 characters as some other database management systems do.

17

Format

You use the Format property to format how the data is displayed. You can use it with Text, Number, DateTime, and Yes/No data types. In the exercise, you created a field called Amount and then selected the Format property to define that it should be displayed as currency. If you have a DateTime field called TimeEntered and you want it to display as hours and minutes, for example, you set the Format to Time.

Input Masks

You use input masks to restrict what kind of data is entered into a field and how it is entered. In the example, you created a field called OrderDate with an input mask of !##/##/####. Input masks use special characters as instructions and placeholders for data. In the example, the first character is an exclamation point, which instructs Access to make the cursor enter the field on the left side and proceed to the right as a person types in the data. This action is opposite of the behavior that Access usually exhibits when entering data in a field.

The pound symbols are placeholders and they restrict data to only numbers and spaces. The forward slash is a standard date separator and automatically appears when the cursor enters the field. Input masks are very powerful because of the level of control it gives you. In the past, you had to write code to achieve the same effect.

Default Values

The Default Values property allows you to set a default value for a field. This can be helpful if you have a field that you don't want to contain null or missing data. By setting the default to zero, you never have null values. Another use is for an area code field in a phone list table. If most of the entries in the table are in the 206 area code, you can define 206 as the default and save a few keystrokes when entering records.

Lookup Fields

The Lookup field is a special property that allows you to limit data input in a field to a list from another table or query. The Lookup field not only makes sure that good data is entered, it also allows the user to select data from a restricted list, rather than enter anything he wants. Figure 17.3 gives you an idea of how to add a Lookup field in the table you created earlier by following these steps:

1. Select the OrdersTable that you created earlier.
2. In the database container window, click the Design button.
3. Click an empty row below the last field in the table.

4. Type ShipVia in the Field Name column. Select Text for the Data Type.

5. Below the grid, click the Lookup tab.

6. Select Combo Box in the Display Control property box.

7. Select Value List in the Row Source Type property box.

8. Enter the following in the Row Source property box: FedEx;UPS;USPS. (Make sure to include the semicolons.)

9. Click the Save button on the toolbar.

When you view the table in Datasheet view, click the ShipVia field to see a combo box. What you have should look like Figure 17.2 earlier in the hour.

Figure 17.3.

Creating a Lookup *field.*

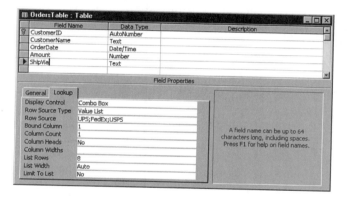

Setting and Changing a Primary Key

Primary keys are what allows Access to relate data between tables in a multitable database. Remember the table you created in the section "Building a Table Using Datasheet View" earlier in this hour? Return to that table and add a primary key to it:

1. In the database container window, select the CustomerTable table and click the Design button.

2. In the first field, click the Primary Key button on the toolbar (the one that looks like a key). You can also select **Edit** | Primary Key or click the right mouse button and select Primary Key from the pop-up menu.

3. To change the primary key, simply select another field and click the Primary Key button on the toolbar.

4. Click the Save button.

17

> When you set or change the primary key for a table that already has data in it, Access checks the quality of the data before allowing you to select it. If Access detects null (missing) data or non-unique values, it warns you and does not allow you to select that field as the primary key.

Indexes

Access uses indexes as road maps to find your data in a timely and efficient manner when you run a query or report or simply browse your tables. Access uses indexes pretty much how you use an index in the back of a reference manual or in a Windows help file to search for a topic or word.

Setting and Changing Indexes

Create an index for the `CustomerName` field in the `OrdersTable` you created earlier:

1. In the database container window, select the `OrdersTable` and click the Design button.
2. Click the Indexes button on the toolbar (the one with a few lines next to a lightning bolt). You should see the Indexes dialog with the `CustomerID` field already entered. Access created this index when you selected the `CustomerID` field as a primary key field.
3. Click an empty row in the Index Name column.
4. Type `CustomerName`.
5. In the Field Name column, click the arrow and select the `CustomerName` field.
6. Close the dialog and click the Save button on the toolbar.

If you enter a lot of records and then run a query or a report based on the customer name, Access is in much better shape to handle the output of the data.

Which Fields to Index

The types of fields to index are not always obvious. Some data types, such as text, seem to always perform better with an index. `AutoNumber` fields and other non-text fields don't seem to gain much benefit from indexing. As a rule of thumb, you should index a `Number` or `DateTime` field in a large table that you are constantly querying. Some database professionals feel that you cannot have too many indexes on a table. It's important to realize, however, that every index placed on a table must be updated whenever records are added, modified, or deleted.

From my experience, performance rather than storage space is the primary factor in limiting indexes.

Setting Relationships Between Tables

In Hour 10, "Modifying an Existing Table," you learned about relationships and how to work with the various properties of table relationships. Access 97 uses relationships to relate the data within various tables. It's similar to how I am related to my in-laws through my wife. Before my marriage, I had no relationship with them. They had their lineage or family tree and I had mine, and there was no connection or link. Our child is the connecting point between the families because she contains the genes, or elements of both genetic lines. In database terminology, the connecting point is called an entity. This example is really more of a mathematical equation, but you get the picture.

Take a look at the two tables again and see how a relationship is established between two tables:

1. Close any tables you might have open and click on the Database container window.
2. Click the Relationships button on the toolbar. Depending on which database you use, you may or may not have some relationships already established.
3. Click the Show Tables button on the toolbar (a yellow plus symbol).
4. Double-click the CustomerTable and OrdersTable, which adds them to the Relationships View window. Click close.
5. Drag the tables around so they are side-by-side with the OrdersTable to the right of the CustomerTable.
6. Now the fun part: Click Field1 in the CustomerTable (the CustomerID field). Now, drag this over to the CustomerID field in the OrdersTable; you need to drop it right over the CustomerID field. You now see the Relationships dialog.
7. Verify that the fields from each table are correct and click the Enforce Referential Integrity box.
8. Click the Create button and the Save button on the toolbar. Figure 17.4 shows how the relationship appears.

Referential Integrity

Access 97 uses referential integrity (RI) to maintain the integrity of the relationships established between tables. RI is how Access prevents orphaned records and other anomalies that can occur in a relational database model. Suppose you have a customer in CustomerTable

17

that has several related records in the OrdersTable. If you delete that particular customer record, orphan records are produced in OrdersTable because they no longer have the relationship to the CustomerTable. By enforcing RI via the Relationships view between the two tables, Access prevents you from creating this type of problem.

Figure 17.4.

Creating a relationship between tables.

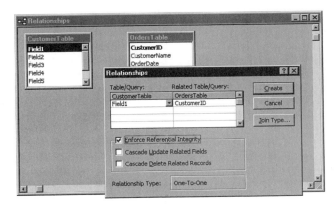

Cascade Updates and Deletes

Another couple of powerful features to help you maintain integrity in your database are the Cascade **U**pdate Related Fields and Cascade **D**elete Related Records options. These options allow you to override the restrictions against updating or deleting data in an RI-enforced relationship. These features are only available if the **E**nforce Referential Integrity option is checked in the Relationships dialog. The way they work is simple. With Cascade **U**pdate, whenever a value in the primary key of a table is changed, any related tables automatically update to the new value. Cascade **D**elete works in a similar way. When a record in the primary table is deleted, any and all related records are automatically deleted.

Types of Relationships

Access 97 relates between tables (also referred to as joins) in three ways. On the Relationships dialog is a button called Join Type. Clicking this button opens a dialog with the three options for joins:

- ☐ Only include rows where the joined fields from both tables are equal—a one-to-one join.

- ☐ Include all records from Customer and only those records from Orders where the joined fields are equal—a one-to-many join.

- ☐ Include all records from Orders and only those records from Customer where the joined fields are equal—a many-to-one join.

The type of join you use will make a big difference in how Access 97 stores and displays your data. The first join type (one-to-one) is the most restrictive, but it helps ensure referential integrity by not allowing unmatched records in your database.

To get a better idea of how each join will affect your data, look at the following data. First, assume you have the following records in the Customer table:

CustomerID	Customer
BENJ	Benjamin's Bagels
HILL	Hillside Cafe
JUMP	Jumping Java

And in the Orders table, you have these records:

OrderID	Customer
JUMP	
JUMP	
BENJ	
13	JACK

If you select the first join type, one-to-one, your data when joined, would look like this:

Customer	Order		
BENJ	Benjamin's Bagels	12	BENJ
JUMP	Jumping Java	10	JUMP
JUMP	Jumping Java	11	JUMP

Notice the customer record for Hillside Cafe is missing. This is because there are no order records for this customer.

If you select the next join type with a one-to-many join on the Customer side, your records would be related like this:

Customer	Order		
BENJ	Benjamin's Bagels	12	BENJ
HILL	Hillside Cafe		
JUMP	Jumping Java	10	JUMP
JUMP	Jumping Java	11	JUMP

Now you see all the customers; but where is the data for the other customers in the Orders table? There is none for the Hillside Cafe.

17

Finally, if you select the join type that is a one-to-many on the Orders side, you will see the following:

Customer	Order		
JUMP	Jumping Java	10	JUMP
JUMP	Jumping Java	11	JUMP
BENJ	Benjamin's Bagels	12	BENJ
		13	Jack

You now see all the orders; but where there is no match for the Customer, there is a blank or Null data. Create your joins carefully and wisely, and they will help to keep your database useful.

Summary

In this hour, you saw how simple it is to use the power of Access 97 to create tables. Access 97 provides several different ways to create objects. The method you choose will be based on your experience and the needs of the system you are designing, but all the methods can be valuable as you build your database. I also touched on some fairly advanced features and topics. Although I only touched on some of the more complex ideas such as referential integrity, you have learned enough information to create and customize your tables to fit your design requirements.

Workshop

The Workshop is designed to help you anticipate possible questions, review what you've learned, and begin thinking ahead to putting your knowledge into practice. The answers to the quiz are in Appendix A, "Quiz Answers."

Q&A

Q When is it appropriate to use a table wizard instead of using Datasheet or Design View mode?

A Access wizards are great for producing simple, cookie-cutter solutions. They are useful for quickly creating a prototype model, which you can then go in and modify to fit your needs. However, as you gain experience creating tables from scratch, it's likely you will want to give up the ease and flexibility that Access 97 allows.

Q **I created a table using the Datasheet View, and I entered the following numbers in a column 4500, 6325, and $3456. When I saved the table, Access 97 selected Text as the data type for this column. Why did Access create it as a text field?**

A Access 97 is pretty smart about selecting the correct data type. However, if you enter a mixture of data types—in this case general numbers and a currency number—Access will pick a data type that they will all fit into, which is usually the Text data type. If you had entered the currency number in the first row, Access would have selected Currency as the data type.

Q **When creating a table in Design View, what is the Description column used for?**

A The Description column is valuable for a couple of reasons. First, it is a way to document your fields when you create them. Sometimes when creating tables, developers create names that are short and meaningful, but which a year or two later don't make much sense. Second, descriptions show up in the status bar at the bottom of the screen when you enter that field in Datasheet View, and are a handy way of reminding your users about the purpose of that field.

Quiz

1. Which method would you use to create a table if the original data source was in an outside database and you wanted to update the original data when you changed the data in Access 97?

2. What is the data type that you use when you want Access 97 to automatically update for you?

3. How would you restrict data in a field to only dates?

4. How do you prevent orphaned or unmatched records between two related tables?

17

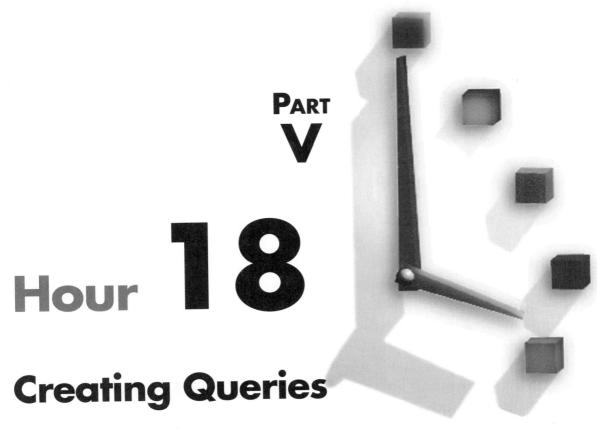

Hour 18

Creating Queries

by Rob Newman

In this hour, you will learn how to create queries from scratch using Access's Design Grid. In Hour 11, "Modifying and Using Existing Queries," you learned how to modify an existing query. Compared to many other database management systems, creating queries in Access is a pleasure with the Design Grid, expression builders, and other powerful query tools that Access 97 provides. Some of the things you will learn in this hour are

- ☐ The Design Grid
- ☐ Steps in creating a query
- ☐ Creating generic queries with parameters
- ☐ Querying multiple tables

As you saw in the previous hour and throughout this book, Access 97 generally gives you several ways of doing something. Queries are no exception to this. You have five different options when you click the New button on the Query tab in the Database window. You also can import queries through the Import Tables option; why this option is not presented through the new query options is anyone's guess, but it is another option you need to be aware of. Take a look at each way you can create a new query in Access 97:

Design View	This method is the equivalent of creating a new table in Design View. It's also the one that gives you the most power and flexibility to create a query.
Query Wizard	Another one of Access 97's many wizards guides you through the creation of a simple query. When they say simple, they mean it. The only options are for which table and fields you want in your query. The Query Wizard is okay for a quick select query, but it doesn't offer much more than simply browsing a table in Datasheet View mode.
Crosstab Wizard	This wizard leads you through the creation of a crosstab query. A crosstab query is a special kind of query that enables you to present your data in a multidimensional mode, similar to an Excel spreadsheet. Its data is defined in both columns and rows, and where they cross, or intersect, is a cell containing something that is significant to both measures.
Find Duplicates	This wizard helps you create a query that finds duplicate values in a single table or query.
Find Unmatched	This wizard helps you find unmatched or orphaned records in a multitable relationship. Hour 17, "Creating Tables," discussed how to use referential integrity to prevent orphaned records. A Find Unmatched query is useful prior to creating a join that enforces referential integrity.

The Query Design Grid

When you select the Design View method to create a new query, you see Access's now-famous Query Design Grid. The beauty of Access's Query Design Grid is how it uses visual objects to represent your tables, queries, and the joins, or relationships between them. This use of visual objects, coupled with the simple genius of its drag-and-drop interface, makes the Design View a potent tool for getting at your data.

The Design Grid has two main areas. (See Figure 18.1.) First, the upper portion is the area where Access 97 displays the tables or queries that you've selected for this query. You can move tables and queries around, resize them to allow you to view more fields, and so on. The lower portion is the grid portion of the window where you define the structure of your query by entering fields, selection criteria, calculations, sorting commands, and so on. The Design

18

Grid window has many other parts, some of which I cover in the following sections. Features such as action queries and crosstab queries are discussed in Hour 24, "Publishing Access 97 Data on the Web."

Figure 18.1.

Creating a query using the Design Grid.

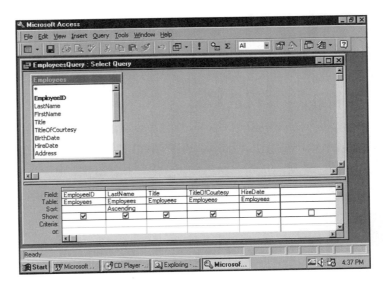

Steps in Creating a Query

Now that you know a little bit about the Design Grid, you can create a new query and learn how to use the exciting features of the Access 97 query form. First, open the infamous Northwind database, the sample database that has been around almost as long as Access (we will be doing all our examples in this database). Now, work through the following steps to create a simple query based on the Employee table in the database:

1. Click the New button while on the Query tab of the database container window or select **I**nsert | **Q**uery from the main menu.

2. Select the first option for Design View.

3. You are now asked to select a table, query, or both. Click the Employee table. Click the Add button. Access leaves open the Show Table dialog in case you want to add more tables or queries. Click Close for now, and you see the Employee table in the upper portion of the query form.

JUST A MINUTE

If you accidentally select more than one table or if you add a table other than the Employee table, you can easily remove it by clicking the table and pressing your delete key.

4. Start adding a few fields. Click the `EmployeeID` field and drag it down to the first column on the grid.

TIME SAVER

> You also can double-click the field, and you can even insert by going to the Field section in the grid where you see a down arrow that allows you to select a field from a drop-down list.

5. Add the following fields: `LastName`, `Title`, `TitleofCourtesy`, and `HireDate`.

6. To view the query, click the View button on the toolbar (it looks like a grid or spreadsheet). You see all the employees with the information from the fields you selected. After viewing the result, click the Save button, type in `EmployeeQuery` for the name, and click OK to save it.

Specifying a Sort Order

As it is, the query you just created is only marginally better than viewing the same table in Table View. It has fewer fields, but other than that change, the query is really no different. One very useful purpose for queries is showing the data sorted in different ways—by last name or title, for example. You can sort in either ascending or descending order.

1. Now, go to the grid and under the `LastName` field, click the Sort box. You see an arrow appear. You can sort either in ascending or descending order.

2. Select Ascending order and then click the View button on the toolbar. Notice that the records appear in order of their last names, whereas before, they were sorted by the `EmployeeID` field by default.

After viewing the query, click on the View button to return to Design view. Keep the query open for the next section.

Specifying Criteria

Now that you have a simple query that is sorted by the employees' last names, take a look at the most common use of a query, which involves providing a parameter or criteria. By specifying criteria, you can look at subsets of data that allow you to work with smaller, more defined recordsets. Enter a real easy criteria and examine the results. Imagine you want to see all employees that have the position of Sales Representative.

1. To do this, click the `Title` field in the Criteria box below the checkbox.

2. Type the words `Sales Representative` just as they appear here (case is not important). Check Figure 18.2 to see how to enter this.

18

Figure 18.2.

Entering criteria in a query.

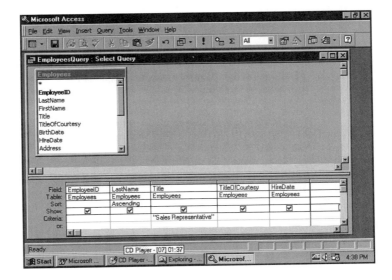

3. Click the View button to see the results. You should see only employees who are sales representatives. You can close this query without saving it.

Showing and Excluding Fields

When you are in the Design Grid, you notice a small checkbox just under the Sort box in each column on the grid. (Refer to Figure 18.2.) When this box is checked, which is the default for each field you select, the field appears in your result set. If you do not want a field to appear, you simply click the box to hide it from showing in your result set. This is useful for a couple of reasons. The primary reason is when using a summary function in your query, you can have conflicting results if you include certain fields. Another time you might not want to display a field is if you specify a certain parameter in a date field, for example, you might not want to display that field, because it's going to have the same value for each record in the recordset, which is redundant.

Using Advanced Options in Queries

By now you have learned some of the principal but basic uses of queries in Access 97. Sooner or later, however, you are going to need to go beyond a simple sorted list. Fortunately Access 97 provides some advanced querying options such as wildcards, parameters, and calculations, and in this section you will see how easy it is to use these advanced options.

Wildcards

One of the problems you might encounter in creating queries involves partial or unknown words, phrases, or other data. What if you want to search your data for a particular value, a name perhaps, but you aren't certain of the spelling?

Access 97 provides several wildcard characters that can either act as placeholders or specify the beginning or ending characters of a text field. Table 18.1 explains some of the wildcards and their usage.

Table 18.1. Access 97 wildcards.

Symbol	Usage	Example	Result
*	Use to match any number of characters in a field either at the beginning or the end of the field.	An* *an	Anne; Andrew Buchanan; Callahan
?	Use to match a single character in a field.	Ro?	Rob; Ron; Rod
#	Use to match any single number in a field.	7#7	727, 737, 747, 757, 767, 777
-	Use to find a single character within a range of characters you specify.	J[a-o]N	Jan, Jen, Jon

Comparison Operators

When you specify criteria in a query, Access needs to know how you want to see the result in relation to the criteria you enter. You specify the relationship with comparison operators, which are common algebraic operators you learned in grade school. For example, if you enter a greater-than symbol (>) in a date or numeric field, Access displays all records with a value greater than the one you specify. You can use them in text, numeric, or date and time fields, but you generally use them to query date and numeric values. Table 18.2 shows the Access comparison operators.

Table 18.2. Access 97 comparison operators.

Symbol	Description	Example	Result
<	Less than	`<12/31/96`	12/30/96
<=	Less than or equal to; includes the value you specify	`<=5000`	5000,4999
=	Equal to	`="Janet"`	Janet
>	Greater than	`>1000`	1001
>=	Greater than or equal to; includes the value you specify	`>=1/1/95`	1/1/95,1/2/95
<>	Not equal to	`<>"Bill"`	Janet

Look at an example of using wildcards and comparison operators. Suppose you want to search for an employee who you know has a first name that begins with the letters An. You enter `An*` in the `FirstName` field. You're not sure of the person's title, but you know this person is not a doctor. You enter `<>Dr.` in the TitleOfCourtesy field. Figure 18.3 shows how this query looks.

Figure 18.3.

Using wildcards and comparison operators in a query.

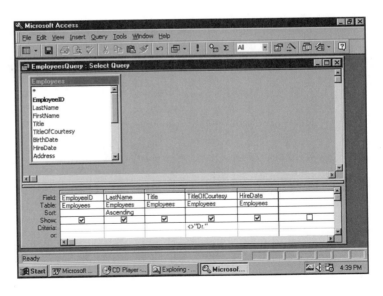

18

Creating Generic Queries with Parameters

One great feature of Access queries is the capability to create generic queries using parameters. Parameters are simply criteria, just like you learned about in the previous section. The difference is that you enter parameters each time you run the query, not at the time you create the query. When you view the query, you are presented with a "fill in the blank" input box, which then inserts the value into the placeholder you specified in the query. Walk through this powerful feature using the EmployeeQuery you created earlier. First, open the query in Design View mode and follow these steps:

1. Double-click the City field from the Employee table. This inserts this field into the query grid.
2. Click the Criteria box below the City column.
3. Type the following: [Enter the City to search for]. Make sure to include the brackets before and after the text.

Now, click the View button. You see a small dialog box asking you to input a city name. (See Figure 18.4.) Enter London, click the OK button, and you see a list of employees who reside in London.

Figure 18.4.

Using parameters in a query.

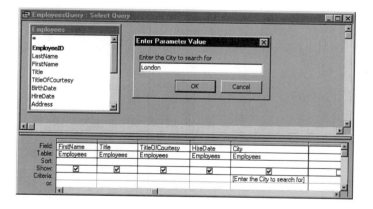

The beauty of parameters is that rather than create a query for each city, you now have one query you can use to query any city. This saves a lot of time, not to mention storage space on your computer.

Adding Calculated Fields

Another extremely useful feature of Access queries is the calculated field. Calculated fields, which can take many forms, are useful for performing analysis on a table. Take a look at how you can manipulate some numeric data to get some useful figures. Suppose you have a table full of orders in your retail business and you want to calculate the revenue. For this, you need to create a new query based on the Order Details table in the Northwind database. Create a new query using the Design View mode and select all the fields.

JUST A MINUTE

Access uses special characters in queries to distinguish Access objects such as fields, tables, queries, and so on in an expression. These identifiers are the left ([) and right (]) bracket symbols. You must put these identifiers around your field and table names when creating a calculated field or other expression.

Follow these steps to create your calculated field:

1. After you insert all the fields in the query, click the blank column to the right of the last field on the grid.
2. Click the Criteria box below the City column.
3. Access allows you to type directly into this field, so simply enter the following text:
   `[UnitPrice]*[Quantity]-([UnitPrice]*[Discount])`.
4. Click the View button to see the results. (See Figure 18.5.)

Figure 18.5.

Using calculations in a query.

Order ID	Product	Unit Price	Quantity	Discount	Expr1
10248	Queso Cabrales	$14.00	12	0%	$168.00
10248	Singaporean Hokkien Fried M	$9.80	10	0%	$98.00
10248	Mozzarella di Giovanni	$34.80	5	0%	$174.00
10249	Tofu	$18.60	9	0%	$167.40
10249	Manjimup Dried Apples	$42.40	40	0%	$1,696.00
10250	Jack's New England Clam C	$7.70	10	0%	$77.00
10250	Manjimup Dried Apples	$42.40	35	15%	$1,477.64
10250	Louisiana Fiery Hot Pepper S	$16.80	15	15%	$249.48
10251	Gustaf's Knäckebröd	$16.80	6	5%	$99.96
10251	Ravioli Angelo	$15.60	15	5%	$233.22
10251	Louisiana Fiery Hot Pepper S	$16.80	20	0%	$336.00
10252	Sir Rodney's Marmalade	$64.80	40	5%	$2,588.76
10252	Geitost	$2.00	25	5%	$49.90
10252	Camembert Pierrot	$27.20	40	0%	$1,088.00
10253	Gorgonzola Telino	$10.00	20	0%	$200.00
10253	Chartreuse verte	$14.40	42	0%	$604.80

Record: 1 of 2155

CalcFieldsQuery : Select Query

18

You created a field that is the product of the UnitPrice field times the Quantity field minus the product of UnitPrice times the Discount field—in other words, price×qty–discount=gross.

You can also handle calculations such as this in reports, but it is fairly easy to do them in a query if you need some quick figures. Another common use of calculated fields is to create a compound field or concatenated field made up of several text fields. An expression such as [LastName]+", "+[FirstName] creates a single field with the last name, a comma, and the first name fields together.

Additional Query Features

The previous sections covered the more standard uses of a select query. Getting familiar with these uses and practicing them by trying various wildcard selections, parameters, and so on provide you with the skills you need to process the majority of your query needs. However, you should be familiar with a couple of other ways to use a query and the common ways of viewing and analyzing your data. These features are usually turned off when you create a new query. To enable them while in Design View mode, click the Totals button on the toolbar; it looks like the Greek Sigma character (Σ), and it is common to Excel and other Windows applications. This inserts a new row called Total into the Design Grid for performing Group By, Sum, Average, Count, and other summary functions. Take a look at a couple of these features, which are described in the following sections.

Group By Queries

A Group By query is a way to view your data arranged in groups by whatever fields you specify. When you use the Group By option, Access combines all records with the same values into a single record. Suppose you create a query showing the CustomerID and ShipCity fields that is sorted by the CustomerID field (from the Orders table in the Northwind database). When you run it, you see that the first records are identical. (See Figure 18.6.)

Figure 18.6.

A query result showing ungrouped records.

18

Now, return to the query, click the Total button, and run the query again. (Access automatically assigns the Group By option to the fields.) You see that each record with duplicates is combined or grouped into one record (as shown in Figure 18.7).

Figure 18.7.

The same query showing the effect of using Group By.

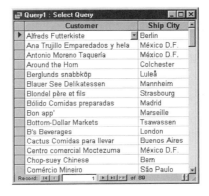

Totals Queries

Access can perform several other summary options using the total feature in a query. Among them, the sum and count functions are used quite often. You use the sum option in Access just as you do in an Excel spreadsheet. The count option is helpful for doing analysis on your data when you want to see a count of the number of records for a certain criteria. Suppose you want to see the number of employees hired for the year 1993. This is easy to do with a query that looks like the screen shown in Figure 18.8.

Figure 18.8.

Using the count function.

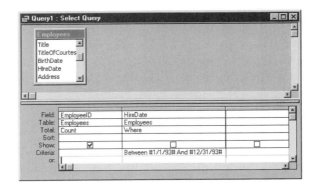

You create this query using the count function on the `Employee` field because you know it is the primary key for the table and therefore contains a unique value for each record in the table. In the `HireDate` field, you enter the date range using the Between operator. When you run the query, you get an answer of 3.

18

Querying Multiple Tables

Up to this point we have been working with a single Access table. One of the principal design features of Access 97 is the capability to support the "Relational Model," which is the primary concept of relating disparate data tables to one another. In Hour 17 you learned how to relate tables to each other using the Relationships design window. You learned about the different join types and how they affect your data. Let's see how we can use these related tables to query data from more than one source. Open the Northwind database and follow along.

1. Create a new query using Design view.
2. From the Show Tables dialog, select (double-click) the Customer and Orders tables. Click Close. You should notice that Access inserted both tables, with a black line connecting them.

JUST A MINUTE

If there is no line connecting the two tables, you can add it by clicking the `CustomerID` field in the Customers table and dragging it over to the `CustomerID` field in the Orders table.

3. Add several fields from each table and click on the View button.

That's all there is to it. There are many advanced queries you can create using multiple tables. Things like outer joins, sub-queries, self-joins, and so on. These types of queries get quite complex, but Access 97 can produce them with ease.

Summary

In this hour, you learned the power of Access 97 queries and some of the ways you can use them to view and manipulate your data. You saw that an Access query makes a fascinating tool. The powerful features of the Query Design Grid make Access shine above its competitors in the desktop database world.

Workshop

The Workshop is designed to help you anticipate possible questions, review what you've learned, and begin thinking ahead to putting your knowledge into practice. The answers to the quiz are in Appendix A, "Quiz Answers."

18

Q&A

Q **What is the star (asterisk) at the top of each table when in Query Design mode?**

A This is the symbol for ALL. Just like the wildcard character. You can insert this field in your query (by double-clicking) and when you view the query, all the fields in the table will be displayed.

Q **How do I enter more than one criterion per field in a query? For example, I want to search for customers in London and Paris.**

A In the Design Grid window you will notice in the lower section of the grid, you have a row called Criteria:. Below that is a row called or:. You can enter as many criteria as you want simply by entering a criterion on each row.

Q **I have a query that has a lot of duplicates in it. How do I select only unique records?**

A While in Design View mode, select **View** | Properties from the menu. Click on the property for Unique Values. Change this to Yes.

Quiz

1. How would you sort a query first by Title from lowest to highest, then by Hire Date from highest to lowest?

2. Which wildcard symbol would you use to match a single character in a field?

3. What does the >= operator mean?

4. How do I get the total of all the values in a field (Quantity Sold, for example)?

18

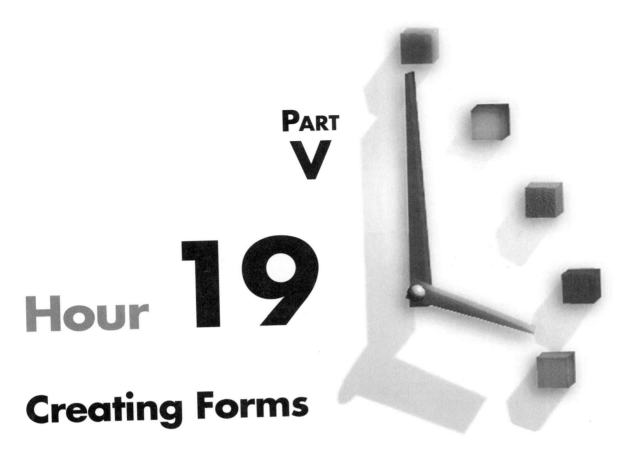

Hour 19

Creating Forms

by Timothy Buchanan

In this hour, you create forms from scratch. You take a couple forms from the Northwind database and re-create them to give you a better understanding of forms and form design. Some of the topics covered in this hour are

- ☐ Types of forms
- ☐ Types of controls
- ☐ Creating and adding controls
- ☐ Setting control properties
- ☐ Creating expressions
- ☐ Creating and linking subforms
- ☐ Aligning and sizing controls
- ☐ Adding graphics

JUST A MINUTE

Earlier in Hour 15, "Adding to a Database Using Wizards," you learned how to create forms using wizards. This hour concentrates on building forms from scratch without using wizards. This gives you a better understanding of the design and inner workings of a form.

Types of Forms

As discussed in Hour 12, "Modifying an Existing Form Design," there are six basic types of forms:

- [ ] Single column
- [ ] Tabular
- [ ] Datasheet
- [ ] Main/subforms
- [ ] Pivot table forms
- [ ] Graphs

You will concentrate on creating single column, tabular, and subforms in this hour. You will look at some forms in the Northwind database and then learn how to re-create them from scratch.

Types of Controls

As discussed in Hour 12, there are three basic types of controls:

- [ ] Bound controls are controls whose source of data is a field in a table or query. When you enter a value into a bound control, that value is updated to the bound table's current record.
- [ ] Unbound controls are controls that do not have a source of data. These controls retain any values you enter but do not update any field in the table.
- [ ] Calculated controls are controls whose source is an expression instead of a field in a table or query. These controls are based on expressions or calculations. Calculated controls do not update any table fields, so they are also a type of unbound control.

Adding Controls

19

Figure 19.1 shows the Customers form from the Northwind database. You will re-create this form from scratch to learn how to create your own forms.

Figure 19.1.

The Customers form from the Northwind database.

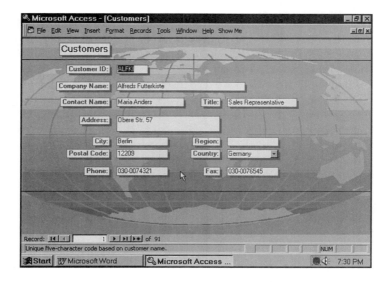

Designing a Form

Look a little closer at the Customers form before you attempt to re-create it. As you can see in Figure 19.1, the Customers form lists all the information about the customer: ID, name, address, phone number, and so on. Each page of the form lists the information about one single customer. The Country field has a drop-down list box to allow the user to select the customer's country. A globe graphic is in the background to spruce up the appearance. When you select the Design View button in the upper-left corner, the display changes to the Design view. There are a couple ways to tell what table or query the form is linked to. If it is not already visible, click the Properties tool to display the property sheet. If you select the form, the property sheet displays the properties for the form, as shown in Figure 19.2.

19

JUST A MINUTE

The toolbox is the menu on the form design screen on the far left side of the screen. This menu consists of the following buttons from top to bottom: Mouse Selector, Wizard, Label, Text Box, Option Group, Toggle Button, Option Button, Check Box, Combo Box, List Box, Command Button, Image, Unbound Object Frame, Bound Object Frame, and a More Controls button. Selecting one of these buttons and clicking one of the sections of the form will create that control wherever you click. This is the easiest way to create new controls.

Figure 19.2.

The property sheet for the Customers form.

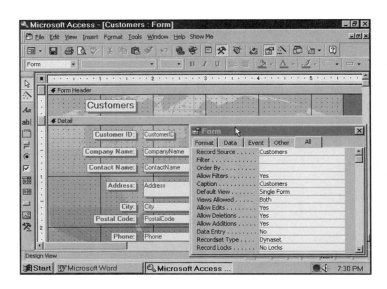

The first property listed is Record Source. As you see in Figure 19.2, the record source for the Customers form is the Customers table. You also can see this by clicking the Field List button on the toolbar. This displays the field list box, as you can see in Figure 19.3. This shows the table or query the form is based on and the fields that are in that table or query.

Figure 19.3.

The field list box for the Customers form.

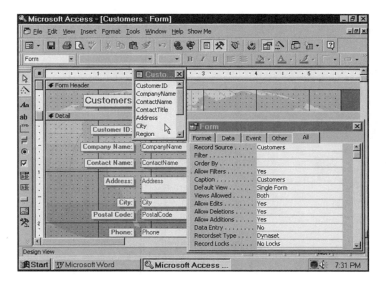

19

Now that you know which table the query is based on and what the form is designed to display, take a look at the table to which the Customers form is linked. Close the Customers form and click the Tables tab in the Database window. Double-click the Customers table to open it in Datasheet view. You should see a screen similar to Figure 19.4. By scrolling to the right, you can see that all the information you saw on the Customers form is stored in this table in datasheet form. The Customers form is a good example of a form that makes tasks such as data entry much easier. Now that you know which table has the information you need and how you want that information to be displayed, create the form.

Figure 19.4.

The Datasheet view of the Customers form.

Customer	Company Name:	Contact Nam	Title:	Address:
ALFKI	Alfreds Futterkiste	Maria Anders	Sales Represent	Obere Str. 57
ANATR	Ana Trujillo Emparedados y	Ana Trujillo	Owner	Avda. de la Constitución 2
ANTON	Antonio Moreno Taquería	Antonio Moren	Owner	Mataderos 2312
AROUT	Around the Horn	Thomas Hardy	Sales Represent	120 Hanover Sq.
BERGS	Berglunds snabbköp	Christina Bergl	Order Administra	Berguvsvägen 8
BLAUS	Blauer See Delikatessen	Hanna Moos	Sales Represent	Forsterstr. 57
BLONP	Blondel père et fils	Frédérique Cite	Marketing Manac	24, place Kléber
BOLID	Bólido Comidas preparadas	Martín Sommer	Owner	C/ Araquil, 67
BONAP	Bon app'	Laurence Lebik	Owner	12, rue des Bouchers
BOTTM	Bottom-Dollar Markets	Elizabeth Linco	Accounting Mana	23 Tsawassen Blvd.
BSBEV	B's Beverages	Victoria Ashwo	Sales Represent	Fauntleroy Circus
CACTU	Cactus Comidas para llevar	Patricio Simps	Sales Agent	Cerrito 333
CENTC	Centro comercial Moctezume	Francisco Char	Marketing Manac	Sierras de Granada 9993
CHOPS	Chop-suey Chinese	Yang Wang	Owner	Hauptstr. 29
COMMI	Comércio Mineiro	Pedro Afonso	Sales Associate	Av. dos Lusíadas, 23
CONSH	Consolidated Holdings	Elizabeth Brow	Sales Represent	Berkeley Gardens
DRACD	Drachenblut Delikatessen	Sven Ottlieb	Order Administra	Walserweg 21
DUMON	Du monde entier	Janine Labrune	Owner	67, rue des Cinquante Ote

Record: 1 of 91

Unique five-character code based on customer name.

JUST A MINUTE

When you create your own forms, you should spend some time thinking about how you want your form to look and what you want your form to accomplish before you begin the actual steps to create it in Access. It is a good idea to sketch on paper what you want the form to look like and then use this as your blueprint when you actually create the form. This advance design work is very beneficial when you actually start to create the form.

19

Creating a New Form

Now you are ready to create a new form. Make sure the Northwind database is open, select the Forms tab from the Database window, and click the New button. A dialog box appears, as shown in Figure 19.5, that asks you for details about the form you want to create.

Figure 19.5.

The dialog box that appears when you want to create a new form.

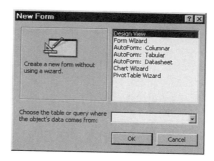

The dialog box asks you to open a blank form or to select the table or query you want to base the form on and whether to use a form wizard. Because the Customers form is based on the Customers table, select the Customers table from the dialog box drop-down list. Now click the Blank Form button to create a blank form that is linked to the Customers table. You should see a blank form view similar to the one shown in Figure 19.6. This blank form shows the property sheet open, as well as the field list box.

Figure 19.6.

A blank form with the property sheet and field list box open.

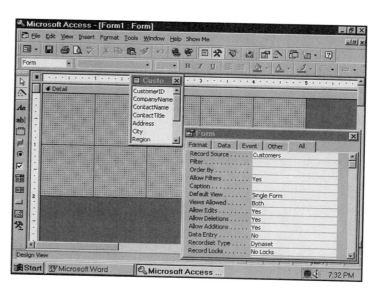

The first step you need to do is add the controls to the form. Looking back to Figure 19.1, notice that all the controls except the Country control are regular text boxes used to display the data. The Country control is a drop-down list box. You need to add all the fields from the Customers table as text boxes, except the Country field. Make sure that the field list box is open and your screen is similar to Figure 19.6.

There are a couple ways to add all the controls to the form. To do this easily, click the Text Box button on the toolbox and then click the Tool Lock button at the bottom of the toolbox. This locks the text box tool in the On position until you are ready to return to the regular mouse tool. Now you can click and drag each of the fields from the field list box to the detail section. For a quicker addition, you can drag the fields all at once. To do this, select the text box tool, click the first field in the field list box, and then scroll down. While holding down the Shift key, select the last field in the list. All the fields are selected. Click the first field in the field list box and drag to the detail section of the form. Drop the icon in the upper-left corner of the detail section, allowing enough room for the text box and label to be displayed to the left of where you drop the icon. Your screen should be similar to Figure 19.7.

Figure 19.7.

The new form after adding the text box controls.

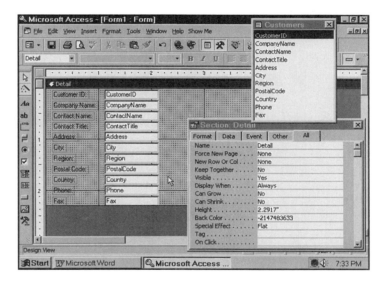

You must delete the Country text box because you will be creating a list box for that field. Scroll down until you see the Country text box. Click the text box and press the Delete key. Now you need to move the controls around and resize them to look like the screen in Figure 19.1. Don't worry about getting things perfect or matching Figure 19.1 exactly. Make sure to leave room for the Country control.

JUST A MINUTE

To select a large group of controls at once, click your mouse pointer on a clear area of the form and drag a square around the controls you want to select. This is useful to size all the controls on this form at one time.

After you resize and rearrange your controls, your form design screen should be similar to the one shown in Figure 19.8. Now you add the Country field as a combo box to allow the drop-down list box to select the country from a list. To add the Country combo box, click the Combo Box icon on the toolbox and then click the Country field in the field list box, drag it to the detail section of your form, and place it near its correct position. When you release the mouse button, the Combo Box Wizard loads, as shown in Figure 19.9.

Figure 19.8.

The form with all the controls added except the Country drop-down list box.

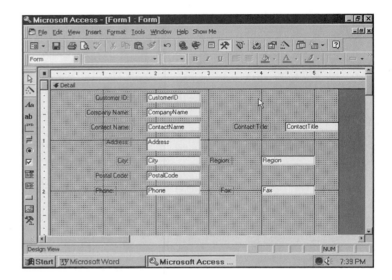

Figure 19.9.

The Combo Box Wizard loads automatically when you place the control on a form.

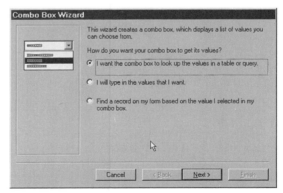

This wizard walks you through setting up a drop-down list box for the Country field. The first screen, shown in Figure 19.10, asks you to tell Access where it should get the values you have to choose from in the list box. Because you want the values already stored in the table, click the Next button to continue.

19

Now, Access asks which table or query you want to base the values on. Select the Customers table, as shown in Figure 19.10.

Figure 19.10.

The first menu that appears when using the Combo Box Wizard.

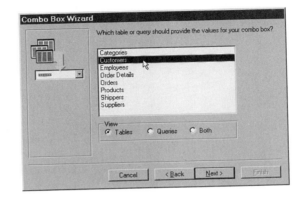

The next screen, shown in Figure 19.11, asks you to choose which field in the table you selected should be used to make the list box. Again, choose the Country field, click the right arrow to add that field to the list, and click the Next button.

Figure 19.11.

The second dialog box of the Combo Box Wizard.

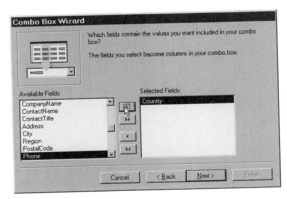

Now Access asks you to select the width of the list box. The default should be fine, and you can always change it later. This is shown in Figure 19.12.

Access asks whether you want to remember the value for later use or to store the value in the chosen field. You want the value to tell you what country the customer is from, so you want Access to store the value in the Country field. This is the default, as shown in Figure 19.13, so click the Next button.

Figure 19.12.

*The third dialog box of
the Combo Box Wizard.*

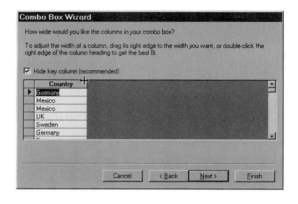

Figure 19.13.

*The fourth dialog box of
the Combo Box Wizard.*

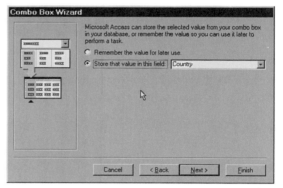

Access asks what name you want to give to the label for the list box. It picks Country as the
name, as you see in Figure 19.14; click the Finish button to continue.

Figure 19.14.

*The fifth dialog box of
the Combo Box Wizard.*

19

You need to add the title to the top of the form. You must add a form header to place the title. To add a form header, select **V**iew | Form Header/Footer from the main menu. This adds the header and footer to the form. You will add a label with the title to the header. To do this, you add an unbound label and enter the title you want to use. Click the Label button on the toolbox, and click the detail section at the top where you want the title to be. Access adds an unbound label control with a blinking cursor for you to add your title. Type the title Customers and press Enter. Change the font to bold and the size to 12 by clicking the Font Size box in the toolbar and clicking the Bold button on the toolbar. You can manually resize the label box to fit the new font size, or you can double-click the border of the label box. That automatically resizes the box to fit your data. (See Figure 19.15 for the final results.)

Figure 19.15.
The new form with all
the controls added.

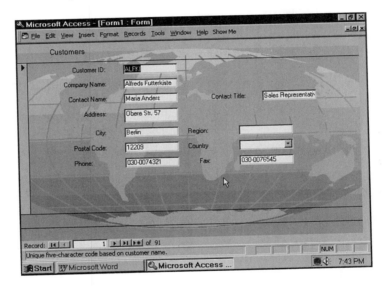

The only thing left to add is the graphic behind the form. As is usually the case with Access, you have several ways to add graphics. The quickest way is to select the form by clicking the gray box with the black center that is located where the vertical and horizontal rulers meet. Click the Properties tool on the toolbar if the property sheet is not already open. Make sure the All tab is selected, and scroll down to the Picture property. Click in this field and then click the Builder button, the button with the three dots in it located next to the property field. Access asks you where the graphic you want to insert in your form is located. The default location with Office 97 for the globe graphic is C:\MSOFFICE\ACCESS\BITMAPS\STYLES\GLOBE.WMF. If your setup is different, the graphic may be located elsewhere on your hard drive. Select Globe.wmf and click OK. The form shows the globe graphic in the background, but it is too small and misaligned. Grab the corner handle on the graphic box and resize it to fill the whole screen. You need to change the Picture Size Mode property to Stretch to get the graphic to fill the whole form.

JUST A MINUTE

> You can add many types of pictures to your forms and reports. Access 97 comes with a few default pictures, and you can import your own. Remember that adding graphics does take up more system resources, and can slow down the speed of your database.

Your form should look like the form in Figure 19.1. You have successfully re-created the Customers form from the Northwind database. Exit your form. Access asks you whether you want to save your changes. Click the OK button, and Access asks you to give your form a name. Do not name it Customers because that overwrites the original form. Give it a different name that you will remember.

Another Form Example

One more control that is used often on forms is calculated expressions. These are controls whose source is an expression instead of a field in a table or query, so they are unbound controls. None of the Northwind forms has an adequate example, so you will quickly create your own. Open a new form in design mode and base the form on the Products table. Add the Unit Price field to the form as a bound control text box. Now select the Text Box button again, but instead of dragging a field onto the form, just click the form and create an unbound text box. You will calculate the total price of an item with 6 percent sales tax. In the Control Source property field in the property sheet, type the following formula: =[unitprice] * 1.06. The next field in the property sheet is the format field. Select Currency from the drop-down list box in this field. Now, take a look at the form in Form view. Your form should be similar to Figure 19.1.

JUST A MINUTE

> You also can add other options to the page header and footer. Remember from Hour 12 that page headers and footers are only visible in the printed version. In an unbound text box, you can use several Access functions, such as =Date() and =Page() to add the date, time, page number, filename, and other information. Look in Help under functions for more details and a list of functions.

Summary

19

This hour was devoted to studying forms and their design. You examined a form in the Northwind database and re-created it using a variety of controls and properties. You now should have a good understanding of the basics of forms and be able to create your own forms from scratch.

Workshop

The Workshop is designed to help you anticipate possible questions, review what you've learned, and begin thinking ahead to putting your knowledge into practice. The answers to the quiz are in Appendix A, "Quiz Answers."

Q&A

Q What are subforms?

A A subform is a form within another form. It is usually used to show data from a table or query that has a one-to-many relationship.

Q What is a pivot-table form?

A A pivot table is an interactive table that performs the calculations you choose, such as sums and counts, based on how the data is arranged. You change layouts to analyze the data in different ways.

Q What is a graph form?

A You can add graphs to any form, using your own data or using data from a table or query.

Quiz

1. What are the six types of forms?
2. What are the three main types of controls?
3. What should you do before creating a form?
4. How do you add the current date or page number to a form?

19

Hour 20

Creating Reports

by Timothy Buchanan

This hour provides more detail on reports. You need to think about several things before you begin to design and create your first report. I discuss some of these issues and show you how to create a new form from scratch and add some more advanced controls to your report. In the course of this hour, you re-create a report from the Northwind database. Topics covered this hour are

- ☐ Designing reports
- ☐ Sorting and grouping data
- ☐ Re-creating a Northwind report

Controls and properties are the fundamental building blocks of forms, as well as reports. You must understand these concepts before you begin to design and develop reports.

Designing Reports

There are nine important steps in designing a report:

1. Design the appearance and function of your report.
2. Determine what data is needed.
3. Create the table or query in which the report will be bound.
4. Create a new report and bind it to the table or query.
5. Place the relevant fields on the report by using text controls.
6. Add other labels and text controls for other fields as necessary.
7. Modify the size, appearance, location, and size of the various controls.
8. Define sorting and grouping options.
9. Use graphics and other special effects to enhance your report.

Take a closer look at these nine steps. Then, you will use these steps to re-create the "Sales Totals by Amount" report from the Northwind database.

Design the Appearance and Function of Your Report

Reports display your data on screen and on paper. Before you design a report, you need to know what information you want your report to display and what source you will use to get this information. For example, if all the information you need is in one table in your database, the report can be based on that table. If the information is in more than one table, you must base the report on a query. Designing the table or query properly is just as important as designing the report. If the report does not have an easy way to receive valid data, the report will be useless.

Determining What Data Is Needed and Creating a Query

If more than one table has the information you want to display in the report, select a query that contains all the information that is needed. If a query that contains the information you need does not exist, you have to build a new query specifically for that report. Reports can have only one source of information. In other words, reports can be based on only one table or one query. Creating a query that incorporates all the information from several tables is the only way to use information from more than one table in a report.

Creating a New Report and Adding Controls

After you determine what data will be displayed on the report and you create the table or query that will be bound to the report, you can create a blank report, link the report to a table or query, and begin adding controls. As discussed in Hour 9, "Displaying Data in Reports," report controls can be bound, unbound, or calculated. The original source of the data a control displays is a good factor to help determine what type of control is needed. You use bound controls when the control gets its values from a field in the underlying table or query. You use unbound controls when the data the control displays does not exist anywhere else in the database. Some examples of unbound controls are captions and titles. A calculated control uses an expression instead of a field to determine the data displayed. Report controls are the same as the controls that are used on forms. After you add the text boxes for your form, you can begin adding other controls, such as labels and other text boxes as needed. Then, you can change the size and appearance of the controls to fit the design you had in mind for the report.

Sorting and Grouping

Sorting data allows you to determine the order in which the data is displayed in the report. This allows you to easily identify the relationships between the groups. You also can use sorting and grouping to enhance readability and ease understanding of complex data. You can sort or group the data in the underlying query, but sorting in the report allows you to change the query without affecting the sort order in the report.

Adding Special Effects

A report with nothing but pages and pages of plain black and white text can be boring and unreadable. You can improve reports with graphical elements such as lines, boxes, graphics, and images. These elements enhance the readability and appearance of a report. You can use the rulers at the top and side of the page and the background grid to help with the placement of controls and objects to make the report look its best. Adding other sections, such as headers and footers, can also improve readability and appearance. These sections also are useful for displaying totals for grouped or sorted data.

Designing and Creating a New Report

Now that you understand some of the basic ideas of reports, take a look at a report from the Northwind database and re-create it from scratch. This lets you see all the steps you need to consider when designing and creating your own reports. The report you will work with from the Northwind database is "Sales Totals by Amount," which is shown in Figure 20.1.

Figure 20.1.

The Sales Totals by Amount report from the Northwind database.

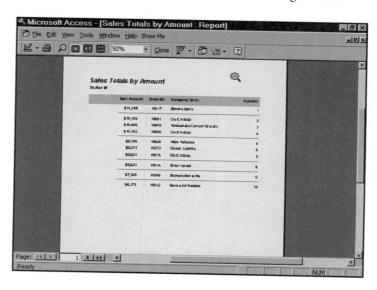

The first step you need to take is to determine what you want the report to display. The "Sales Totals by Amount" report displays all the sales totals, the order ID, the company name, and a counter ID. The totals are sorted by the sale amount and grouped into $10,000 sections. The title and date appear at the top of the first page, the column names appear at the top of every page, and each page has the total sale amount for that page only at the bottom of the page, along with the page number and total number of pages. You want to display only the sales that are greater than $2,500. You also want only the sales that were shipped during 1995. You first need to create a query that gives you the information you need.

The information the report needs is stored in three places: the Customers table, the Orders table, and the Order Subtotal query. You need to combine these three objects to form the query for the report.

20

1. Open the Northwind database if it is not already open.
2. Select the Query tab and click the **New** button. (See Figure 20.2.)

Figure 20.2.

The dialog box Access displays when creating a new query.

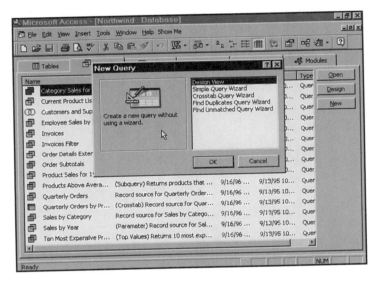

3. The default choice is to create a new query without using a wizard.
4. Click the OK button to continue.

Access asks you which tables or queries you want the query to use. You know that the Orders and Customers tables and the Order Subtotal query are what you need.

5. Double-click each of these to add to the query builder and then click the Close button.

Your screen should now look like Figure 20.3.

JUST A MINUTE

> Notice that the tables already have the proper relationships displayed. The CustomerID field in the Customers table has a one-to-many relationship with the CustomerID field in the Orders tables, and the OrderID field in the Orders table has a one-to-one relationship with the OrderID field in the Order Subtotal query. You have to set your own relationships in the tables and queries that you design from scratch.

Now you need to add the fields you want to use in the report. You first need the sale amount from the Order Subtotal query.

Figure 20.3.

The Access query builder with the tables and query added to create the new query.

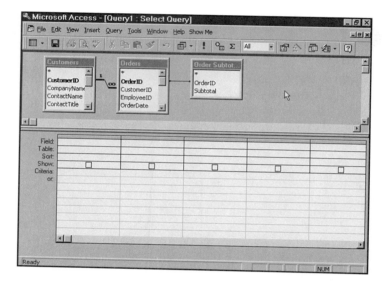

1. Drag the Subtotal field from the Order Subtotal box to the first query line.

2. You want only the sales that are greater than $2,500, so add the text >2500 in the Criteria field.

3. You want this field to have a different name in the report—and although you can change the label in the report design, it is easier to change the name at this stage. You want this field name to be Sales Amount instead of Subtotal.

4. To make the change, click in the Query field and type Sale Amount: before the name Subtotal, as shown in Figure 20.4. This displays all the sales totals from the Order Subtotal query that are greater than $2,500.

5. Now add the OrderID field from the Orders table, which is used to display the order ID on the report. To add this field, drag the OrderID field from the Orders table to the second query line.

6. Now, your screen should be similar to Figure 20.5.

7. The next field you need is the company name, which is stored in the CompanyName field in the Customers table. Drag this field to the third query line.

20

Figure 20.4.

The new query with the first field added and formatted.

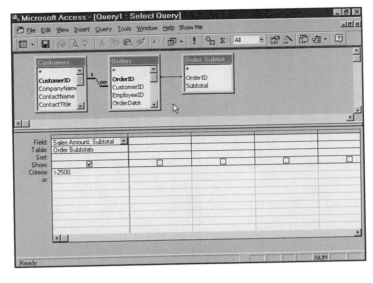

Figure 20.5.

The new query with the first two fields added and formatted.

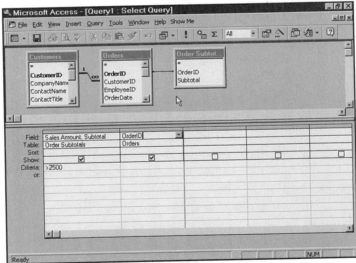

20

Figure 20.6 displays the query with three fields entered.

Figure 20.6.

The new query with the first three fields added and formatted.

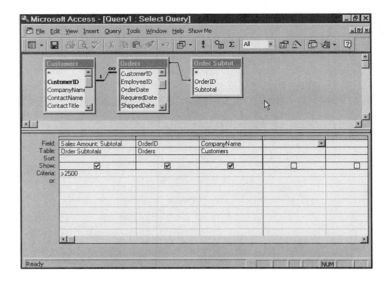

The fourth and final field you need on the report enables you to display only the orders that were shipped during 1995. This field is not displayed on the final report but determines what records the query returns. The date information is stored in the ShippedDate field in the Orders table.

8. Drag the ShippedDate field to the fourth query line.

9. You want only the orders from 1995, so you need to add a line to the Criteria field. To do this, you use the Between..And function. Type the following into the Criteria field: Between #1/1/95# And #12/31/95#. Using this criteria displays only the records with a ship date occurring during 1995.

10. Your screen should now look like Figure 20.7.

JUST A MINUTE

> The width of the query lines has been changed to display all the text entered to make it easier to understand what the query is designed to accomplish.

The query is now finished. To test the query, first save it, naming it New Sales Totals by Amount. Click the Run button on the menu toolbar (the button with the exclamation point). Your datasheet should look like Figure 20.8.

20

Figure 20.7.

The new query with all four fields added and formatted.

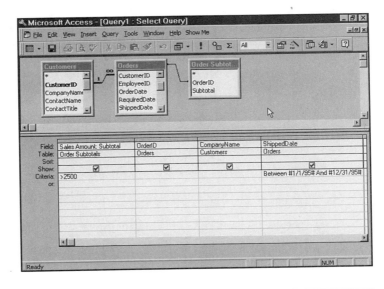

Figure 20.8.

Datasheet displaying the information you designed the "New Sales Totals by Amount" query to display.

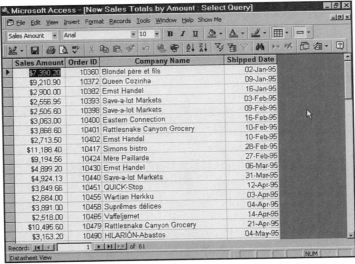

20

Now that you are satisfied that the new query displays the information you need for the report, you can design the report.

1. Close the new query, making sure that it was saved.

2. Click the Report tab and click the **New** button.

   Access displays the New Report dialog box and asks you what table or query you want to link to the new report.

3. Select the "New Sales Totals by Amount" query and click OK.

   Access now displays a blank report that is bound to the new query. According to Figure 20.1 with the original report, the first thing you need to add is the title and the date that are displayed in the report header.

4. To add the report header, select **View** | Report Header/Footer from the menu.

   You can add both of these elements with an unbound text box placed in the report header.

5. Select the text box tool from the toolbox and click in the Report Header section.

6. Type Sales Totals by Amount in the label section.

7. Move the label to the top-left corner of the report header, change the font size to 18, and make the text bold.

8. Increase the size of the label box to display all the data. You can use a separate label to display the title, but using the label that is provided automatically to the unbound text box saves you a step or two.

9. Now, you want the text box to display the date. Add text =date() to the text box.

10. Change the font size to 10 and make the text bold.

11. Resize and place the text box directly under the title label, and align the left sides.

12. To match the date format of the original report, click in the Format property for the text box and select the Medium Date format.

13. Scroll down to the Text Align property and select Left.

Your screen should now look like the one shown in Figure 20.9. Now, you are ready to add fields to the Page Header and Detail section.

You add the data from the fields Sales Amount, OrderID, and CompanyName to the Detail section and labels for these fields to the Page Header section. The labels act as column titles and are printed on each page. The data displayed on the text boxes is printed on each page of the report.

1. Select the text box tool from the toolbar and drag the three fields from the Field list box to the Detail section of the report.

2. Select the label tool, click in the Page Header section, and type the name of each of the three labels.

3. Change the label font to 10 and make the text bold.

4. Line up the labels similar to the report in Figure 20.1 and align the text boxes in the Detail section below the labels.

5. Change the Text Align property of the OrderID text box to Center to display the information in the middle of the text box instead of the right.

20

Figure 20.9.

The new report with the first two fields added to the report header, displayed in Design view.

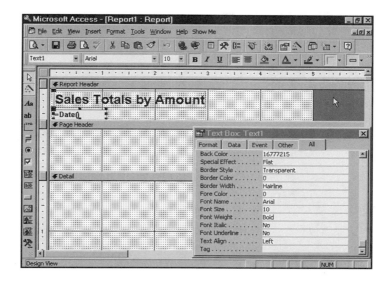

6. Change the Decimal Places property for the Sales Amount text box to zero to round up the values.

7. Add another label in the Page Header and type Counter: in the label.

8. Add an unbound text box in the Detail section directly under the Counter label and type =1 in the text box.

9. To change the background color of the Page Header, click the Page Header section and click the button with the three dots next to the Back Color property in the Property sheet.

10. Select the light gray color for the background of the page header.

Your screen should now be similar to Figure 20.10.

You want to sort the sales amount in descending order and group the sales amount in $1,000 increments.

11. To do this, select the Sorting and Grouping button on the toolbar.

12. In the top line under Field/Expression, click the drop-down list and select Sales Amount.

13. To the right under Sort Order, select Descending to sort the values in descending order.

14. You want a line to separate each group, so select Yes for Group Footer in the Group Properties field in the lower section of the Sorting and Grouping box.

20

Figure 20.10.

The new Sales Totals by Amount report with the Report Header, Page Header, and Detail sections added and formatted.

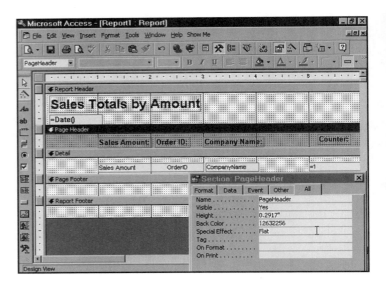

15. You want to group on an interval of $1,000, so select Interval for the `Group On` property and select 1000 for Group Interval.

16. Add a horizontal line running the width of the report in the Sales Amount footer, using the Line button from the toolbox.

Your screen should be similar to Figure 20.11, with the property sheet open and the Sorting and Grouping menu open. Figure 20.12 shows the form without these menus open.

Figure 20.11.

The new Sales Totals by Amount report with the Report Header, Page Header, Detail, and Sales Amount Footer sections added and formatted.

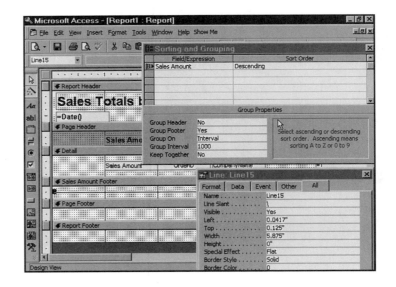

20

17. The next step is to change the `Running Sum` property of the Counter unbound text box to Over All.

18. The next thing you need to do is add the page number box in the Page Footer.

19. Add an unbound text box to the lower-right corner of the Page Footer and delete the label.

20. Add the following text to the `Control Source` property for this text box: `="Page " & [Page] & " of " & [Pages]`.

    This uses the concatenation function to add the words `Page` and `of` to the current page number and total page numbers.

21. Change the size of the font of this text box to `10`, and line it up all the way to the right of the Page Footer.

22. Add a horizontal line to the entire width of the Page Footer. Click the line and change the `Border Width` property to `3` and the `Border Color` to `light gray`.

These last few steps allow the `Counter` field to display a new number for each sequential record. That way, this report prints only 10 records per page and sums only the totals for each page.

Now, the report is finished and ready to preview. Your screen should look like Figure 20.12.

Figure 20.12.

The new report with all the controls added and formatted.

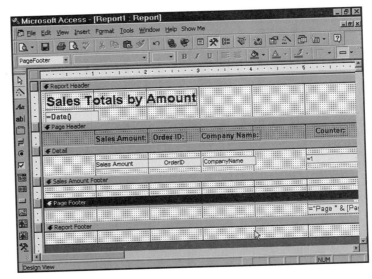

Save the report as New Sales Totals by Amount Report and select the Print Preview view. Your new report should be similar to the one shown in Figure 20.13.

Figure 20.13.

The new report shown in Print Preview.

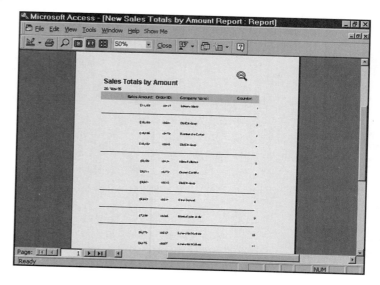

Congratulations; you just designed and created your first report, a complex combination of several tables and queries that display exactly the information you need to know.

Summary

This hour discussed more detail on reports. I discussed several steps you need to take before you can design and create a report. You re-created a report from the Northwind database from scratch while learning many of the design issues you need to think about when designing and creating reports.

Workshop

The Workshop is designed to help you anticipate possible questions, review what you've learned, and begin thinking ahead to putting your knowledge into practice. The answers to the quiz are in Appendix A, "Quiz Answers."

Q&A

Q **What is a good way to learn more about creating reports?**

A Do exactly what you did in this hour. Pick a report that does something similar to what you want to do and examine all the parts of that report. After you get an idea of how the report works, you can use that information to help you create a new report.

Q **What other calculations or expressions can you add to a report?**

A Many more calculations and expressions can be added, such as a running sum, average, and other arithmetic calculations.

Quiz

1. What are the fundamental building blocks of reports?
2. What kind of special effects can be added to a report?
3. What are the nine steps in designing a report?

20

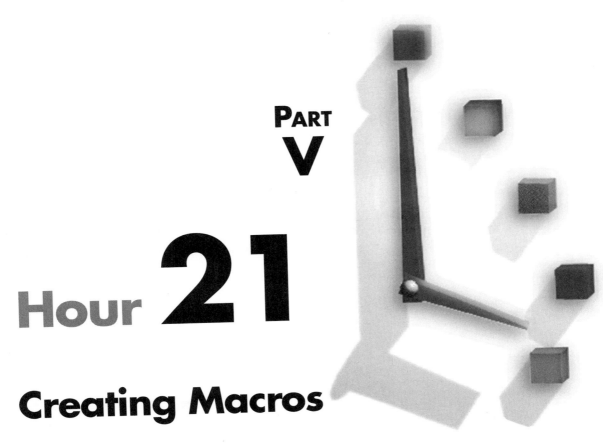

Hour 21

Creating Macros

by Timothy Buchanan

This hour introduces macros. Macros help automate tasks that are performed frequently or repetitively in your database. You can use macros by themselves or in combination with other objects in your database. You can automatically run macros using *events*. How macros work and how you integrate them into your databases is the focus for this hour. The topics covered this hour are

- ☐ What a macro is
- ☐ The uses of macros
- ☐ The Macro window
- ☐ Creating and editing macros
- ☐ Running macros
- ☐ Conditional macros
- ☐ Debugging macros
- ☐ Events
- ☐ Self-executing macros
- ☐ Integrating macros and forms

What Is a Macro?

A macro is an Access object that executes certain tasks or a series of tasks. Each of these individual tasks is called an *action*. Access 97 allows you to select and perform dozens of different actions in a macro.

When you run a macro, Access uses the objects and data that were specified in the actions of the macro to execute the actions in the sequence in which they are listed. For example, you can design a macro that automatically opens two forms that are used often in your database. Your macro would have two actions that would tell Access to open the forms in the order you list them. You also can use macros for other functions, such as validating complex data, creating custom menu bars, or triggering other macros.

CAUTION

Macros can change the data in your tables! Make sure you make a backup copy of your database before you attempt to create your own macros.

The Uses of Macros

You can use macros for any repetitive task or series of tasks you do in your database to save time and effort. Macros also add accuracy and efficiency to your database by performing the actions you specify in the exact same way every time they are run. You can use macros to perform a wide variety of tasks, such as

- Opening a table, form, query, or report in Design view or Datasheet view.
- Opening multiple forms and reports together.
- Closing tables, forms, and reports that are open.
- Using data validation forms to ensure data accuracy.
- Opening and preview or print reports.
- Running action queries.
- Moving data between different tables.
- Executing any commands from the Access menu bar.
- Setting values of controls on forms and reports.
- Performing certain actions when you click a command button or press a key.
- Moving, minimize, maximize, size, or restore any window.
- Displaying information, such as warnings to the user.

- [ ] Renaming database objects.
- [ ] Starting other applications.

There are many ways to integrate macros into the design of your database. Any task that is repetitive or used often is a good task to be used as a macro. The following list outlines some important ways that you can use macros:

- [ ] Allow forms and reports to work together.
- [ ] Use buttons linked to macros to print automatically a report that is based on the current form. You also can use buttons to open one form that is related to the form you are currently using.
- [ ] Set values in form and report controls.
- [ ] Set the values on a form or report using macros. Using the results of calculations or using a value from another table, a macro can set the value in the form or report.
- [ ] Set properties of forms and reports and their controls.
- [ ] Set or change most form and report properties and their respective controls using macros.
- [ ] Find specific records or filter records automatically.
- [ ] Use macros to accelerate the process you use to find specific records.
- [ ] Check data accuracy using validation forms.
- [ ] Use macros to validate data on forms. You can use macros to ensure accuracy of the data being entered in the form.
- [ ] Automate transfers of data.
- [ ] Use macros to import or export data automatically.

The Macro Window

The Macro window is the graphical design workplace used to create macros. It is very similar to the Design window of other Access objects. To open the Macro Design window, click the Macro tab in the Database window, select a macro from the list, and click the Open button. Figure 21.1 shows the list of macros in the Northwind database. Figure 21.2 shows the Customers macro from the Northwind database displayed in Design view.

21

Figure 21.1.

The list of macros available in the Northwind database.

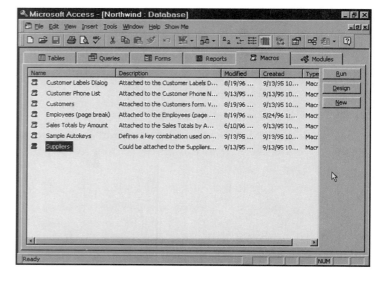

Figure 21.2.

The Customers macro from the Northwind database, opened in Design view.

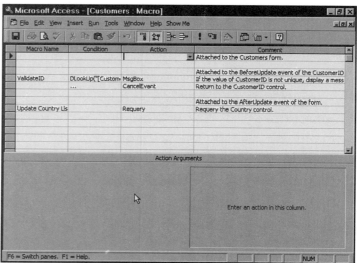

To create a new macro, click the Macro tab on the Database window and click the New button. Figure 21.3 shows a blank macro in Design view. Notice that the Design window is separated into four parts. The menu and toolbar are located at the top of the screen, similar to the other Access objects. The upper section of the Macro window is where the macro is designed. This section has two columns, Action and Comment. You use the Action column

21

to add the actions for each step of the macro. You use the Comment column to add a description of each action. The data in the Comment column is ignored by Access; it is only there for your reference.

Figure 21.3.

A blank macro opened in Design view.

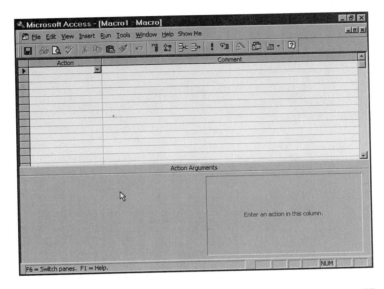

JUST A MINUTE

You can display two additional columns in the upper section of the Macro window. You can display the Macro Name and Condition sections by selecting **V**iew | **M**acro Name and **V**iew | **C**ondition. You also can click the icons on the toolbar to view these sections.

JUST A MINUTE

The Comment column is a good place to document the actions of a macro. You can make comments about each action of the macro for future use. Documenting your code is an important programming tool.

The lower section of the Macro window specifies the arguments for each action. Most actions need more information about the objects you specify before they can be performed. Access uses these arguments to get more information about how to perform each of the actions. In Figure 21.4, the Customer Labels macro from the Northwind database is open, and an action that opens a report is selected. Notice that the action is OpenReport. The lower section lists the arguments for the OpenReport action. The Report Name is the report to be opened. In

21

this case, the Customer Labels report is specified. The View is the view in which the report is to be opened. In this case, the Customer Labels report is to be opened in Print Preview. Each action has different arguments it needs before it can execute properly.

Figure 21.4.

The Customer Labels macro from the Northwind database is opened in Design view, and the OpenReport action is selected.

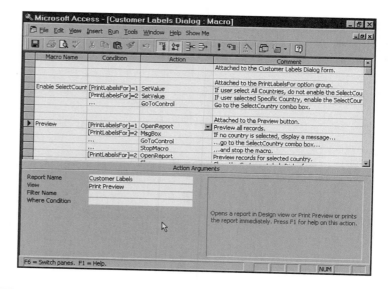

You can easily and quickly move between the upper and lower sections by pressing the F6 key.

JUST A MINUTE

Creating and Editing Macros

When creating a macro, you must use both sections of the Design window. After you add the actions and arguments, you can save the macro to use another time.

Adding Actions

There are several ways to add an action. You can enter the action name directly in the Action column of the Macro window. You can select an action from the drop-down list box in the Action column. You also can drag and drop an action from the Database window into the Action column. You can add more than one action to a macro. Access performs the actions in the order in which the actions are listed. The next step is to add a description of the action in the Comments column. Adding a description is not mandatory but is considered a good programming practice. Now, you must specify the arguments for the action listed in the

Action column. After the action is selected in the Action column, the lower section displays the arguments that you can select for that specific action. You can manually type a value into the argument or select a value from a drop-down list.

Editing Actions

When you have a macro with multiple actions, you might need to change the order of the actions. To move an action, select the row selector to the left of the action name. Click the highlighted row and drag it to the place in the macro where you want it to be performed. You can also delete macro actions. Select the row selector to the left of the action name, and press the Delete key or select **E**dit | Delete **R**ows from the menu. Macros are run in the order in which they are listed in the macro screen, from top to bottom. If you call another macro from your original macro, the macro you call is run in its entirety, and the control is returned to your original macro. Then, the remaining macro actions are performed.

Saving Macros

You must save a macro before you can run it. If you attempt to run a macro that was not saved, Access asks you whether you want to save it. After the macro is saved, it is listed with the other macros under the Macro tab in your Database window.

TIME SAVER

> The easiest and fastest way to save a macro is to press the F12 key and type the macro name.

Running Macros

After you create a macro, several different places in Access allow you to run the macro. You can run the macro from the Macro Design window by clicking the Run button in the toolbar, which has an exclamation point icon. You also can choose **R**un | **R**un from the Design menu. Another way to run a macro is from the Database window. Select the macro from the macro list under the Macro tab in the Database window, and click the Run button. You can also double-click the macro you want to run.

JUST A MINUTE

> You also can run a macro within another macro. The action RunMacro enables you to run any other macro in your database.

Conditional Macros

In some cases, you might want to perform a certain action or actions only if a specific condition is true. For example, you might want to display different information to the user depending on what value the user enters. In these cases, you can use a condition to control the flow of a macro.

A condition is a logical expression. In other words, it can only be true or false. The macro follows a path that is dependent on the condition of the expression. When the condition is true, the macro follows the true path; when the condition is false, the macro follows the false path. The Customer Labels macro from the Northwind database, displayed in Figure 21.4, has several actions that depend on the condition of the PrintLabelsFor variable. To add a condition to a macro, you must have the Condition column visible. Click the Condition button on the toolbar to view this column. You enter the conditions for each action in the Condition column in the Macro Design window. If the condition is true, Access performs that action. Access can also execute a series of actions if the condition is true.

Type an ellipsis in the Condition column of the actions that immediately follow that condition. The ellipsis is shown in the Customer Labels macro from the Northwind database in Figure 21.4. When you run a macro, Access examines each expression in the Condition column and determines whether the condition is true or false. If the expression is false, Access ignores the action and moves to the next row that does not have an ellipsis. If the expression is true, Access performs the action that is beside the expression and all the following actions with an ellipsis in the Condition column. If the Condition column is blank, Access performs that action and continues to the next expression, where the cycle continues.

Debugging Macros

Access provides two tools to help you troubleshoot problems in your macros: single stepping and the Action Failed dialog box.

Single Step

You use single-step mode when you receive unexpected results from your macro and you want to examine the macro's actions more carefully. Single stepping moves through the macro's actions one step at a time, pausing between each action. Single stepping allows you to take a look at the result of each action and determine which action or actions are causing the incorrect results. To use the single-step mode, click the Single Step button on the toolbar or select **R**un | Single Step. Run the macro as you usually do by clicking the Run button on the toolbar. You have three options when single stepping:

21

□ Step performs the action listed in the dialog box. If no errors occur, the next action appears in the dialog box.

□ Halt stops the execution of the macro and closes the dialog box.

□ Continue turns off the single-step mode and continues to run the remainder of the macro.

Turning on single-step mode opens all macros in the single-step mode. Turn off single stepping if you want to run any macros as usual.

JUST A MINUTE

Action Failed Dialog Box

When a macro is run and an action causes an error, an error message appears. The error message appears in a dialog box that looks just like the macro single-step box, but the only option available is the Halt button. Choose Halt and return to the macro window to correct the problem.

Events

Another way that you can run macros is to base the activation of a macro on a user action. You can run a macro based on an *event*. An event is the result of some user action. An event can occur when a user clicks a button in a form, closes a report, moves between records in a form, and many other cases. Access databases are event-driven. Access objects respond to many different events. Access 97 has eight different groups of events.

□ Data events occur when data is entered, deleted, or changed, or when the focus moves from one record to another.

□ Error and timing events are used for error handling and synchronizing data.

□ Filter events occur when you apply or create a filter on a form.

□ Focus events occur when a form or control loses or gains focus or becomes active or inactive.

□ Keyboard events occur when you type on the keyboard or when you send keystrokes using the SendKeys action.

□ Mouse events occur when a mouse action happens.

□ Print events occur when a report is printed.

□ Window events occur when you open, resize, or close a form or report.

21

You can trigger a macro when a user performs any of the approximately 50 events that Access recognizes. Access recognizes these events through the use of special properties in forms, reports, and controls. There are no event properties in tables or queries.

Self-Executing Macros

A good example of a macro that uses an event to trigger the macro execution is a self-executing macro. The most common self-executing macro is the AutoExec macro, which is automatically executed every time you open your database. To create the AutoExec macro, simply create the macro you want to run every time you open the database. Save the macro and name it AutoExec. Every time you open that database, the AutoExec macro runs, which is useful if you want to display an opening screen to your users or open a main switchboard menu.

JUST A MINUTE

To bypass the AutoExec macro, hold down the Shift key as you select the database in the Open Database dialog box and continue holding it while the database loads.

Integrating Macros and Forms

When you use a form in your database, Access recognizes certain events that occur on the form. Some events that Access recognizes are moving from one record to another and double-clicking a control. You can use macros on forms to respond to these types of events. Form events have corresponding event properties. Macros specify how each control or form responds to any event. The form or control property is linked to the macro. When creating a response to an event, you must first identify the control or form event that the macro responds to. If the macro you want to link to this event does not exist, you have to create it first. Then, you set the event property to the name of the macro. You can use the Macro Builder to create a macro, and it sets the event property automatically. You can use the Macro Builder for any event property. To use the Macro Builder, select the control property you want to change and click the small button with the ellipsis (three dots) on it. Select the Macro Builder button, and you can create and save the macro without leaving the form or report you are currently working on. Access help offers more information on the Macro Builder. You can use macros and forms to do the following:

- ☐ Help make forms work together
- ☐ Synchronize forms
- ☐ Print forms
- ☐ Filter records

21

- ☐ Use command buttons to open and close forms
- ☐ Set values
- ☐ Find records
- ☐ Validate and synchronize data
- ☐ Display messages
- ☐ Navigate between records, controls, and pages

Summary

This hour introduced the topic of macros. How macros work and how you can integrate them into your databases was the focus for this hour. I explained what macros are, as well as when and why to use them. Macros is a very large topic, and much of the use and information about macros are beyond the scope of this book. However, this hour is a good introduction to macros and how to use them.

Workshop

The Workshop is designed to help you anticipate possible questions, review what you've learned, and begin thinking ahead to putting your knowledge into practice. The answers to the quiz are in Appendix A, "Quiz Answers."

Q&A

Q What are some more uses for macros?

A Macros can be used to display messages to the user, run other applications, set values in tables, and so on.

Q Can you do anything more advanced than macros?

A Yes, you can, using Microsoft's Visual Basic for Applications. Much of what you can do with macros can be done with code, and code has the advantage of being faster and more powerful. And you can trap any errors that occur.

Quiz

1. What is a macro?
2. Why should I use a macro?
3. What are events?
4. Why use events to trigger macros?

21

PART
VI

Additional Topics

Hour

Hour 22

Exchanging Data with Word 97, Excel 97, and Other Applications

by Craig Eddy

You're almost done. You've made it to Hour 22 in the quest to teach yourself Access 97. You've learned all about using, extending, and creating an Access 97 database. Now it's time to learn how to use that database in some real-world situations.

This hour covers the basics of using Microsoft's Office Links. These are built-in wizards that assist you in using information from one Office application in another. The Office Links included with Access 97 are Merge It with MS Word, Publish It with MS Word, and Analyze It with MS Excel. You'll also learn about the Label Wizard for generating labels and about exporting data from Access 97 to other file formats or even other database systems.

> You must have the appropriate Office 97 applications installed on your computer to use the Office Links.

JUST A MINUTE

In this hour we'll use the Northwind database that's included with Access 97 as a sample database. If you want to follow along with the examples in the text, open that database now.

Using Access 97 Data for Word 97 Mail Merge

Perhaps the most useful tool in the Microsoft Office suite is Word 97's mail merge. Performing a mail merge involves creating a Word document that contains special merge fields and then combining this document with a data source. The data source is used to replace the merge fields with real data. A separate document is created for each record in the data source.

You can use the Merge It with MS Word Office Link on the data contained in tables or returned by a query. You cannot use this Office Link with forms and reports.

To use the Merge It Office Link, follow these steps:

1. Activate the database window and select the table or query that will provide the data for the mail merge. For our example, select the Customers table.

2. Use the **T**ools | Office **L**inks | **M**erge It with MS Word menu item.

3. The Microsoft Word Mail Merge Wizard appears as shown in Figure 22.1. This dialog allows you to choose between merging to an existing document or creating a new document. For now, choose to create a new document and click OK.

Figure 22.1.

The Microsoft Word Mail Merge Wizard.

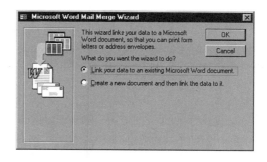

22

4. Microsoft Word loads a new document and turns on the Mail Merge toolbar, as you can see in Figure 22.2. In Figure 22.2 I have clicked the Insert Merge Field to drop down the list of available merge fields. As you can see, this list matches the fields available in the Customers table.

Figure 22.2.

Microsoft Word prepared for the Customers table mail merge.

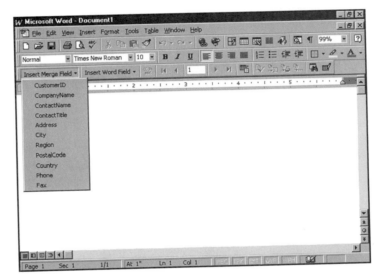

5. Create the document as you normally would in Microsoft Word, inserting the fields from the Customers table as appropriate.

6. After you've finished creating the document, you should save it for future use.

7. To see the merged document, click the View Merged Data button (the one labeled ABC) that resides to the right of the Insert Word Field button on the Mail Merge toolbar. The data from the Customers table is merged with the document, replacing the merge fields with the appropriate data. The example document I created is shown in Figure 22.3.

8. You can use the record locator buttons on the Mail Merge toolbar to display other records in the merge document. To print the merged document, use the **File | Print** menu.

Now that you've created a merge document for the Customers table, you can use this file for future mail merges by choosing the Link your data to an existing Microsoft Word document option on the initial Mail Merge Wizard dialog. When you do so, Access will present you with a Select Microsoft Word Document file open dialog box. Simply locate the appropriate file using this dialog and then continue with step 5 above.

Figure 22.3.

The final merged document.

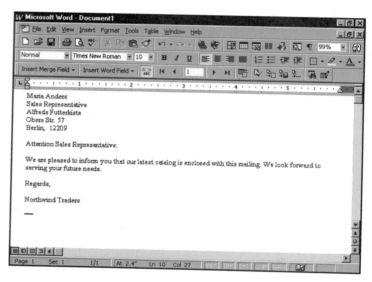

You can also use the Save **A**s/Export feature, discussed later in this hour, to save the data in a table or query into a form Word 97 can use for mail merge. Doing so, however, does not allow you to select the document to be used for the merge nor does it allow you to create a new document.

Publishing Access 97 Components Using Word 97

The Publish It with MS Word Office Link allows you to quickly create a Word document from the datasheet view of tables, queries, and forms. It can also create a document from a report. This Office Link creates a file in the Rich Text Format (RTF) and immediately launches Word 97 with this document.

Using this Office Link is simple. Simply select the table, query, form, or report you want to use as the source for the new document. Then use the **T**ools | Office **L**inks | **P**ublish It with MS Word menu item.

Access will choose the name for the file based on the name of the object. If the filename already exists, Access will ask you whether you want to replace the existing file. If you answer no, a File Save dialog will appear allowing you to choose a different name or folder for the file. If you answer yes, the existing file will be replaced with the new one.

22

For tables, queries, and forms, the Publish It Office Link will produce a document that uses a table to display the data. For a report, the document will closely resemble the printed report, except that charts embedded in the report will not be ported to the Word document.

Figure 22.4 shows the document produced when the Publish It Office Link was used on the Sales by Category query.

Figure 22.4.

The results of the Publish It Office Link used with the Sales by Category query.

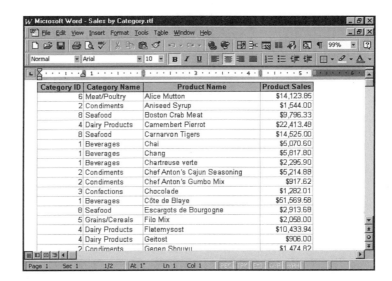

Analyzing Access 97 Data Using Excel 97

The final Office Link is the Analyze It with MS Excel Office Link. This Office Link allows you to transfer your tables, queries, forms, and reports to an Excel spreadsheet. Most of the formatting in the datasheet views, forms, and reports is preserved in the spreadsheet. Forms are saved using their datasheet views. If you have grouping levels in your reports, they are saved as outline levels in the spreadsheet.

To use this Office Link, select the component you want to transfer to Excel. Use the **Tools** | Office **Links** | **A**nalyze It with MS Excel menu item. Like the Publish It Office Link, Access will choose the name for the file based on the name of the object. If the filename already exists, Access will ask you whether you want to replace the existing file. If you answer no, a File Save dialog will appear allowing you to choose a different name or folder for the file. If you answer yes, the existing file will be replaced with the new one.

Figure 22.5 shows the Excel spreadsheet produced when the Sales by Category report was used with the Analyze It Office Link.

Figure 22.5.

The results of the Analyze It Office Link used with the Sales by Category report.

	A	B	C
	X Microsoft Excel - Sales by Category.xls		
	File Edit View Insert Format Tools Data Window Help		
A1	= Sunday, February 16, 1997		
1	Sunday, February 16, 1997		
2	CategoryName		
3	*Beverages*		
4		ProductName	ProductSales
5		Chai	$5,070.60
6		Chang	$5,817.80
7		Chartreuse verte	$2,295.90
8		Côte de Blaye	$51,569.58
9		Guaraná Fantástica	$1,571.62
10		Ipoh Coffee	$10,034.90
11		Lakkalikööri	$7,883.10
12		Laughing Lumberjack Lager	$868.00
13		Outback Lager	$5,663.40
14		Rhönbräu Klosterbier	$3,670.24
15		Sasquatch Ale	$2,079.00
16		Steeleye Stout	$5,955.30
17	*Condiments*		
18		ProductName	ProductSales
19		Aniseed Syrup	$1,544.00
20		Chef Anton's Cajun Seasoning	$5,214.88

Using the Label Wizard to Produce Labels

As you've seen so far in this hour, Access 97 is full of features that assist you in using the data entered into your databases. This section covers another very useful feature, the Label Wizard. The Label Wizard is a report generator that can create a variety of printed labels from the data in a table or query. Typically, labels are created for mailing purposes. However, you can just as easily create product labels, tape labels, or any other type of label you want.

To create a new set of labels using the Label Wizard and the Northwind database, follow these steps:

1. Open the Northwind database, activate the Database window, and select the Reports tab.

2. Click the **N**ew button to open the New Report dialog, shown in Figure 22.6.

Figure 22.6.

The New Report dialog box.

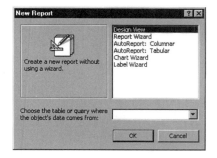

22

3. Select Label Wizard in the list box at the right side of the dialog.

4. In the drop-down list box at the bottom of the dialog, select the table or query that contains the data to be used for the labels. In this example, select Customers.

5. Click OK to launch the Label Wizard. The first dialog of the wizard, shown in Figure 22.7, appears.

Figure 22.7.

The initial dialog of the Label Wizard.

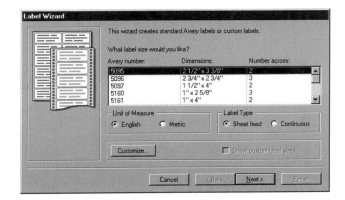

6. Select the label style you're using or click the Customize button to create a new label style. The styles included are the styles for the Avery brand of labels. For this example, select 5164. Click **N**ext when you've chosen the proper label style.

JUST A MINUTE

> If you have created custom labels and checked the box labeled Show custom label sizes, the standard labels will not appear in the list of available labels. Only the custom labels will appear. Simply clear the check box if you need to use a standard-sized label.

7. The next dialog allows you to choose the font name, font size, font weight, and font style, as well as the color for the label's text. After choosing appropriately click **N**ext.

8. This dialog, shown in Figure 22.8, is where you'll do the field layout for the label. Select the field in the list of available fields and click the > button to move it to the prototype label on the right side of the dialog. In the prototype label, you can type static text as well as use the Ctrl+C, Ctrl+X, and Ctrl+V copy, cut, and paste shortcut keys. After the label is laid out properly, click **N**ext to continue.

Figure 22.8.

The label layout dialog.

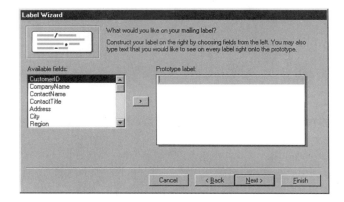

9. The next dialog is where you choose how to sort your labels. This is useful if you're doing bulk mailings, for example, because the postal rates are lower for sorted mail. Select the field or fields you want to sort and move them to the Sort By list by either double-clicking them or clicking the > button. You can add all fields by using the >> button. To remove a field, select it in the Sort By list and click <. To remove all fields, click <<. When you're finished here, click **N**ext to continue.

10. This is the final dialog. Here you'll set a name for the report and instruct Access what to do when you click **F**inish. For our example, change the name to `Customer Labels (5164)` and click **F**inish. The resulting report is shown in Figure 22.9.

Figure 22.9.

The finished `Customer Labels (5164)` *report.*

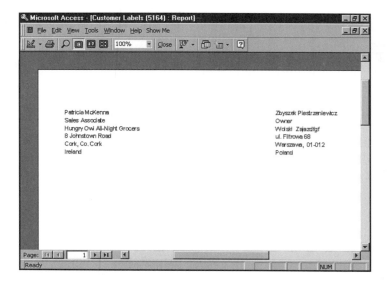

22

Exporting Data to Other Sources

22

In addition to the means already discussed in this hour, Access 97 provides a way to manually export data from your database to an external file or database. The available recipients for this export feature depend on the options that you installed when Access 97 was installed. Likewise, different components have different possible export capabilities. For example, forms and reports cannot be exported to other database systems but tables and query results can.

JUST A MINUTE

If an external file type or database is not available when you follow along in this section, it simply means you haven't installed that option. To do so, return to Hour 2, "A Quick Tour of Access 97," for instructions on installing Access 97.

To export an entity to an external file, follow these steps:

1. Select the entity in the Database window.
2. Use the **F**ile | Save **A**s/Export menu item or right-click the entity's name and select Save **A**s/Export from the shortcut menu. The Save As dialog box shown in Figure 22.10 appears.

Figure 22.10.

The Save As dialog box.

3. Because we're saving to an external file or database and not making a copy of the selected entity within the current database, leave the default option button selected and click OK.
4. The Save *Entity Name* In dialog shown in Figure 22.11 opens. On this dialog you specify how and where you want to save the entity.
5. Select the type of file to which to save the entity using the Save as **t**ype drop-down list box at the bottom of the dialog. Open the list box to see which types are available on your system. Select the type desired.
6. Use the top portion of the dialog to specify the location and filename for the file to export to and click Export.

Figure 22.11.

The Save In dialog box.

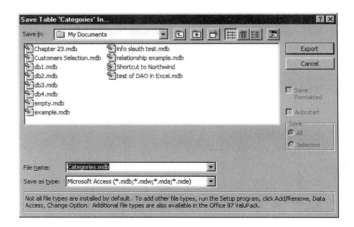

NEW TERM *ODBC* refers to an *Open Database Connectivity*. ODBC defines a standard means of connecting to an external data source. The interface to the outside world is identical for every ODBC-compliant database. ODBC drivers, which perform the actual access to the data, are built for each ODBC-compliant data source.

If you're exporting a table or query to another database using ODBC, follow the above steps through step 4, then continue as follows:

5. Select `ODBC Databases()` in the Save as **t**ype drop-down list.

6. In the Export dialog that appears next, specify a name to use for the entity in the destination ODBC database. Click OK.

7. The Select Data Source dialog appears. Specify or create an ODBC data source name for the database you're exporting to. The choices of databases and ODBC drivers available varies greatly from system to system.

8. Click OK and the data is exported to the specified data source. If any errors occur during this process, you will receive the appropriate message boxes informing you of the problem.

Access can also export to a variety of Internet formats, including creating Active Server Pages based on your database. Publishing data on the Web is the subject of Hour 24, which is appropriately titled "Publishing Access 97 Data on the Web."

Summary

Hopefully by now you've discovered a wealth of ways to put the data in your database to good use. This hour has shown you how you can create Word and Excel documents from your data, how to create labels using the Label Wizard, and even how to export your data to just about any other file or database.

22

Access 97 really removes the limits as to what you can do with data after it's placed in your database. In other words, the data is not stuck in the database serving little to no purpose. You can always act upon and use your data in the way that best matches how you operate.

Workshop

The Workshop is designed to help you anticipate possible questions, review what you've learned, and begin thinking ahead to putting your knowledge into practice. The answers to the quiz are in Appendix A, "Quiz Answers."

Q&A

Q I have an existing database system I'd like to export data to. Where can I find the ODBC drivers for this system?

A Access 97 ships with quite a few ODBC drivers. If the driver you're looking for isn't currently on your system (use the 32-bit ODBC Control Panel applet to find out which drivers are installed), try running the Access 97 setup again to see whether it's available within Access 97. If it isn't, contact the database vendor to see if they have a 32-bit ODBC driver available. Chances are most commercial database systems have such a driver available. You can also check Microsoft's ODBC Web site at `http://www.microsoft.com/ODBC` for additional drivers.

Quiz

1. What is the main difference between the Merge It and the Publish It Office Links?

2. When using the Merge It Office Link, does the document to be merged with have to already exist?

3. What size labels can be created using the Label Wizard?

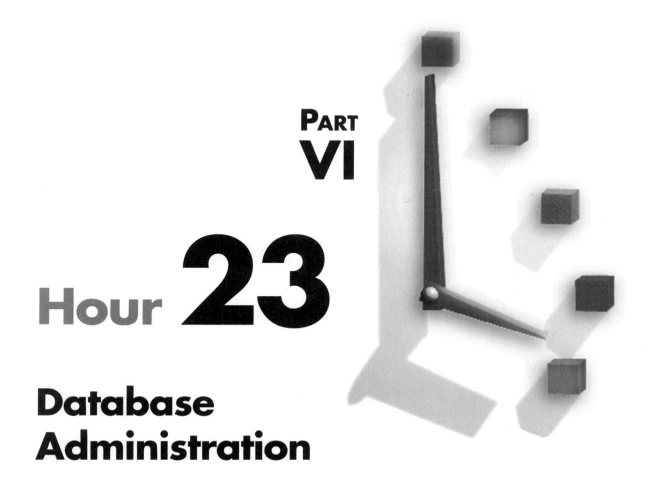

Hour **23**

Database Administration

by Timothy Buchanan

This hour discusses the topic of database administration. Above and beyond the design of your database and the overall scheme of how it works, you need to know several things about your database and how to manage several of its aspects. Such things as how to compact your database and how to repair your database are very important. Access 97 provides several utilities that make it easy to manage your database. The topics covered this hour are

- ☐ Compacting a database
- ☐ Repairing a database
- ☐ Backing up a database
- ☐ Encrypting and decrypting a database
- ☐ Converting a database
- ☐ Securing a database

Compacting a Database

When deleting records from a table or deleting objects from your database such as tables, queries, forms, or reports, Access does not reduce the size of your database. When the database becomes fragmented, it does not use the drive space efficiently. Access does not reduce the size of the database every time you delete something because it can be very time-consuming. When you reduce the size of a database file, all the objects in the database are recopied. This can take considerable time, which greatly affects the speed in which your database operates. Access provides a utility that allows you to explicitly compact the database and eliminate wasted disk space. The easiest way to tell whether your database needs to be compacted is if the current size of your database is much larger than its previous size, and few objects have been added to it since.

To compact the database that is currently open, select **Tools | Database** Utilities | **Compact** Database from the menu, as shown in Figure 23.1.

Figure 23.1.

The menu option to compact a database that is currently open.

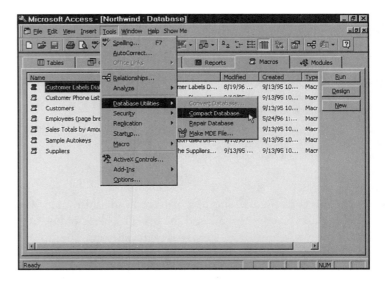

To compact a database that is not currently open, make sure no databases are open in Access. Select **Tools | Database** Utilities | **Compact** Database from the menu as shown in Figure 23.1. Specify the database you want to compact in the Database to Compact From dialog box, which is shown in Figure 23.2. Click **Compact** to continue. In the Compact Database Into dialog box, you specify the name of the compacted database and where to store it on your drive. (See Figure 23.3.) Click **Save** to continue; Access compacts your database and writes the compacted database to the location you specified.

23

Figure 23.2.

The Database to Compact From dialog box is where you select the database you want to compact.

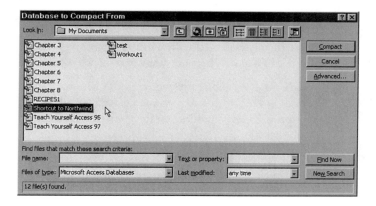

23

Figure 23.3.

The Compact Database Into dialog box is where you select the name and location for the compacted database to be written.

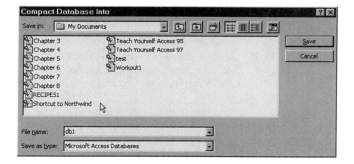

JUST A MINUTE

You can use the same name as the original database, but make sure to have a backup copy of your database. If you choose the same name and location as the original database, Access overwrites the original database with a compacted version.

JUST A MINUTE

Compacting a database from a previous version of Access does not convert it to Access 97 format.

JUST A MINUTE

It is usually a good idea to compact a frequently used database on a regular basis, especially those databases that create and delete a large number of records or objects on a regular basis, such as inventory databases.

Problems When Compacting a Database

Compacting a database usually consists of waiting for Access to finish the job. Sometimes a problem can occur. There are a few reasons why a database does not compact.

If you do not have enough storage space on your hard drive, the database does not compact. You must have roughly twice as much space available as the size of the database you are trying to compact. Delete any files you do not need and attempt to compact the database again.

Compacting the database fails if you do not have Modify Design or Administer permissions for all the tables in the database. If this database is not your own and was created by someone else, you must contact the original creator and get permissions on all the tables. If this database is your own, you must update permissions on all the tables. Search for help in Access under the topic "Compacting Database" for more information.

CAUTION

If you attempt to compact a database from Access version 1.x and an object in this database includes a backquote character (') in its name, the database does not compact. Use Access 1.x to rename the object or update the database to Access 97.

Repairing a Database

A database can become corrupted when a user turns off the PC without first exiting from Access or a power surge or other related problem prevents the user from exiting Access properly. Access usually detects a corrupted database when you try to open or compact a database and gives you the option to repair the database at that time. You cannot open or compact a database that is corrupted; you must first repair it.

  A database is *corrupted* when the database is improperly closed or exited, leaving certain Access files open. Access cannot open databases that are corrupted, and will give an error message when you try to open one.

To repair the database that is currently open, select **T**ools | **D**atabase Utilities | **R**epair Database from the menu, as shown in Figure 23.4.

  When Access *repairs* a database, it fixes and closes the files that were left open when the database was improperly closed. Most of the time the repair will be completely effective.

Figure 23.4.

The menu option to repair a database that is currently open.

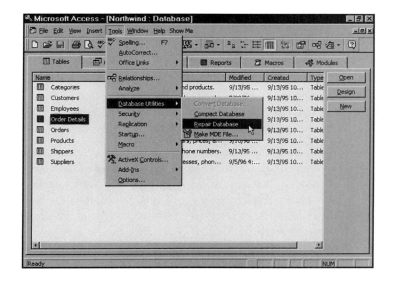

To repair a database that is not currently open in Access, first close any open databases. Select **T**ools | **D**atabase Utilities | **R**epair Database from the menu as shown in Figure 23.4. Enter the name and location of the database you want to repair in the Repair Database dialog box. (See Figure 23.5.) Click **R**epair to continue. Access repairs the database.

Figure 23.5.

You choose the database you want to repair in the Repair Database dialog box.

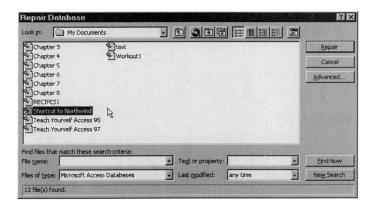

JUST A MINUTE

If your database is behaving erratically, you might need to repair it. As with compacting, it is a good idea to repair important databases that are frequently used. Your database might need to be repaired if nothing happens when buttons are selected, information is lost, or the system experiences sudden crashes.

Backing Up a Database

Backing up databases was covered in Hour 2, "A Quick Tour of Access 97," but I will cover it again quickly and discuss how to restore a database from the backup copy.

All important databases must be backed up frequently on a regular schedule. A good rule of thumb is to back up those databases that you don't want to re-create from scratch. For most of us, that is every database.

Make sure the database is closed. If you are on a network environment, backing up a database is as easy as copying the database file to a drive on the network. If you are not on a network, backing up a database is still very simple. Choose a location or backup medium in which to place a copy of your database. You can use Windows Explorer, the MS-DOS Copy command, or My Computer to copy the .MDB database file to the location you choose. Make sure there is enough room in this new location for the database to be written. Choose a location that will not be affected if the current database is accidentally erased or permanently corrupted. If you have the option, save a copy of the database to your network at work, or save a copy on floppy disk. You want to have a copy of the database in at least two separate locations and hardware mediums to ensure complete protection.

Restoring a Backup Database

If your original database has been corrupted or destroyed, you can restore your backup copy of the database. Simply copy the backed up database from its location to your database folder. You also can choose to run the database from the backup copy location.

JUST A MINUTE

If you copy the backup database to the same location as the original database and they both have the same name, the backup database overwrites the original database. If you want to save the original copy of the database, rename one of the databases before you copy the backup file.

Encrypting and Decrypting a Database

Sometimes you want to shield the contents of a database from unauthorized users. Encrypting a database might sound complicated and powerful, but it is actually very simple and not extremely effective. Encrypting a database makes the database information unreadable to word processors or utility programs. Encrypting a database also compacts a database

23

first. The database is still readable by anyone with Access and a copy of the database. To restrict access to the database, you must define user-level security. Securing a database is covered later in this hour in the "Securing a Database" section. Decrypting a database reverses the encryption of the database.

To encrypt or decrypt a database, first make sure the database is closed. You cannot encrypt or decrypt an opened database. After the database is closed, select **T**ools | **S**ecurity | Encrypt/ Decrypt Database from the main menu. Choose the database you want to encrypt or decrypt and click the OK button. Figure 23.6 shows the Encrypt/Decrypt Database dialog box. Choose the location where you want to write this encrypted or decrypted database and its name, and click the OK button.

Figure 23.6.

The Encrypt/Decrypt Database dialog box is where you choose the database you want to encrypt or decrypt.

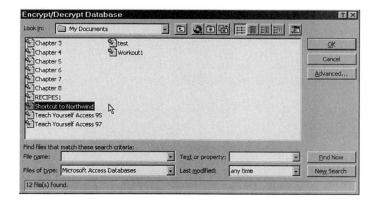

JUST A MINUTE

You can use the same name as the original database, but make sure to have a backup copy of your database. If you choose the same name and location as the original database, Access overwrites the original database with the encrypted or decrypted version. If there is an error when encrypting or decrypting the database, Access does not delete the original database file.

JUST A MINUTE

The errors or problems that can occur when encrypting or decrypting a database are the same as when compacting a database. Refer to the section "Compacting a Database" earlier in this hour, for more details.

Converting a Database

If you have used a previous version of Microsoft Access, you probably have databases that were created in a version other than Access 97. Access 97 databases use a file format different from any previous version of Access. You can open a database from any previous version with Access 97, but the database is opened in read-only mode, and you cannot make changes to the database. You must convert the database to Access 97 if you want to make any changes.

To convert a database from a previous version of Access to Access 97, select **Tools** | **D**atabase Utilities | Conver**t** Database from the menu, as shown in Figure 23.7. Choose the database you want to convert in the Database to Convert From dialog box. (See Figure 23.8.) Choose the name and location for the converted database in the Convert Database Into dialog box, as shown in Figure 23.9. You must choose a new filename or location for the converted database in the Convert Database Into dialog box. You have two databases when you are done: one in the older version of Access and one in Access 97. Make sure the converted database was correctly converted and delete or rename the older version of your database. This ensures there is no confusion between the two databases.

Figure 23.7.

The menu selection to convert a database to Access 97.

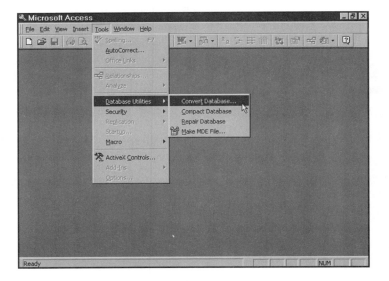

Figure 23.8.

The Database to Convert From dialog box is where you specify what database you want to convert.

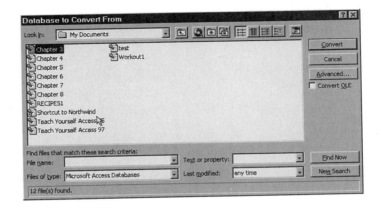

Figure 23.9.

The Convert Database Into dialog box is where you specify the name and location of the converted database.

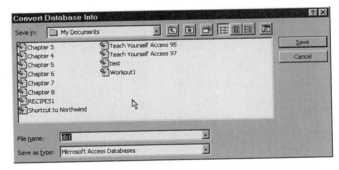

JUST A MINUTE

After you convert the database to Access 97, it cannot be converted back into an earlier version, and it cannot be used by older versions of Access. Keep a copy of the older version only if someone who has not upgraded to Access 97 might need to use it. If you are in a network environment and more than one user uses the database, make sure all users have upgraded to Access 97 before you convert the database. Keeping an older version of a database active is dangerous, considering that Access is not easily backward-compatible. It would be a good idea to make the older version read-only, and to create a warning to those users informing them that they are using an older version.

JUST A MINUTE

When you open a database that was created in an earlier version of Access, you are prompted to choose if you want to convert the database or open it in read-only format. (See Figure 23.10.)

Figure 23.10.

The dialog box that appears when you open a database that was created in an earlier version of Access.

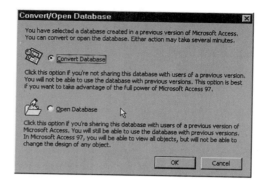

Securing a Database

Methods on how to secure a database were covered in Hour 4, "Understanding Someone Else's Database." This section outlines a brief summary of those methods.

Encrypting a database does nothing to prevent a user with Access 97 on his computer from opening a copy of your database. To prevent this, Access 97 provides two methods of adding security to your database. You can set a password for your database that prevents anyone who does not have the password from opening the database. You also can use user-level security to control which parts of the database the user can access or which parts the user can change.

Access 97 provides two general types of database security. The first and simplest is password security. Databases that have this type of security display a password screen when you try to load the database.

If you do not enter the correct password, you cannot open the database. If you enter the correct password, you are allowed to open the database and you also have the rights to view and edit all objects in the database.

JUST A MINUTE

Do not use database passwords if the database will be replicated. Replicated databases will contain errors and cannot be synchronized when database passwords are enabled.

The second type of security is called user-level security, and it is more flexible and extensive than simply setting a password. This form of security is similar to a network system's security. Users must enter a user ID and password when they open these databases. Each user is defined as a member of a group in the Workgroup Information file. Each group is given permissions that regulate what they are allowed to do with each object in the database.

23

There are some good reasons to use user-level security in databases that are distributed to a number of users. One reason is to protect the intellectual property of your database design and code. Users outside your company should not be able to determine how you designed your database and wrote your code. Another reason to use user-level security is to prevent users from accidentally changing the design or code of your database. Simple errors that users make can prevent your database from working properly or cause unexplained errors. A very good reason to use user-level security is to protect sensitive data you might have stored in your database. Unauthorized users should not have access to important data.

JUST A MINUTE

> You can find more information about removing this type of security by searching for the help topic "Removing User-Level Security."

Summary

This hour discussed the topic of database administration. I covered the utilities that Access 97 provides to make it easy to manage your database. How to compact, repair, back up, encrypt and decrypt, convert, and secure your database were discussed in this hour. Although some of these utilities might seem trivial, they can be the most important steps in designing and managing your database. You should now know how to administer your databases.

Workshop

The Workshop is designed to help you anticipate possible questions, review what you've learned, and begin thinking ahead to putting your knowledge into practice. The answers to the quiz are in Appendix A, "Quiz Answers."

Q&A

Q What versions of Access databases can be converted to Access 97?

A Any previous version of an Access database can be converted to an Access 97 database.

Q Can other databases be converted to an Access 97 database?

A Yes, some databases created using other applications can be imported or converted as Access 97 databases. See Access 97 Help under Converting Databases for more information.

Q What is replication?

A Replication is a new feature of Access 97 that allows a database to be used at two different locations, but allows changes made at one location to be reflected at the other locations. This subject is beyond the scope of this book, but is covered in Help, and other Sams publications.

Quiz

1. Why should I compact my databases?
2. How often should I compact my databases?
3. How does a database become corrupted?
4. Where should I back up my databases?

23

PART
VII

Advanced Topics

Hour

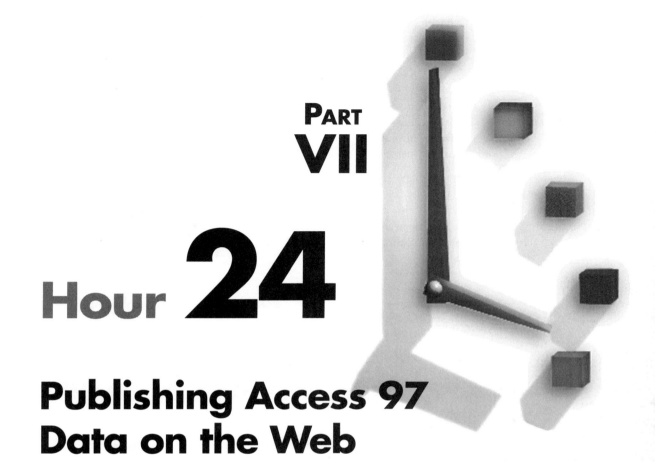

Hour 24

Publishing Access 97 Data on the Web

by Craig Eddy

By far, the hottest news in computing during the second half of this decade has been the Internet and World Wide Web. Microsoft has promised that its products will make publishing information on the Internet in general and the Web in particular accessible to everyone. The Office 97 suite, including Access 97, goes a long way to making this promise a reality.

Access 97 has many features useful in publishing your data on either the Internet or an intranet. These features include the capability to export tables, queries, forms, and reports to HTML format and to create dynamic links to your Access database. Access 97 also provides useful tools for actually publishing the files to your Web server. All these topics will be touched upon in this hour. Hold on to your seat, you're about to blast into cyberspace!

An *intranet* is a TCP/IP network set up for local access only. It's an internal Internet where you may have Web servers, FTP servers, and other Internet-related servers installed. However, unlike the Internet, which is accessible to everyone else on the Internet, an intranet is accessible to only a select group of computers and users.

NEW TERM *Hypertext Markup Language (HTML)* is a special format of text file interpreted by Web browsers and other viewers designed to display HTML files. HTML allows you to create a document that can be rendered (displayed) on any type of system from a text-based terminal to a high-powered graphics display. HTML is the language used to create most of the documents found on the World Wide Web.

> I'll once again be using the Northwind database to illustrate the steps in this hour. If you want to follow along, make sure you've installed the sample databases (refer to Hour 2, "A Quick Tour of Access 97").

JUST A MINUTE

Setting Up a Web and FTP Server on Your Computer

The Internet in general and the World Wide Web in particular have gained popularity because of their capability to provide a medium of information exchange. On the Web, this information exchange typically takes place by a Web browser application (acting as a client) requesting a specific page from a Web server application. The Web server then returns that page, assuming that the page exists and that the browser has the right to retrieve the page.

In the past, setting up a Web server required a great deal of knowledge about computers and networking. Now, assuming you already have an Internet or TCP/IP network connection, it's simple to install and operate a small-scale Web server.

Microsoft provides three levels of Web server: the Personal Web Server (PWS), the Peer Web Services, and the Internet Information Server (IIS). The Personal Web Server is designed for single connections or small networks and can run on Windows 95. The Peer Web Services are included with NT Workstation 4.0 and are designed for supporting small networks on an NT platform. Finally, the IIS is designed for large-scale networks and for the Internet. It is included in NT Server 4.0.

For our purposes we'll stick with the Personal Web Server. You can download the required software from Microsoft's Internet Explorer Web site at `http://www.microsoft.com/ie/default.asp` or purchase Microsoft's Internet Explorer Starter Kit, which includes the PWS software.

24

The Personal Web Server will run on any machine capable of running Windows 95. You will need to ensure that you have enough free disk space to hold the Web content (pages) that will be available on your PWS, but beyond that the system requirements will be met by any computer currently running Windows 95.

After you've installed the software and restarted your PC, the Web server is probably up and running. By default, the PWS is set to run automatically when you turn on your computer. You can verify this by checking the task bar for the PWS task bar icon. Briefly hold the cursor over each icon in the task bar and its tooltip will appear. If you find an icon whose tooltip says Personal Web Server, your Web server is running. Double-clicking the icon will bring you to the server's Properties dialog where you can check the server and make sure it's set up to your liking. Also, if you don't want the PWS running when you start the computer, the Services tab of the Properties dialog allows you to change Personal Web Server's startup behavior.

To test your Web server, start Internet Explorer and enter `http://localhost` in the address box. If everything is operating properly, the default Web page installed with the PWS will display. You're now ready to begin publishing your Access data onto your Web site!

The PWS creates a content directory to hold your Web pages. The default folder for this is `c:\Webshare\Wwwroot`. You can make files available to the Web server by copying them to this directory. Note that Web browsers will have access to any files that you place in this directory. Only put files that are all right to be seen by everyone in this directory and any subdirectories.

To start the FTP server on your machine, follow these steps:

1. Double-click the PWS task bar icon.
2. Select the Services tab.
3. Select FTP in the Services list box and click the Start button. The FTP server is now operating on your computer.

JUST A MINUTE

To have the FTP service run whenever you start your computer, click the **P**roperties button and select the **A**utomatic (FTP service starts up automatically) option button. Then click OK. The FTP service will now start automatically the next time you start your computer.

Exporting Data to an HTML File

Now that you've seen how to open a database stored on an FTP server, it's time to investigate actually publishing data onto the Web. The remainder of this hour will be devoted to taking data from your Access 97 databases and publishing it in a form suitable for the Web.

Access 97 provides several ways to publish your data to the Web. You can either publish static data or dynamic data. Static pages never change; they always display the same data. Dynamic pages, however, generate queries against your Access databases and produce Web pages on-the-fly, using current data from the database. This section discusses creating static Web pages. The section that follows explains how to publish dynamic Web pages.

Creating an HTML Template File

Access 97 can create Web pages from datasheets, forms, and reports without any input from you. However, you can also specify an HTML template file to be used in creating these Web pages. This template file allows you to specify your own standards for the Web page to be created. You can also add graphics such as company logos and backgrounds, as well as specify text colors, link colors, and background colors.

You can use any text editor or even a specialized HTML editor such as Microsoft's FrontPage 97 to create the HTML template file. Store it in a common directory so that you'll have no trouble locating it when you perform an export. If you installed the sample databases when you installed Access 97, a sample template for the Northwind database is installed in the same directory as the MDB file. It's named `NWINDTEM.HTM` and can be opened using Internet Explorer or Notepad.

Template files can also contain tokens which Access replaces with appropriate material as shown in Table 24.1.

Table 24.1. HTML template file tokens.

Token	Replacement
`<!--AccessTemplate_Title-->`	The object name is placed in the Web browser's title bar.
`<!--AccessTemplate_Body-->`	The exported data.
`<!--AccessTemplate_FirstPage-->`	A link to the first page.
`<!--AccessTemplate_PreviousPage-->`	A link to the previous page.
`<!--AccessTemplate_NextPage-->`	A link to the next page.
`<!--AccessTemplate_LastPage-->`	A link to the last page.
`<!--AccessTemplate_PageNumber-->`	The current page number.

Performing the Export

To perform the export to an HTML format, follow these steps:

1. In the Database window, select the object to be exported.

2. Use the **File** | Save **A**s/Export menu item.

3. Select To an External File or Database on the dialog that appears.

4. On the Save dialog that appears, select HTML Documents in the Save as type drop-down list.

5. Select the location to save the HTML file to and enter the name of the file. If you want to use an HTML template file, check the box labeled Save Formatted. Click Export.

6. If you elected to use an HTML template file in step 5, a dialog box will appear where you specify the location of the template file. You can either type the file's name or use the Browse button to locate the template using the familiar file's dialog.

   If the component you selected requires any user input before being displayed (such as a report with date parameters for example), you will be prompted to enter the required information. The HTML file is then created in the location you specified. You can use Internet Explorer to view its contents. Figure 24.1 shows the Northwind Customers table exported using the `NWINDTEM.HTM` template file.

Figure 24.1.

The Customers table exported to HTML.

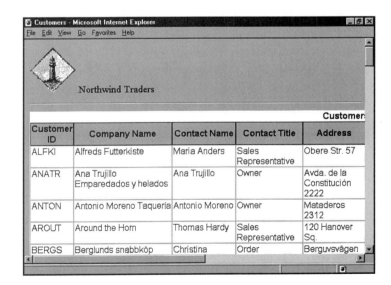

Using the Publish to the Web Wizard

In addition to the manual process of exporting data to HTML, discussed in the previous section, Access 97 sports a Publish to the Web Wizard. This wizard assists you in publishing your data to the Web in a variety of manners: static HTML as seen in the previous section, dynamic HTML using Microsoft's Internet Database Connector, and dynamic HTML using Microsoft's Active Server Pages.

The Internet Database Connector (IDC) is a specialized application that can be installed on either the Personal Web Server or the Internet Information Server. Using the IDC, you can produce Web pages that display live data. The IDC uses a template file which contains tokens for each database field and a script file which contains the information necessary to retrieve the data from the database. The template files have an extension of .HTX while the script files have an extension of .IDC. When you create a link to an IDC page, you should link to the IDC file. The Web server application (if IDC has been properly installed) knows to provide the requestor with the database-aware Web page when the requestor attempts to retrieve an IDC file.

The Active Server Pages run on Internet Information Server 3.0. These pages contain some scripting language, typically (but not necessarily) VBScript, which executes on the Web server. After the script executes, it returns a Web page to the requestor but doesn't return any of the script code that executed. Active Server Pages can access any ActiveX-compatible component installed on the server machine, including database-aware components and ActiveX controls.

Using Active Server Pages, you can create an entire Web-based application, and the details can become quite complicated. For our purposes in this hour, we'll concentrate on creating static HTML and using the Internet Database Connector.

Creating Static HTML Pages

Although Access 97 allows you to quickly create an HTML page using the **File** | **S**ave As/ Export menu item, the Publish to the Web Wizard provides you greater flexibility. You can select multiple tables, queries, forms, and reports to export, and you can automatically launch the Web Publishing Wizard (discussed in the next section) to transfer your HTML pages to a Web server.

To use the wizard to create static HTML pages and store them on your hard drive, follow these steps:

1. Use the **File** | Save **As** HTML menu item. One of the wizard's dialogs allows you to specify which components of the database to export, so it doesn't matter which component you have selected in the Database window.

24

2. The first dialog is an introductory dialog that explains what's about to happen. It also allows you to select a previously saved profile. The last dialog in the wizard provides you with the capability to save the steps you're about to complete in a profile that can be used again by selecting it in this dialog. Click the **N**ext button to continue.

3. The next dialog, shown in Figure 24.2, is where you'll specify what components to export. You can click the tabs to select which type of component to export, and then select the specific items to export by clicking the check boxes or the **S**elect and Select **A**ll buttons. You can remove items by using the **D**eselect All button or by clearing their check boxes. For this example, I've selected the Current Product List query. After you've selected the items you want to export, click the **N**ext button to continue.

Figure 24.2.

Publish to the Web Wizard's component selection.

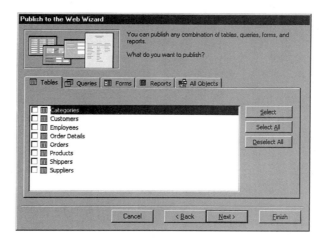

4. In the next dialog you specify the HTML template file to use if you want to use one. You can type the filename or use the Browse button to locate it. If you have selected multiple items on the previous dialog, you can use the I want to select different templates for some of the selected objects check box. If you select this option, the next dialog will present you with a list box where you can specify different template files for each of the exported objects. I've selected the Northwind sample template. Click the **N**ext button to continue.

CAUTION

If you use a template file that contains graphics, make sure that the graphics exist in the folder you specify as the output folder in step 6. Otherwise, the graphics will not be loaded when you open the pages in a browser.

5. This dialog is where you specify how the export file should be created. For this example, leave the Static HTML option button selected. Again, if you wanted to create different types of export for the different objects you've selected, there is a check box that allows you to do so in the same manner as specifying the HTML template file. Click the **N**ext button to continue.

6. The next dialog allows you to specify where to publish the exported objects. The text box is where you enter the name of the folder into which Access will place the HTML files. You can type the folder name or use the Browse button to locate the folder. If you were going to move the files to a Web server as well, you'd select one of the Web Publishing Wizard option buttons in the middle of the dialog. For now, leave the default selected. It is best to store all your Web content in a single folder or in subfolders of a specific folder. This will make it easier to manually copy the content to your Web site or to use the Web Publishing Wizard described later in this hour. After you've selected the folder to export to, click the **N**ext button to continue.

7. This dialog allows you to specify whether a home page is created for your exported data. If you choose to create a home page, you should specify the name for the file in the text box provided. The home page will contain links to the individual pages created for each object you export. Because we're only doing a single object right now, leave the check box unchecked and click **N**ext to continue.

8. On the wizard's final dialog you can instruct the wizard to save the answers to the previous wizard dialogs into a publication profile. You can then use this profile in future uses of the Publish to the Web Wizard, and your current choices will already be selected for you. It's also a great way to figure out what steps you took to create the Web page if you forget. After you've made your choice on this dialog, click **F**inish to create the HTML files.

9. Launch Internet Explorer and use the **F**ile | **O**pen menu to locate the HTML file created. It will be placed in the folder you specified in step 6. The resulting page for the Current Product List query is shown in Figure 24.3.

JUST A MINUTE

Figure 24.3 shows how Microsoft Internet Explorer displays the resulting page. I have turned off the toolbars in order to maximize Internet Explorer's viewing area.

24

Figure 24.3.

The Web page produced for the Current Product List query.

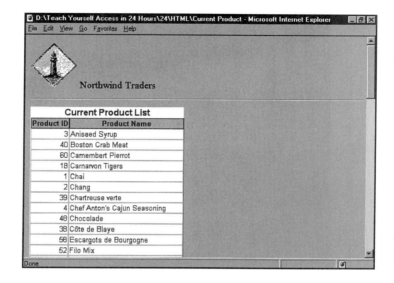

Creating Internet Database Connector Pages

Now that you've seen how easy it is to create a static HTML page based on data in your database, it's time to learn about dynamic Web page creation. The process you'll use is nearly identical to the steps for creating static HTML pages.

The first difference is that instead of selecting the Static HTML option button in step 5 you'll select the Dynamic HTX/IDC option button. When you do so, the dialog that appears when you click Next is where you'll specify an ODBC data source name to use when someone requests the IDC file. This dialog is shown in Figure 24.4.

Figure 24.4.

The dynamic Web page properties dialog.

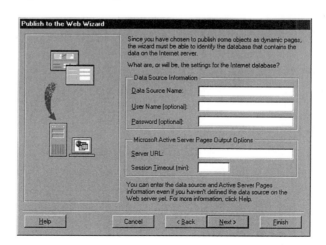

Here you'll enter an ODBC data source name. The actual data source specification does not need to exist yet; you can create it later. Unless you have secured your Access database using the techniques discussed in the preceding hour, you can leave the User Name and Password boxes empty.

To create a Microsoft Access ODBC data source, follow these steps:

1. Launch Control Panel and double-click the 32-bit ODBC icon.
2. Click the Add button. Select Microsoft Access Driver and click **F**inish.
3. The ODBC Microsoft Access 97 Setup dialog appears. Here you assign the name for the data source, select the database to be used, set any advanced options, and perform some database utilities. All that is required is a data source name and a database filename. When you've entered the required information, click the OK button to add the data source.

The second difference from creating static HTML pages is that you must store the files in a directory accessible by a Web server. Otherwise, when you open the files using Internet Explorer you'll see only the actual contents of the files, not the data from the database.

Figure 24.5 shows the results of the IDC page created for the Customers and Suppliers by City query. As you can see, it doesn't look any different from the other pages we've created. The difference, though, is that if data in the database changes, the next time this page is loaded it will automatically show the updated data.

Figure 24.5.

The results of an IDC page created for the Customers and Suppliers by City query.

City	CompanyName	ContactName	Relationship
Aachen	Drachenblut Delikatessen	Sven Ottlieb	Customers
Albuquerque	Rattlesnake Canyon Grocery	Paula Wilson	Customers
Anchorage	Old World Delicatessen	Rene Phillips	Customers
Ann Arbor	Grandma Kelly's Homestead	Regina Murphy	Suppliers
Annecy	Gai pâturage	Eliane Noz	Suppliers
Århus	Vaffeljernet	Palle Ibsen	Customers
Barcelona	Galería del gastrónomo	Eduardo Saavedra	Customers
Barquisimeto	LILA-Supermercado	Carlos González	Customers
Bend	Bigfoot Breweries	Cheryl Saylor	Suppliers
Bergamo	Magazzini Alimentari Riuniti	Giovanni Rovelli	Customers
Berlin	Alfreds Futterkiste	Maria Anders	Customers
Berlin	Heli Süßwaren GmbH & Co. KG	Petra Winkler	Suppliers
Bern	Chop-suey Chinese	Yang Wang	Customers
Boise	Save-a-lot Markets	Jose Pavarotti	Customers
Boston	New England Seafood Cannery	Robb Merchant	Suppliers
Bräcke	Folk och fä HB	Maria Larsson	Customers
Brandenburg	Königlich Essen	Philip Cramer	Customers
Bruxelles	Maison Dewey	Catherine Dewey	Customers

24

Using the Web Publishing Wizard

Now that you've created all these wonderful Web pages, you might want to publish them to a Web server so that the rest of the world (or perhaps just others on your company's intranet) can view the data as well. Microsoft Office 97's ValuPack includes a Web Publishing Wizard that can be used to transfer Web content to a Web server.

You can use the Web Publishing Wizard in one of two ways: Launch it automatically while using the Publish to the Web Wizard or launch it from the Start menu. To use it with the Publish to the Web Wizard, select one of the Web Publishing options discussed in step 6 of the section "Using the Publish to the Web Wizard" earlier in this hour.

When using the Web Publishing Wizard from the Publish to the Web Wizard, the first dialog you'll see is shown in Figure 24.6. This dialog is where you'll specify to which Web server to publish the files.

24

Figure 24.6.

The Web Publishing Wizard's server selection dialog.

We're going to create a new server specification for the Personal Web Server we installed earlier in this hour. Then we'll publish the pages to the server. To do all this, follow these steps after the Web Publishing Wizard launches:

1. Click the New button.
2. In the dialog that appears, enter a friendly name to identify the Web server. The default (My Web Site) is fine for our purposes. Because we're using the Personal Web Server, leave <Other Internet Provider> selected in the list box for selecting Internet service providers. Click **N**ext.
3. The next dialog is for the Internet address of the Web server. We'll enter http://localhost. Click **N**ext to continue.
4. In this dialog, you choose the connection type for the Web server. Because we're using the PWS, select Use Local Area Network (Intranet). Click **N**ext to continue.

5. The Web Publishing Wizard verifies the accessibility of the Web server. If all goes well, you'll see a dialog with a **F**inish button. Click it, and your Web pages will be copied to the Web server.

Summary

This final hour has shown you another extremely useful way to put your Access 97 databases to work. You've learned the basics of using Access 97 to generate HTML files, either in a static or a dynamic format. You've also learned how to publish those files onto a Web server. Hopefully Access 97, in particular, and the whole Office 97 suite, in general, will live up to the promise of providing everyone with the capability to publish information on the Web. This hour has given you the knowledge required to take advantage of this promise.

Workshop

The Workshop is designed to help you anticipate possible questions, review what you've learned, and begin thinking ahead to putting your knowledge into practice. The answers to the quiz are in Appendix A, "Quiz Answers."

Q&A

Q My Internet service provider has told me that the Web server runs on a UNIX machine. Does this mean I cannot use the tools in this hour to publish Access data to the Web?

A Yes and no. You won't be able to produce IDC or Active Server Pages files (unless a UNIX-based Web server capable of handling IDC and ASP files has been produced since this writing) on the Web server. However, you will still be able to create static HTML and use the Web Publishing Wizard even on a UNIX server.

Q If I create an IDC or an ASP file attached to my database, is it possible for someone to gain unwanted access to the data?

A No. Because the IDC and ASP files will use ODBC to open and query your database, you do not need to make them accessible to the Web server itself. This means you can (and should) store the database in a directory that is not referenced by your Web server's configuration and is, therefore, not made accessible via the Web server.

Quiz

1. What is the primary difference between pages created for static HTML and pages created for either IDC or ASP?

2. Which of the Web servers mentioned in this hour is designed for use on the Internet?

3. How can you standardize the Web pages created using the techniques of this hour?

24

PART
VIII

Appendix

A   Quiz Answers

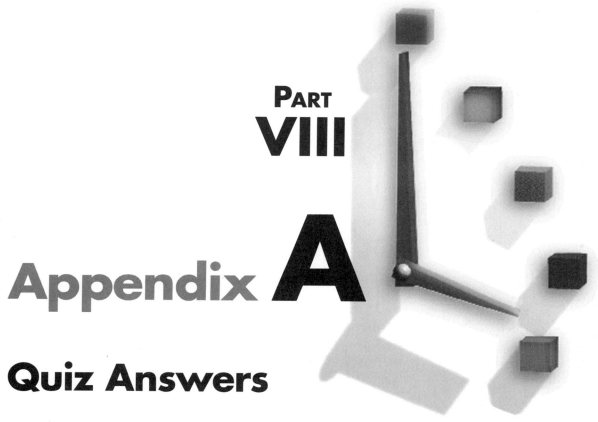

Appendix A

Quiz Answers

This appendix lists the answers to the quiz questions in the Workshop sections at the end of each hour.

Hour 1

1. Access 97 is a *relational desktop database.*

2. Indexes speed up the execution of searches by creating an ordered list of the data contained in the index's fields.

3. Queries are used to search, summarize, and analyze the data stored in a database.

4. 1.2GB.

Hour 2

1. You need 14 to 45 megs of hard-drive space to install Access 97 on your PC, depending on what options you choose to install.

2. The six main database objects in Access are tables, queries, forms, reports, macros, and modules.

3. You can save your database in Access by simply exiting Access. Access will save your database changes automatically, and ask you to confirm any changes made to database objects if they are open when you exit Access.

Hour 3

1. Yes. Microsoft has many Web pages on various Microsoft products. You will need to have an Internet browser program, and access to the World Wide Web. With a browser program, such as Microsoft Internet Explorer, you can access Web pages with more help and news on Access 97 and other Microsoft products. Simply point your browser to http://www.microsoft.com or choose **Help** | Microsoft on the Web.

2. The easiest way is to press F1 or click the Office Assistant.

3. Yes. Open the Help Topics window or search by using the Office Assistant.

4. The tip of the day is a helpful tip about Microsoft Access 97 that you can view separately every day, or browse through to learn more about Access.

Hour 4

1. Press Shift while the database is loading.

2. Click the Relationships button on the toolbar.

3. Yes. Just choose **File** | Save **As** Table.

Hour 5

1. Filter. Find searches the entire set of records in the datasheet and locates only one record at a time. Filter removes all records from the datasheet except the ones that meet your criteria. You can then print these records using the standard datasheet printing.

2. Yes, as long as the columns are adjacent to one another in the datasheet. You can move columns by clicking once in the column header and then using click and drag to move the column to the desired location.

Hour 6

1. Open the table in Design view. The fields that define the primary key are denoted with a key icon in the leftmost column of the grid at the top of the Design View window.

2. The `Validation Rule` property.

3. Yes, but doing so might require special handling when the field is being referred to in an Access expression such as a query definition or a code module.

Hour 7

1. The `InputMask` property. The `Format` property is used to specify how the data should look when the field is displayed in a datasheet or on a form.

2. Set the query's `Output All Fields` property to `Yes`.

3. Whenever the cursor is positioned in a field whose data type is Hyperlink.

Hour 8

1. Single Column, Datasheets, Tabular, Subforms, Pivot Table, and Graphs.

2. Forms provide a much easier and more flexible interface to view and edit data.

3. A query or table stores and supplies the information to a form.

Hour 9

1. They are the best way to present a customized view of information from tables and queries.

2. They are the best way to distribute printed information.

3. Tabular, Single Column, Mail-Merge, and Mailing Label.

4. Reports are used to view data onscreen and on paper; forms are usually used to make data entry easier and more reliable.

Hour 10

1. A standard edit box, a drop-down list box, and an edit box with a Builder or Wizard button are available.

2. Open the table in Design view and choose **View | Indexes** to display the Indexes window.

3. Yes. Access attempts to convert existing data to the new data type. If any of the existing data cannot be converted, Access gives you the option of deleting that data or reverting the data type back to the original type.

Hour 11

1. The Format property. The InputMask property specifies the format for data when it is entered into the field.

2. These lines represent a relationship between the two tables. For more information on table relationships, see the section "Querying Multiple Tables" in this hour or refer to Hour 17, "Creating Tables."

3. Use the Criteria rows for the fields involved in the query or use the query's Filter property.

Hour 12

1. Any object on a form, such as a text box or a label.

2. Provide an easy way to enter and display values.

3. Option groups contain two or more toggle buttons, option buttons, or check boxes, and provide a way to select one option from many choices.

Hour 13

1. Design view and Print Preview view.

2. Queries and tables.

3. Report header, page header, group header, detail, group footer, page footer, and report footer.

Hour 14

1. A data model describes which tables are to be included in the database, what the properties of those tables are, and what relationships exist between the tables.

2. For both display elements (such as forms) and reports. You can specify different styles for each of these.

3. No, you can modify the field names by selecting the field in the wizard's initial dialog and clicking the Rename Field button.

Hour 15

1. You can create everything from scratch, but wizards save time and effort and can also help you avoid errors. You can also look at the end result and learn more about creating objects.

A

2. The Table Analyzer Wizard helps you create a more efficient database by splitting up tables that store duplicate data into separate, related tables.

3. There are four query wizards: the Simple Query Wizard, Crosstab Query Wizard, Find Duplicates Query Wizard, and Find Unmatched Query Wizard.

4. There are 22 databases you can create using the New Database Wizard.

Hour 16

1. Primary, composite, and foreign.

2. A primary key serves as the unique identifier in a table. A foreign key is used in another table to establish a relationship between a record in the other table and a record in the table in which the matching field is the primary key.

3. One-to-one, one-to-many, and many-to-many.

4. The modification of a database's structure so that it meets the requirements of a fully relational database.

5. A repeating group. The multiple fields could be broken into a separate table which contains a field for the foreign key reference back to the original table, a field to describe the type of phone number, and a field for the actual phone number.

Hour 17

1. Use the Link Table method.

2. AutoNumber.

3. Use an input mask.

4. Select the Enforce Referential Integrity checkbox in the Relationships dialog.

Hour 18

1. In Query Design view, click on the Sort row for Title and select Ascending. Then click on Hire Date and select Descending. Also make sure the order is correct. Title must be to the left of Hire Date.

2. The question mark.

3. Greater than or equal to.

4. Use the Sum function—that is, `Sum(Quantity)`.

Hour 19

1. Single column, tabular, datasheet, main/subform, pivot table, and graph.
2. Bound, unbound, and calculated.
3. Think about the overall design of the form. On paper, draw a blueprint of how you want the form to appear on screen.
4. You can use the `=Date()` and `=Page()` functions.

Hour 20

1. Controls and properties.
2. Lines, boxes, graphics, and images.
3. The nine steps are as follows:
    - ☐ Design the appearance and function of your report.
    - ☐ Determine what data is needed.
    - ☐ Create the table or query in which the report will be bound.
    - ☐ Create a new report and bind it to the table or query.
    - ☐ Place the relevant fields on the report by using text controls.
    - ☐ Add other labels and text controls for other fields as necessary.
    - ☐ Modify the appearance, location, and size of the various controls.
    - ☐ Define sorting and grouping options.
    - ☐ Use graphics and other special effects to enhance your report.

Hour 21

1. A macro is an object that executes tasks or a series of tasks when run.
2. A macro helps with any repetitive task to save time and effort, and performs difficult actions with ease.
3. Events are the result of some user action, such as clicking a button, pressing a key, or moving from one field to another.
4. Events make great starting places for macros to be run, such as clicking a button to start a macro or moving into a field to run another macro.

Hour 22

1. The Merge It Office Link allows you to combine data from the database with a Word document. The Publish It Office Link merely exports the data into a new Word document.

2. No. Access gives you the option to create a new document or open an existing document.

3. Any size. If you don't have a standard Avery brand label, you can create your own custom sizes by clicking the Customize button on the initial dialog of the Label Wizard.

Hour 23

1. Compacting your databases saves room on your hard drive and increases database speed.

2. It depends on the size and frequency of use, but once a month is a good place to start.

3. When you close or exit Access improperly, such as turning off your PC without exiting Access.

4. Preferably on a separate computer network or on a floppy disk.

Hour 24

1. The IDC and ASP pages are dynamic—they retrieve up-to-date data from the database each time they are requested.

2. The Internet Information Server.

3. By using an HTML template file and placing within this file the standard elements and properties for your Web site.

INDEX

N-O

P